Imprisoned in English

Imprisoned in English

THE HAZARDS OF ENGLISH AS A DEFAULT LANGUAGE

Anna Wierzbicka

OXFORD
UNIVERSITY PRESS

OXFORD
UNIVERSITY PRESS

Oxford University Press is a department of the University of Oxford.
It furthers the University's objective of excellence in research, scholarship,
and education by publishing worldwide.

Oxford   New York
Auckland   Cape Town   Dar es Salaam   Hong Kong   Karachi
Kuala Lumpur   Madrid   Melbourne   Mexico City   Nairobi
New Delhi   Shanghai   Taipei   Toronto

With offices in
Argentina   Austria   Brazil   Chile   Czech Republic   France   Greece
Guatemala   Hungary   Italy   Japan   Poland   Portugal   Singapore
South Korea   Switzerland   Thailand   Turkey   Ukraine   Vietnam

Published in the United States of America by
Oxford University Press
198 Madison Avenue, New York, NY 10016

Library of Congress Cataloging-in-Publication Data
Wierzbicka, Anna.
Imprisoned in English : the hazards of English as a default language / Anna Wierzbicka.
pages cm
Includes bibliographical references and index.
ISBN 978–0–19–932150–6 (pbk. : alk. paper)—ISBN 978–0–19–932149–0 (hardcover : alk.
paper) 1. English language—Social aspects. 2. English language—Influence on foreign
languages. 3. Multilingualism—Social aspects. 4. Language and languages—Globalization.
5. Language and languages—Philosophy. I. Title.
PE1074.75.W54 2013
306.44—dc23
2013019336

9 8 7 6 5 4 3 2 1
Printed in the United States of America
on acid-free paper

For my grandchildren
Elizabeth, Nicholas, Catherine and Therese

CONTENTS

ACKNOWLEDGMENTS

The main purpose of this book is not to argue with others but to point to what I see as a serious problem in contemporary social sciences, and to propose a solution. Since this problem, however, is a blind spot in the social sciences (or so I contend), perhaps inevitably, it is also a polemical book—and it owes a great deal to many people who will disagree with it. The idea that English—which is understandably widely perceived as history's gift to the world—can also be a conceptual cage, especially for scholars, has sometimes been the object of derision, incredulity, and scepticism for some of my colleagues. These negative reactions have been a great stimulus to me to write this book.

The title of this book came to me in the course of an informal discussion of these matters in January 2012, at a linguistic party on a farm near Canberra, when my colleague David Nash said to me, with friendly Australian sarcasm, "I know, I know, I'm a prisoner of English". What a great title for a book, I thought—and I started to write this book (only slightly adjusting the title) on the same day. I'd like to thank David for provoking me in this way. I am also grateful to other colleagues, who created a milieu within which thoughts developed in this book could be tested and contested. In particular, I'd like to mention in this context Avery Andrews, Nick Evans, Harold Koch, Patrick McConvell, Andy Pawley, Alan Rumsey, and Jane Simpson.

I am also indebted to some more distant interlocutors who over the years have engaged in controversy with me and thus pushed and provoked me to sharpen my ideas and arguments—to mention a few, Paul Kay, Rolf Kuehni, Paul Ekman, the late Richard Lazarus, Carroll Izard, Rupert Stash, Leonard Katz, Kristen Lindquist, Ray Jackendoff, Dirk Geeraerts, Asifa Majid, Nick Riemer, Jan Wawrzyniak, and Daniel Everett.

When I look deeper into the recesses of my heart and mind, I must acknowledge that I am also indebted to some fellow linguists who have studiously avoided mentioning my work (when writing about linguistic relativity, language universals or the relationship between languages and cultures).

Having one's ideas ignored or marginalised can also have a stimulating effect on one's thinking and writing. We do need intellectual friends, but we also need our opponents, detractors,, and bêtes noires. They can all fuel the fire of what philosopher Peter Goldie (editor of the *Oxford Handbook on Philosophy of Emotions*) calls "affect in intellectual activity", and consequently increase our passion and motivation.

Goldie quotes the French psychologist Theodule Ribot (1897), according to whom, "Malebranche [seventeenth-century French philosopher, A.W.] was nearly suffocated by palpitations of his heart when reading Descartes" (2012: 122). Ribot doesn't say what these thoughts and passions provoked by the reading of Descartes were, but whatever they may have been, it is clear that they were stimulating and motivating for Malebranche.

I don't mean to compare myself to Malebranche and I don't think that I have ever experienced "palpitations of the heart" while reading scholarly literature, but I have often felt strong emotions—not always positive, but always motivating. The message that I have been trying to put across—that to reach a non-ethnocentric perspective on languages and human beings we need to get out of the historically-shaped conceptual vocabulary of English—is a challenge. In my view, facing that challenge can bring anyone great intellectual benefits, but it necessitates getting out of the comfort zone of familiar Anglophone academese. It should not be surprising that not everyone wants to hear this message. But this, too, can increase the desire to try to make this message heard by those whose ears can be open to it.

Having acknowledged my indebtedness to many opponents, as well as to colleagues who are valued interlocutors without being intellectually very close, I now want to thank my closest intellectual friends. Cliff Goddard's support for this book, and his input, were essential to its progress from start to finish. I'm grateful to Cliff, and for Cliff, more than I can say. I am also very grateful to, and for, my other friends who share the over-all approach to meaning, culture and the human mind that underlies this book and with whom I was able to talk frequently while writing it, or who made their presence felt through their work, especially Helen Bromhead, Anna Gladkova, Carsten Levisen, Bert Peeters, Carol Priestley, Catherine Travis and Zhengdao Ye. Among linguists outside Australia whose friendship and support has been particularly nourishing to me, I'd like to mention Andrzej Bogusławski and Jerzy Bartmiński in Poland, Juri Apresjan, Lena Paducheva and Aleksey Shmelev in Russia, and Igor Mel'čuk in Canada.

Apart from linguists, I have derived a great deal of encouragement from the support of philosophers David Chalmers, James Franklin, Rom Harré and Thomas Mautner; historians David Hackett Fischer and Darren McMahon; anthropologists Roy D'Andrade, Doug Jones, Naomi Quinn and Richard Shweder; theologian Wacław Hryniewicz; psychiatrists Christopher Dowrick and Horacio Fabrega; sociologists Stanisław Obirek and Douglas Porpora; political scientist Richard Collin; literary and translation scholars Adam Potkay and Birgit Stolt; and novelist J.M. Coetzee.

I am grateful to my daughter Mary (Besemeres), whose 1998 article on Eva Hoffman's *Lost in Translation* and 2002 book *Translating One's Self* continue to be a source of inspiration for me in thinking about the role of English in self-translation of "language migrants" as well as in the habitual thinking of "native Anglos". I was fortunate to be able to talk to Mary about these themes throughout the writing of *Imprisoned in English*.

I have been sustained, as well as challenged, by the semantic workshops held twice yearly at the Australian National University and organised by Cliff Goddard and myself (and recently, also by Zhengdao Ye), and also, by discussions with several cohorts of students in my Seminar on Semantics at the ANU. The search for semantic understanding in dialogue with colleagues and students is a joy, and both these workshops and these seminars are times of very intensive and fruitful engagement with others. My heartfelt thanks to all the participants.

It has often been said (following Humboldt) that to learn to think outside the mold of one's native language one needs to move into another language. Up to a point, this is true, and this is why perspectives on the world arising from bilingual experience are invaluable. But there is also another path: not **out** of one's language and into another one, but **down**, deep down, to that core of simple words and concepts where all languages meet. As this book illustrates, relying on that shared human store of simple concepts (what Leibniz called the "alphabet of human thoughts") one can articulate complex thoughts precisely and clearly. But thinking and talking about any subject in very simple words is not easy for an adult, and perhaps especially for an academic. I've had great opportunities to practice this difficult art in talking about the world with my grandchildren, Elizabeth, Nicholas, Catherine and Therese. (Lizzie, the eldest, has also acted on many occasions as my special consultant and sounding-board.) This book is dedicated to them, with love.

My husband John has helped me, as usual, by editing my writing and at times softening my polemical tone, which after forty years of living in Australia still tends to follow Polish rather than mainstream Anglo cultural scripts of self-expression and engagement with others. "Intellectual emotions", Peter Goldie says, are good. But as the pejorative meaning of the English word "heated" testifies, a "heated" tone is usually seen as being out of place in post-Enlightenment Anglo intellectual discussions, and a tone of calm, understated, impersonal rationality is still generally required, even in these times of growing internationalisation and "inter-culturalisation" of scholarship. (Relatedly, if I were writing in Polish, I could say that I thank all those mentioned in these Acknowledgements "gorąco", that is, 'hotly', but in English, I can only thank them "warmly".)

Two people who deserve very special thanks are my two priceless Research Assistants, Helen Bromhead (in a different hat) and Kathleen Jepson. Helen assisted me throughout the work on the book, prepared the final version of the manuscript for publication, and produced the index, whereas Katie worked with me through the copy-edited manuscript and through the proofs. I am in awe of their computer skills, their competence and their professionalism.

Last but not least, I'm grateful to my editors at Oxford University Press, Peter Ohlin and Hallie Stebbins for their support, advice and guidance, and to my production manager, Peter Mavrikis, for his efficiency, patience and understanding. Thank you all very much.

Imprisoned in English

PART ONE

Every Language Draws a Circle...

1

Recognizing the Contingency of One's Own Language

"We don't see things as they are—we see them as we are" (Anaïs Nin). This is true not only of individuals, but also of human groups, especially groups defined by people's native language. As individuals, we often see things differently because we are different persons, with different interests, preoccupations, and assumptions. As speakers of different languages we see them differently because every language equips its speakers with a particular set of cognitive tools for seeing and interpreting the world. This applies both to the literally visible world of colors and light, and the "invisible" world of emotions, relationships, social structures, and mental life.

In his book *The Island of the Colorblind*, Oliver Sacks writes revealingly about the ways of seeing the world characteristic of the color-blind people on the Micronesian atoll Pingelap, where the prevalence of color blindness is exceptionally high. As Sacks says, the vegetation on the island, which for him and his "colour-normal" companions "was at first a confusion of greens," to the color-blind people on the island "was a polyphony of brightnesses, shapes, and textures, easily identified and distinguished from each other" (1996: 37). When asked how they can distinguish, for example, the yellow bananas from the green ones, the achromatopic islander James replied: "[Y]ou see, we don't just go by colour. We look, we feel, we smell, we know—we take everything into consideration, and you just take colour!" (ibid.)

Speakers of languages that have no color words as such, and have instead a rich visual vocabulary focusing on brightness and visual patterns (such as the Warlpiri people in Central Australia, cf. Hargrave 1982; Laughren et al. 2006; Munn 1973; Wierzbicka 2008a) are not color-blind, but they, too, "take everything into account," not just color—not because their physical perception is different but because, for cultural reasons (including their way of life), their interest in the visual world is different.

As the condition of achromatopsia shows, there is indeed a neuro-physiological basis to color perception. But perception is not the same thing as *attention*—and Oliver Sacks, for one, carefully distinguishes between "forms of perception" and "forms of attention" (see, e.g., 1996: 12). In different societies, the predominant "forms of attention" may be different, depending on people's way of life, economy, technology, and culture; this is what linguistic evidence from diverse languages tells us.

Like any other language, English, too, has its own in-built culture-specific "forms of attention"—and native speakers of English are often blind to them because of their very familiarity. Often, this blindness to what is exceedingly familiar applies also to Anglophone scholars and leads to various forms of Anglocentrism in English-based human sciences, not only in description but also in theory formation.

In an arresting passage of his *Philosophical Investigations*, Ludwig Wittgenstein wrote:

> The aspects of things that are most important for us are hidden because of their simplicity and familiarity. (One is unable to notice something—because it is always before one's eyes.) The real foundations of his enquiry do not strike a man at all. Unless that fact has at some time struck him.—And this means: we fail to be struck by what, once seen, is most striking and most powerful. (1953: 50)

I quoted this passage in one of my earlier attempts to challenge what is one of the most influential theories in human sciences in recent times, Berlin and Kay's theory of "colour universals" (cf. Wierzbicka 2008a). My purpose was, of course, to draw attention to the way our native languages can blind us to the world as it presents itself to other people.

> This applies, above all, to our native language: often, we are unable to notice the spectacles that we are always wearing. To many scholars working through English, English words on which they rely most (e.g., *reality, fact, evidence, mind, emotions, anger, self-esteem, fairness, reasonable, rights, privacy,* and so on) are simply invisible—as invisible as a pair of glasses that one never takes off. Often, such words constitute the real foundations of their inquiry—never examined and never noticed. The same applies to the word *colour.* (Wierzbicka 2005: 217)

Since I wrote this, the glow of the "B&K colour theory" has dimmed considerably (though it still has many adherents); but the blinding power of English as the global language of science and the unquestioned tool for interpreting the world has only grown.

The goal of this book is to try to convince speakers of English, including Anglophone scholars in the humanities and social sciences, that while English is a language of global significance, it is not a neutral instrument or one that, unlike other languages, carves nature at its joints; and that if this is not recognized, English can at times become a conceptual prison.

Anthropologist Ward Goodenough, in his 1970 book *Description and Comparison in Cultural Anthropology,* wrote, with special reference to kinship and family:

> The use of one's own culture as a negative standard lies behind the entire set of evolutionary sequences formulated by nineteenth-century theorists. If we begin with ourselves as representing the most advanced state of human society and culture, then other societies can be readily conceived as falling on a continuum according to how similar in form to our family their nearest functionally equivalent institution appears to us. (p. 5)

Of course no one speaks anymore of "ourselves as the most advanced state of human society and culture." Yet the practice of implicitly treating the English language as a standard in relation to which all other languages and cultures can be analyzed and interpreted is still very widespread.

Speaking of a woman's progress through three marriages and three languages, the British writer Zadie Smith describes language, concisely and aptly, as "shared words that fit the world as you believe it to be" (2009: 5). Let me try to illustrate Smith's insight and the intimate relation between selective "forms of attention" and language-specific word meanings with a handful of examples from linguist Ken Hale's (1974) elementary dictionary of the (already mentioned) Australian language Warlpiri prepared for practical purposes (for use in the Yuendumu Warlpiri language program). I'll cite these examples under three headings: 1. Environment, 2. Animals, 3. Human relations and emotions.

1. Environment

> *jarrarlpa*—"natural shelter, overhang"
> *japi*—"entrance to sugar ant's nest"
> *laja*—"hole or burrow of lizard"

From a Warlpiri speaker's point of view, words like these identify no doubt important features of the environment (potential sources of shelter and food), but there are no corresponding words in European languages (and, of course, in many other languages in other parts of the world).

2. Animals

> *kuyu*—"meat; meated animal" [including edible birds, but not other birds]
> *jinjirla*—"tail of rabbit bandicoot"
> *karnpi*—"fat under the skin of emu"

> *tarlti*—"contents of animal's stomach"
> *yulu*—"limp, relaxed—of slain kangaroo whose hindleg joints have been
> broken (in preparation for cooking)"
> *papapapa-ma*—"to make the sound of a male emu calling to its chicks"

Clearly, all these words reflect culture-specific forms of attention, often focused
on animals as potential sources of food.

3. Human Relations and Emotions

> *kurrurupa*—"bereaved sibling"
> *papardipuka*—"bereaved elder brother"

Attention to bereavement and emotions related to bereavement is a salient
characteristic of Australian Aboriginal cultures, as is also attention to the
order of birth among the children of the same parents.

As these examples illustrate, the words of a language reflect the speakers' special interests. For the speakers of a particular language, their words "fit the
world" as they see it—but how they see it depends, to some extent, on what
they want to see and what they pay attention to. This is true also of European
languages, and English is no exception, either.

   The conviction that the words of our native language fit the world as it
really is, is deeply rooted in the thinking of many people, particularly those who
have never been forced to move, existentially, from one language into another
and to leave the certainties of their home language.

   In her splendid language memoir *Lost in Translation: A Life in a New
Language*, Eva Hoffman (1989: 106) tells the story of how she became aware
of "the relativity of meaning" and the contingency of her own language upon
her family's emigration from Poland to America. In a key passage focusing
on the word *river*, Hoffman invokes Ferdinand de Saussure's doctrine of the
arbitrariness of linguistic signs, and his conception of a word as a union of
two elements: "the signifier" and "the signified," that is, the word and what this
word stands for.

> mostly, the problem is that the signifier has become severed from the sig-
> nified. The words I learn now don't stand for things in the same unques-
> tioned way they did in my native tongue. "River" in Polish was a vital
> sound, energized with the essences of riverhood, of my rivers, of being
> immersed in rivers. "River" in English is cold—a word without an aura.
> It has no accumulated associations for me, and it does not give off the
> radiating haze of connotation. It does not evoke.

As the passage just quoted reveals, reflecting on her own experiences, Hoffman was able to look at the relationship between words and their meanings in two different ways at once. As a newcomer to English, she felt keenly that the link between English words and their meanings was "arbitrary": for example, there was no necessary link here between the sound "river" and what it stood for. As an "exile from Polish," however, she realized that for her, the link between Polish words and their meanings was **not** arbitrary; for example, the link between the Polish sound "rzeka" and what it stood for was to her (as she now realized) natural and not at all arbitrary.

As Mary Besemeres (2002: 107) points out, Hoffman's bilingual testimony throws a new light on what Emile Benveniste (1971: 46) says about words being arbitrary from a linguistic perspective but not arbitrary from the point of view of a native speaker:

> For the speaker there is a complete equivalence between language and reality. The sign overlies and commands reality; even better, it *is* that reality [...]. [T]he point of view of the speaker and of the linguist are so different in this regard that the assertion of the linguist as to the arbitrariness of designation does not refute the contrary feeling of the speaker.

As Hoffman's bilingual testimony illustrates, a "language migrant" (Besemeres 2002: 10) can, exceptionally, become aware of both perspectives at once. Benveniste's observation on the "complete equivalence" between language and reality in the mind of the native speaker helps explain why some Anglophone scholars who have not had an experience and illumination similar to Hoffman's may believe in the existence of a perfect fit between English and reality. No doubt the scientific glow and prestige of English contributes to this belief, blinding some speakers to its contingency and threatening to turn it at times from a secure conceptual home into a high-security conceptual prison.

Perhaps no area illustrates this danger better than that of colors, given how much has been written about color categories in different languages and how persistent the conviction is that English color categories fit the world best. Before returning to "rivers," therefore, let me make a digression about some color terms.

English (like most European languages) has two different words for "blue" and "green," whereas many other languages of the world treat these two areas as two shades of the same color and name them with the same word. On the other hand, English has only one word—*blue*—for a range of colors that both Russian and Polish divide into two, each in a different way (*goluboj* and *sinij* in Russian, *niebieski* and *granatowy* in Polish). Similarly, English (like other European languages) has two different words for "red" and "orange," whereas many other languages of the world have one. On the other hand, English has only one word—*red*—for an area that Hungarian divides into two (*piros* and *vörös*). From a language-independent perspective, the division of color space embedded in the English lexicon is just as arbitrary as that embedded in Russian, Polish, and Hungarian. Yet from a native speaker's point of view, these divisions are not arbitrary but simply fit the world.

Linguist Paul Kay, for one, speaks of the colors singled out by English vocabulary as "phenomenologically basic" and suggests that to adequately portray the meaning of color words in other languages that don't fit the English palette (such as the Polish word *niebieski,* the Russian word *goluboj,* or the Hungarian word *piros,* which is lighter than *red* but darker than *pink*), one should describe them in relation to the closest English color words:

> all the analyst needs to do is to take the phenomenally basic colours: black, white, red, yellow, green and blue as primitives and to define other color words such as words for pink and light blue (Russian *goluboj,* Polish *niebieski*) or light red (but darker than pink = Hungarian *piros*) in terms of these. (Kay 2004: 242)

What is particularly instructive about this passage is that the English color words are described here as "phenomenally basic" and are given in Roman type, whereas the Polish, Russian, and Hungarian color words are presented in italics. The implication is that in the case of Polish, Russian, and Hungarian, we are dealing with mere words, whereas in the case of English, no italics are needed, because we are dealing with reality itself. This being so, it is only logical that foreign words which don't match "phenomenally basic" English words should be defined in terms of the latter.

Kay elaborates on these claims by affirming that there is no reason why words like *piros, niebieski,* and *goluboj* "cannot simply mean 'red' (...) and 'blue' at the perceptual and conceptual level." (p. 243)

Commenting on Kay's suggestion in my 2005 article "There are no 'color universals'—But there are universals of visual semantics," I wrote,

> The suggestion that both Russian *goluboj* and Polish *niebieski* should be described in terms of English words *light* and *blue* misses the point (discussed in detail in Wierzbicka [1996]) that the range of use of the Polish word *niebieski* is different from that of the Russian word *goluboj* or that of the English expression *light blue*. Unlike *goluboj* (or *pink*), *niebieski* is not a light color, and it is commonly used in combination with modifiers like 'light,' 'dark' or 'bright': *jasnoniebieski* 'light-niebieski,' *ciemnoniebieski* 'dark-niebieski,' *jaskrawo niebieski* 'bright niebieski.'

Quite apart from its Anglocentrism, Kay's proposal simply does not work: it cannot explain both the similarities and the differences between *blue* and *niebieski*. Nor can it explain the relation between *niebieski* and the two Russian "blue" words, *goluboj* and *sinij,* both as basic to Russians as *blue* is to the speakers of English. (Wierzbicka 2005: 224)

I will come back to the polemic with Paul Kay and his associates later, in the context of a discussion of the (alleged) universality of the concept of "color." But for the moment, let me return to "river," which is an excellent example of that relativity of meanings which Eva Hoffman discovered upon her immigration into the world of English.

In her recent study of the Australian key landscape term *bush*, Helen Bromhead (2011b: 446) writes: "languages and cultures differ as to how they categorize the landscape (...) Individual landscape terms in various languages often have different meanings." Having first illustrated this point with a reference to the French words *fleuve* and *rivière*, she goes on:

> A further example is the term *karu* taken from the Australian Aboriginal language Pitjantjatjara/Yankunytjatjara. The term *karu* refers to mostly dry depressions in the ground which sometimes contain water (Bromhead 2011: 66–68). The meaning of *karu* does not exactly match up with the English words, *river* and *creek*, although these words are often used as glosses (...). Terms for potential sources of water, such as *karu*, in some Australian Aboriginal languages reflect cultures in which water is a scarce resource. Moreover, words of this kind are related to water gathering practices, such as digging in the earth to uncover ground water.

Bromhead is developing here (and also in her larger study, Bromhead 2013) a theme on which the Australian writer of Aboriginal (Noongar) descent, Kim Scott (2007) reflected in his essay "Strangers at home" in *Translating Lives* (Besemeres & Wierzbicka 2007). Scott begins his remarks on this theme by quoting, appreciatively, Australian historian Jay Arthur's (1999) observation that Australians are trapped in the language of the "Default Country" (England).

> Our language is set to the Default Country. The Default Country... is narrow, green, hilly and wet, which makes Australia wide, brown, flat and dry. In the Default Country, the rivers run all the year round... They know how to find the sea.

Scott continues:

> The word 'drought' in a country where rainfall is naturally irregular, says Arthur, encourages disappointment, the sense of being cheated by a hostile land. The word 'river' only approximates what Australians know by that word. Think of the Todd River in Alice Springs for example, or the south coast of Western Australia, where the word 'river' often describes a tenuously linked sequence of ponds barred by sandy dunes from the sea.
>
> Perhaps the English language—yes, even "Australian English"—carries ways of thinking that correspond awkwardly with the country we inhabit. (Scott 2007: 10)

The example of *drought* is particularly interesting given the huge role that this word plays in Australian public discourse, and, in rural areas, in domestic and community talk as well. Yet there is no word meaning "drought" in Australian Aboriginal languages, that is, languages of people who inhabited the continent for thousands of years before British settlement.

Drought means, roughly speaking, that for a very long time there is no rain in some places, that because of this, the ground in these places is very dry for a long time, that things of many kinds can't grow in these places because of that, and that this is very bad for people who live in these places. Clearly, there was no need for such a concept in Australian languages before farming came to this continent. And the farming came here, of course, together with the English language, which, naturally, was for a long time the "Default Language" for the British settlers, and in which—according to Jay Arthur and Kim Scott—Australians are in some ways still trapped.

Continuing with this line of thought, we might ask if the dominant conceptual framework of the humanities and social sciences is not "trapped" in the language of the "Default Country" (England) and the "Default Culture" (Anglo culture). Clearly, the English language carries with it ways of thinking that correspond awkwardly not only with the geography of Australia, but also with the conceptual landscape of the speakers of Australian languages, and indeed, of speakers of most other languages of the world.

Of course, if a language other than English were to be treated as the default language of the humanities and the standard for interpreting other languages and cultures, this would also lead to conceptual distortions. But the fact is that in this day and age it is English, rather than any other language, that is being treated as such a standard.

There are dangers inherent in this, especially if this status of English as the default language of analysis and interpretation is not recognized and if alternative methods of analysis and interpretation are not deployed that would allow English itself to be looked at from a non-English and non-Anglo perspective.

Concluding my chapter in the recent volume *Language and Bilingual Cognition* (Wierzbicka 2010a: 215), I wrote:

> The philosopher van Brakel (2004, p. 21) remarks ironically that the assumption that English is hardwired is pervasive. The good news arising from cross-linguistic semantic investigations is that *part* of English is indeed hardwired—that part which matches the shared core of all other languages; and this good news is compatible both with the well-documented possibility of successful intercultural communication and with bilingual experience. It is on this part of English that a transnational and transcultural science of human cognition can build.

Here, I would go further: not only the science of human cognition, but human sciences in general, need a reliable metalanguage. They can't always find it in the "maxi-English" which carries with it a hidden baggage of history and culture; they can, however, find it in a mini-English, built on that inner core of all languages.[1] I will explain this idea in more detail shortly. First, however, I want to consider some further examples, in order to explain why I think that the "maxi-English" widely used in human sciences as the default language can really be a conceptual prison.

2

Naming the World or Construing the World?

In her study of ethnographical categories embedded in different languages, Helen Bromhead (2013) writes:

> What could be more real than a mountain? To the philosopher John R. Searle, a mountain is the ultimate example of a "brute fact"—a concept which does not depend on human observation. A mountain, or, for example, a star, or a molecule, as a "brute fact" differs from an "institutional fact," which is based on human perception and organization, such as money, or citizenship, or a bathtub. (Searle 1995: 1–4)

Bromhead questions Searle's view of "mountain" as an ultimate example of a brute fact. "What if we look at the concept of 'mountain' from a cross-linguistic point of view?," she asks.

> For example, Mt Woodroffe (Ngarutjaranya) in South Australia is called a *mountain* by English speakers, while Pitjantjatjara speakers call it a *puli*. By contrast, the Australian landmark Uluru (Ayres Rock) is also called *puli* by Pitjantjatjara speakers, although English speakers call it a *rock* or a *monolith*, but not a *mountain*.

Bromhead's conclusion—that "languages and cultures differ as to how they categorize the landscape"—is in keeping with a long line of European and American thought, from Herder and Humboldt to Sapir and Whorf, and from Sapir and Whorf to Conklin, Geertz, Hoffman, and others.

But as Searle's notion of "mountain" as a "brute fact" illustrates, the philosophical implications of cross-linguistic variations in how "nature" is conceptually carved up in different languages are still far from being widely appreciated. What is at issue here is not whether the existence of mountains or rivers is a fact, but rather whether it is a "brute fact" or a fact mediated by the English language. Eighty odd years ago, Sapir wrote: "To a greater extent than the philosopher realizes (…), the mould of his thought, which is typically a linguistic mould, is apt to be projected into his conception of the world" (Sapir 1949[1924]: 157). He warned: "The philosopher needs to understand language if only to protect himself against his own language habits" (1949 [1929]: 165).

It seems, however, that few philosophers in the English-speaking world have paid much attention to Sapir's caution. Many did come to question "language," of course, but more often than not, their distrust was directed at "language" in general rather than at particular languages, and certainly not at English. To many Anglophone scholars, including philosophers, "rivers" and "mountains" still seem to be "brute facts," whatever they might think about *fleuve*-s and *rivière*-s, not to mention out-of-the-way words like *puli.*

Sapir's way of speaking (in particular, his use of "he" in a generic sense) sounds dated today, but the key point that he was making is not dated at all. On the contrary, in view of the ascendency of English in the present-day world, many scholars' (including philosophers') tendency to project English categories and meanings onto the world as they conceptualize it has become, it seems, even stronger.

In fact, when one rereads the warnings of Sapir and Whorf against ignoring or underestimating language, one is struck by the absence of any references to English as a particular problem for philosophy and human science. One is also struck by the fact that when Sapir does refer to English as a language whose speech-forms may "dupe" the philosopher, he mentions it along with Latin and German (1949 [1924]: 157).

But the very fact that eighty or ninety years ago not only English but also Latin and German could have duped many philosophers (and other scholars), whereas today English has achieved a unique and seemingly unassailable position as the language of global science and academic discourse, makes the danger to which Sapir and Whorf tried to draw the world's attention even greater than it was then. Whorf (1956 [1941]: 244) wrote: "Western culture has made, through language, a provisional analysis of reality and, without correctives, holds resolutely to that analysis as final." Since then, science has of course made many correctives to that provisional analysis of reality, and the linguistic investigations of "all those other tongues, which by aeons of independent evolution have arrived at different, but equally logical, provisional analyses" (ibid.) have contributed to these correctives. Nonetheless, some aspects of the provisional analysis of reality made through European languages and especially through English are still widely taken for granted in the human sciences—particularly if they have also entered scientific English.

Nothing illustrates the stranglehold of English (Benedetti and Cook 2011: 147) better than the scholarly absolutization of the concept of "color" and associated concepts such as "blue," "purple," and "orange," adamantly defended over the last forty years or so.

The basic fact is that many languages of the world don't have a word for "color," just as they don't have words for "river" or "mountain" (in the English sense of these words). As anthropologist Harold Conklin noted half a century ago: "Color, in a Western technical sense, is not a universal concept and in many languages such as Hanunóo there is no unitary terminological equivalent."

(1964 [1955]: 189). Commenting on this quote, another anthropologist, John Lucy (1997: 332), asks: "Without such a term, how can we attribute 'color' as a concept to a language?" Lucy also notes, very pertinently, that Conklin "was forced to ask questions such as 'How is it to look at?' and then when his informants responded he asked them to stop providing the sort of terms he did not want, such as shape terms."

Linguist Ken Hale (1959) made a similar point in relation to the Australian language Warlpiri, noting that one cannot ask in Warlpiri, "what color is it?" and that one would normally render it as "Nyiyapiya nyampuju?"—that is, literally, "what is it like?" Thus, for the Warlpiri people, the question "what color is it?" simply does not (did not) arise. Hale (1959: 455) cited in this connection a very interesting definition of the rainbow offered by the Warlpiri consultant:

> We call rainbow that which stands high, *yukuriyukuri* [lit. grass-grass]; then across underneath it' *yalyuyalyu* [lit. blood-blood].

In my own study of Warlpiri visual semantics based on the Warlpiri Dictionary database (Laughren et al. 2006)—in which I analyze the rich Warlpiri visual discourse (Wierzbicka 2008a; see also Hargrave 1982; Munn 1973)—I concluded, as Conklin did for Hanunóo, that in the past (including recent past), Warlpiri speakers did not have a concept of "color" in the English sense of the word. As I argued, the concept was imported into Warlpiri together with the word *kala,* in the context of an influx of shirts, cars, and other kinds of objects that differed from one another in color alone, unlike most things in the traditional Warlpiri environment. In response, Kay and his coauthor Rolf Kuehni (henceforth K&K) accused me of using the word *concept* in an "idiosyncratic" and even "incoherent" way. They wrote:

> If Warlpiri speakers see colours, are sensitive to differences in colours, (apparently) name what we call colours, and yet lack any concept of colour, then the term *concept* is being used in an unusual way. Of course, AW has every right to use terms however she wishes, but the reader inclined to accept AW's argument that lack of a word for 'colour' entails that apparent colour terms are not really colour terms should be aware that the argument depends on an idiosyncratic version of the notion of having a concept. (K&K 2008: 887).

In fact, I was using the term "concept" in exactly the same sense as Conklin (and, I think, Lucy). The real question, however, is not how to use the word *concept* but whether or not Warlpiri speakers think (thought) about the world in terms of "color," and whether or not they ever asked about anything, "what color is it?" It is also a real question what the words *yukuriyukuri* ("grass-grass") and *yalyayalyu* ("blood-blood") mean for them: "green in color" and "red in color," or rather something like "looking like grass" and "looking like blood," as I argued in my article. (See also Wierzbicka, In press b.)

The quote from K&K about the alleged Warlpiri "color concept" is instructive, because it clearly shows their reasoning. The same reasoning could be applied to the French counterparts of *river*:

– Do French people see rivers?—They do.
– Are they sensitive to differences in rivers?—They are.
– Do they (apparently) name what we call rivers?—They do (sometimes as *fleuve,* sometimes as *rivière.*)
– Do French people have a concept of "river"?—They do.

And do English speakers who don't know French have the concept of "fleuve"? Do they have the concept of "bily"—*bily* being the Noongar "word for river," a word that, as Kim Scott (2007: 10) says, "often describes a tenuously linked sequence of ponds barred by sandy dunes from reaching the sea"?

The advocates of the Berlin & Kay paradigm of color studies do not ask such questions about English speakers because they usually do not look beyond English terms. For them, "color" is a brute fact, not a conceptual category encoded in some languages (such as English) but not in others. In my response to Kay & Kuehni's charge of "idiosyncrasy" and "incoherence," I quoted the philosopher Charles Taylor's remark that "The human agent exists in a space of questions" (1989: 29) and commented that some of these questions are universal and some are language- and culture-bound. I also noted that, as evidence suggests, in all languages people can ask questions like "what do you see?" or "what is it like?," because all languages have words meaning "see" and "like," but that in many languages, including Warlpiri, people can't ask: "what color is it?," because they don't have a word for "color," and evidently, are (were) not interested in abstracting "color" from the overall appearance of things in their environment. I also made a broader observation that I will adduce here in full:

K&K's assumption that Warlpiri-speakers can have the concept of 'colour' (even though they have no word for 'colour') is part of a larger phenomenon: the tendency of [many] Anglophone scholars to assume that concepts named in English and fundamental to their own thinking must also be present in the thinking of the speakers of other languages. They simply cannot imagine that it could be otherwise. The reification and absolutization of English concepts is widespread in the literature in English on emotions, values, human cognition, 'personality traits,' and so on (Wierzbicka 2006a; in press [now 2009a, A.W.]).

Thoughts are not directly observable and neither are concepts. We know how people think by observing how they speak. English words such as *fairness, commonsense, democracy, teenager, measure,* and *colour* constitute evidence for the presence of the corresponding concepts in the shared conceptual universe of speakers of English. There are no such words in Warlpiri, and thus there is no evidence of the presence of such concepts in Warlpiri culture. (Wierzbicka 2008b: 887–888)

That exchange between Kay and Kuehni and myself took place in 2008. Since then, the advocates of "basic color terms" (Berlin and Kay 1969) and "color naming universals" (Kay & Regier 2007; Regier et al 2010) have changed their position somewhat and, for example, Regier & Kay (2010: 178) don't talk anymore of "universalist findings," but rather, of "an ultimately universalist finding, but with a relativist twist." Nonetheless, these authors still speak of "universalist tendencies of color naming" (p. 165) and continue to frame their research in terms of "color naming," not in terms of how speakers of different languages actually talk about what they see and about what things that they see look like (the universal discourse of seeing). As I noted in my response to K&K (2008):

> From the outset, the emphasis of the Berlin and Kay approach was on 'naming' and on neurophysiological constraints on 'naming.' 'Naming' implies that there are things 'out there' ready to be named, and the phrase 'neurophysiological constraints' refers to the human body. What was missing from that approach was the level of construal: how speakers of different languages construe (habitually think about) the physical world that presents itself to their eyes and their brains. Yet it is that middle level, that cognitive bridge between the human body and the 'reality' outside the human body, which should be the central concern of cognitive anthropology and anthropological linguistics. To study this middle level (the level of construal), anthropology needs a metalanguage. English (full-blown English) cannot be that metalanguage, because like any other natural language it embodies its own, culture-specific construals. (Wierzbicka 2008b: 888–889)

This is, then, what I saw at that time, and see now, as the key point: English—"maxi-English," with all its "rivers" and "streams," "mountains" and "hills," "colors" and "hues," with its "fairness," "privacy," "frustration," "sense of right and wrong," and all the rest of its vast culture-specific conceptual inventory—cannot be a neutral language for the human sciences. As I will try to show throughout this book, a neutral framework for comparing meanings across cultures cannot be found in external standards described in complex and culture-specific English. It can, however, be found in a mini-English—an English trimmed to the bone and matching the universal "bone structure" (the scaffolding) underlying all the diverse cultural embodiments of the human mind.

A neutral framework for describing languages and cultures is an old anthropological and linguistic dream, often dismissed as a utopia, but nonetheless reappearing from time to time with a new force. In the past, the call for a neutral framework was sometimes explicitly linked with recognition of a need for a neutral set of terms. For example, in his 1970 book *Description and Comparison in Cultural Anthropology,* Ward Goodenough wrote:

> we have to find some set of terms that will enable us to describe other cultures with minimal distortion from ethnocentric cultural bias. And we need

some set of universally applicable concepts that will enable us to compare cultures and arrive at valid generalizations about them. (p. 2)

Other scholars, however, either despairing of ever finding such a neutral set of terms or hoping that some simpler and easier solution might be discovered, have sought for methodologies grounded directly in the external reality rather than in any set of independently justified terms.

A classic example of such a methodology, which tries to bypass language to find a neutral framework in the external reality alone, is the use of the commercially produced Munsell color samples as a basis for cross-linguistic semantics of "color." The chips are shown to informants (the now accepted term "consultants" seems particularly out of place in this kind of mechanical exercise), who are asked to label the items in the array. As anthropologist John Lucy (1997: 323) observed, since the chips vary in hue, saturation, and brightness but exclude other possible aspects of what people can see, "the stimulus array dictated in advance the possible meanings the terms could have since no other meanings were embodied in the sample." As also pointed out by Lucy, "The procedure strictly limits each speaker by rigidly defining what will be labelled, which labels will count, and how they will be interpreted." (p. 344)

The Munsell-based methodology is easy to apply, requires no careful semantic analysis, and, without any difficulties, produces the desired results. Not surprisingly, many critics have suggested that these factors were in fact the main reasons for its enthusiastic acceptance by scores, if not hundreds, of linguistic and anthropological field workers. There can be no doubt, however, that a healthy desire for a neutral framework has also played a large role, as Jane Simpson's (2006) article on the Australian language Warlpiri entitled "How do we know what they see?" clearly illustrates:

> Showing a large number of speakers a large number of Munsell colour chips and asking them how to describe them is a way of reducing the level of bias created by attempts to elicit or understand word meanings through gathering texts and translations of those texts. The stimulus is as close to independence from language as one can get.

As I argued in my (2008a) article on Warlpiri visual semantics, however, the stimulus is not independent from language but has English meanings embedded in it.

> By its very structure it introduces the tacit assumption—alien to Warlpiri-speakers—that 'colour' is a conceptual domain separate from others, and the reliance on this culturally alien preconception blinds researchers to bona fide indigenous meanings, ... Furthermore, the behaviourist reliance on 'stimuli' and 'response to stimuli' (describable in English but not in Warlpiri) precludes treating Warlpiri-speakers as conversational partners capable of understanding the meaning of their own words, and

reduces them to silent objects of the investigations carried out, in English, by Anglo investigators. (Wierzbicka 2008a: 420)

The popularity of Munsell color chips, and of the theory of "colour-naming universals" that goes with it, is now increasingly a thing of the past (although the theory still occupies a large place in undergraduate textbooks, encyclopedias, and handbooks). But the hope of finding a neutral framework in some external stimuli independent of language never dies, and as I will discuss in Chapter 5, is currently strongly represented by the Nijmegen School of linguistics and anthropology.

3

The Givens of Human Life

In his widely read book *The Saturated Self,* social psychologist Kenneth Gergen (1991: 8) writes: "If there is one message writ large within the annals of anthropology, it is to beware the solid truths of one's own culture. If we contrast our views with those of others, we find that what we take to be 'reliably known' is more properly considered a form of folklore."

Like Mary Besemeres (2002: 24), from whom I am borrowing this quote, I would like to distance myself to some extent from Gergen's somewhat extreme position. In particular, I would like to qualify his statement that "what we take to be 'reliable knowledge' is more properly considered a form of folklore" with the word "often." Surely there are some things that we do know reliably: for example, that all people die. Very frequently, however, it is indeed the case that what we take as a given is a form of "folklore"—often "folklore" grounded in the vocabulary of modern English.

Gergen gives an excellent example of this when he writes about emotions (p. 9–10).

> Consider the emotions, for example. In Western culture our emotional expressions can usually be sorted into less than a dozen broad categories. We can legitimately say, for example, that we feel anger, disgust, fear, joy, love, sadness, shame, or surprise (or we can use various alternative terms, such as saying "depressed" instead of "sad"). Further, we treat these emotional terms as representing biological givens. Thus we say that people inherit the capacities for these emotional feelings, and that we can literally "see" the expressions of these emotions in people's faces. Any adult who did not have the capacity to feel sadness, fear, or love, for example, would be considered psychopathic or autistic.
>
> Yet when we look at other cultures, we become painfully aware of just how parochial these "biological givens" are.

I will come back to the example of emotions and the "parochial" character of labels like "anger," "disgust," and "sadness" in Chapter 7. Here, I would like to take up Gergen's more general point concerning "biological givens" and ask some questions about the concept "sex"—first, in the sense of the distinction between "males" and "females," and then, in the sense of "sexual intercourse." **19**

Is it then a given of human life that people can be male or female? In English-speaking countries, all kinds of documents (birth certificates, passports, visa application forms, and so on) assume that this is indeed the case, but in many other countries there is no such assumption, because many other languages don't have words corresponding to *male* and *female*. For example, in Russian, similar documents ask about a person's "pol" (roughly, sex) and offer the options "m" and "ž," for "mužskoj" and "ženskoj"—not quite the same as "male" and "female."

The difference is that the two Russian words apply only to humans and don't bring under a common conceptual denominator the difference between men and women and cows and bulls or geese and ganders. The adjectives *mužskoj* and *ženskoj* are derived from *mužčina* (man) and *ženščina* (woman), but they apply also to boys and girls. They imply that there are two kinds of (grown-up) people, men and women, and that these two kinds are seen as two basic human prototypes. They do not imply, however, that people can be divided into two kinds in the same sense in which domestic (and other) animals can be divided into two kinds ("male" and "female").

The fact that the English words *male* and *female* are demonstrably language-specific is of special significance given that, as discussed in Goddard and Wierzbicka (in press), they play a big role as analytical tools in linguistics and anthropology. When an English speaker is called upon to generalize about what words like *men* and *boys,* or *women* and *girls* have in common, the terms *male* and *female* come to mind almost irresistibly, and their objective, scientific status is never doubted. Nevertheless, in a typological perspective English is the odd language out in having words that can apply broadly across so many different kinds of living creatures as well as people. Comparable concepts in other languages are typically restricted to certain "kinds of animals." For example, the Polish nouns *samiec* (male) and *samica* (female) are typically restricted to (non-human) animals (mostly mammals), and in colloquial language would not be readily applied, for example, to reptiles and insects, and certainly not to people.

I am not saying this in order to suggest that there are no givens of human life, but rather that speakers of different languages tend to think about those "givens" in different ways. Shared words (words with shared meanings) crystallize different ways of thinking, and when ways of thinking change, shared words change, too.

In what follows, I will illustrate the relativity of the "givens of human life" with three words that may all seem to "name" such givens, and that nonetheless sift human experience through particular, language-specific filters. They are *sex, pain,* and *sister.*

Sex in Russian

Is sex a given of human life? "Of course it is, otherwise we would not be here." But if so, then why is it that most languages of the world don't have a word meaning "sex" (as in "talking about sex," or "having sex")?

Russian does have a word meaning "sex" now: *seks*. But, as its form indicates, the word is a loan from English, and a recent one at that. For many speakers, the word *seks* is linked with a famous episode from the pre-perestrojka period, when American talk show host Phil Donahue and Russian journalist Vladimir Posner organized one of the first Soviet-American "tele-bridges." When an American participant in this encounter complained about the use of sex images in American TV ads and asked if the same was the case in the Soviet Union, the Russian respondent, a certain Ivanova (a representative of the "Committee of Soviet Women") replied famously: "U nas seksa net...," "there is no sex in the USSR...", a comment that created a still-popular catchphrase.

According to Posner, the woman meant (and said) "on television," but these last words were drowned out by audience laughter. According to Ivanova herself, she actually said, "In the USSR there is no 'sex,' there is love." Her additional comment on this point is instructive: "Later, people remembered only the beginning of the phrase. (...) But in our country, the word *sex* was really almost a dirty word. We always occupied ourselves not with sex [*seks*] but with love. And this is what I had in mind."

Ivanova's version is confirmed by an opinion survey conducted in 2008 on the subject "The generations of Russian sex [*seks*]" (Žuravleva 2008). Many of the young respondents, who presumably know English to some extent, use the word *seks* in ways comparable to how the word *sex* is used in English. Older respondents, however, offer comments like the following:

> Of course there was no **sex** (*seks*) in the Soviet Union. (...) The process, of course, was there, but there were no words for it, only interjections. Married couples used to say: "Why don't we that, this, y'know what?" (Maria, 78 years old)
>
> It sounds paradoxical, but there was really no **sex** in the Soviet Union. In this country, there was love, and all the rest was just added on. (Valeriy, 63 years old)
>
> At the beginning of the 1980s the air was, it seemed, saturated with **sex**, although the concept as such did not yet exist. (Anna, 45 years old)

Before we consider the differences between the English *sex* and loanwords like the Russian *seks* (as used by the older generation of Russian speakers), however, we need to note that *sex* has several different meanings in modern English and to try to sort them out.

Different Meanings of the English Word "Sex"

Above all, *sex* in phrases like *age, weight and sex*, *regardless of sex*, and *sex discrimination* has a different meaning from *sex* in *sex drive*, *sex life*, and *safe sex*. Thus, broadly speaking, there are two main types of uses of *sex* in contemporary English: *sex* as the difference between two kinds of people based on two main kinds of human bodies, and *sex* as something that people do, or can do, and that is perceived against the background of activities involving two people with two different kinds of bodies (a man and a woman).

To begin with the first use of *sex*, there is the heading "sex" on countless forms that people living in English-speaking countries have to fill out and that offers the respondents the choice between "M" and "F," "male" and "female," and there are many uses of *sex* linked with the distinction between the two categories "male" and "female." The assumption that there are two kinds of people, by virtue of people's anatomy, is reflected in contemporary examples such as the following one from Cobuild:

> Many professional women prefer to deal with members of their own **sex**.

The use of *sex* as, roughly speaking, one of two major categories of people (defined in terms of their anatomy) is closely related to, but not identical with, *sex* as an abstract parameter, distinguishing between those two categories of people. This "parameter" sense of *sex* can be illustrated with the following sentences from Collins Wordbanks:

> Obviously, the intention of banning advertisements which specify age or **sex** is to ensure older people, or women, get a fair go.
> The Stairmaster machine measures your fitness level by testing your ability to walk on the spot for five minutes. By taking into account your age, weight and **sex** it spits out a fitness reading.

The predominantly biological emphasis of the word *sex* used in relation to the features distinguishing two major categories of people has often been perceived as a limitation of this concept as a basic tool for categorizing people and characterizing them—hence the emergence and spread of the word *gender* in modern Anglo usage, especially in feminist discourse, a word that makes room, so to speak, for the psychological and social aspects, in addition to biological ones. But despite the growing use of the word *gender* in some registers of English, especially academic and feminist ones, the word *sex* as a major conceptual tool for categorizing people continues to hold its own.

The predominant contemporary use of *sex*, which focuses on what people *do* with their bodies, is quite recent. The "explosion" of this new use is largely a twentieth-century phenomenon, although phrases like *sex mania* and *sex maniac* started to be used in the late nineteenth century, as the following examples cited by the OED testify:

> **Sex** mania in art and literature can be but a passing phase. (1895)
> **Sex** in modern literature. (1895)

The expression *to have sex* appears to have been popularized, if not introduced, by D. H. Lawrence, in contexts like the following one:

> If you want to have **sex**, you've got to trust, at the core of your heart, the other creature. (1929)

This relatively recent use of *sex* to refer to "what men and women do," rather than to "what kind of people men and women are," developed a large network of collocations during the twentieth century, some of them neutral and lending themselves to positive interpretations (for example, *sex appeal, sex life, sex drive, safe sex,* and *sex education*) and some negative ones (for example, *sex offences, sex offenders, sex slaves, unprotected sex, sex object, underage sex, sex abuse, sex crime,* and so on).

The most prominent contemporary sense of *sex* includes a reference to pleasurable feelings, thus inviting a plethora of phraseological and cultural extensions (from *good sex* to *sex toys* and the like). One of the sentences with *sex* in the Cobuild database reads: " 'Say *cheese,*' photographers used to mutter to get a smile before they switched to 'say *sex,*'" thus highlighting the presence of "good feelings" in the conceptual prototype of *sex.* These potential "good" feelings are evoked not only by the topic (i.e., the thought of the physical activity as such), but more specifically, by the word *sex.*

Despite the reference to "good feelings" in the conceptual prototype implicit in the modern English concept of "sex," what is most striking about this concept from a cross-cultural, cross-linguistic, and also, historical point of view is the largely physical, "behavioristic" characterization of the activity in question, without any reference to human relationships and interpersonal emotional attitudes.

While a reference to seeking pleasure is included in the prototype, it is not accompanied by any allusion to good feelings directed at the other person (not even in the prototype). Of course, phrases (and book titles) like "Love, sex and marriage," which link "sex" with "love," are possible and even common, but by itself *sex* is free of such associations (unlike, for example, the French phrase *faire l'amour*, or indeed its literal English equivalent *to make love*).

In most other languages, for example in Russian or even in French, there is no colloquial equivalent of "they were talking about sex." One could use something euphemistic like *l'amour* ("love"), something vulgar and "in your face" like *baiser*, or something scientific-sounding like *acte sexuel*, but nothing as neutral, matter-of-fact, and colloquial as *sex.* It is this dissociation of physical acts (what people do with some parts of their bodies) from the expectations about the accompanying feelings and attitudes that is the hallmark of the prevalent contemporary use of the English word *sex.*

The lexical dissociation between the body and the emotions, or between physical activities involving the genitals and interpersonal relations, has wide-ranging ramifications in modern English phraseology and discourse.

Expressions such as *good sex, enjoy sex, consensual sex, sex toy, sex games, sex-starved, kinky sex, sex industry, sex workers,* and even *sex education* are translators' nightmares and their untranslatability contributes to the widespread borrowing of the English word *sex* into other languages, and also, to changes in meaning that often accompany such borrowing. The lack of conceptual and cultural equivalents of such phrases in other languages often leads to the perception that "sex" is something specific to Anglo-American culture, something cheap, immoral, and lending itself to commercialization--hence the somewhat pejorative meaning of loanwords such as the Russian *seks* mentioned earlier.

The discourse of *sex* as something separate from human relations and emotions has often been the subject of critical discussions in English itself. For example, Collins Wordbanks includes some critical remarks on a government-sponsored "Safe Sex Guide" promoted by *Cleo* magazine under the motto, "It is not who you have sex with but how safe the sex is that counts." According to the commentator cited in Collins Wordbanks, "The naked truth about the values promoted in this 'Safe Sex Guide' is that sex has nothing to do with relationships, love, other people. (...) If the value of the other person is totally discounted in this most deeply personal human activity, how long can we survive as a human society?"

This is, of course, a commentary that one may or may not agree with. Someone else might take the view that the largely "behaviorist" character of the prevalent modern English meaning of *sex* (with its connotations of potential pleasure rather than interpersonal connectedness) reflects a healthy attitude toward the body, without "hang-ups" of any kind, and that the same applies to publications like the "Safe Sex Guide" promoted by *Cleo*. Whatever view of the modern English "discourse of *sex*" one takes, it needs to be recognized that this discourse—which is now spreading, through English, across the global world—is a new cultural phenomenon, entrenched in, and transmitted through, contemporary English.

Pain in French

Is pain a given of human life? Surely, one might think, if anything is, pain is. But *pain*, too, is an English word, which carries with it a certain way of looking at the phenomenon that it refers to. This way of looking is different from that reflected in the French *douleur* (and its frequently used plural form *douleurs*), and often *douleur* cannot be felicitously translated into English as *pain*, and vice versa.

As I have discussed in detail in my chapter on "Pain" in *Words and Meanings* (Goddard and Wierzbicka In press), in James Grieve's English translation of Marcel Proust's (1982) *À la recherche du temps perdu* most instances of *douleur* have in fact been rendered with words other than *pain*. (For many other such case studies, see Wierzbicka, 2012c and 2012e).

This is consistent with the observation that while at first sight, the French *douleur* may seem identical in meaning to the English *pain*, a closer look reveals that there are significant differences between the two. To begin with, while both *douleur* and *pain* can range over emotional as well as physical experiences, *douleur* evokes emotions far more than *pain* does. One piece of evidence for this difference comes from the opposites of the two words. While *pain* is routinely contrasted in English with *pleasure*, which can be physical,*douleur* is frequently contrasted with *bonheur*, "happiness." For example, in Camus's novel *The Plague*, when one of the protagonists, Rambert, becomes reunited with his wife, he cries, and he doesn't know himself if his tears come from his present *bonheur* or from the preceding and long suppressed *douleur* (Todd 1996: 360). Here are some fuller examples from French websites:

> *Tu enfanteras dans la **douleur**, tu allaiteras dans le **bonheur**.* "You will give birth in *douleur* [pain?], you will nurse your child in happiness."
>
> *Mon accouchement: de la **douleur** au **bonheur** le plus total.* "My experience of giving birth: from *douleur* [pain?] to the most complete happiness."
>
> *Ma vie est tristement belle. Des averses de **bonheur**. Des cyclones de **douleur**.* "My life is sadly beautiful. Showers of happiness. Cyclones of *douleur* [pain?]."
>
> *Le **bonheur** de Jean-Pierre est un affront à la **douleur** qui les habite et dont ils lui attribuent la responsabilité.* "Jean-Pierre's happiness is an insult to their continuing *douleur* [pain?], which they blame him for."
>
> *Sans apprentissage de la **douleur**, le **bonheur** n'est pas solide.* "Without an apprenticeship in *douleur* [pain?], there can be no solid happiness."
>
> *Mon enfant, ma **douleur**, mon **bonheur**.* "My child, my *douleur* [pain?], my happiness."

The French counterpart of *pleasure, plaisir*, is not normally contrasted with *douleur*, just as the English word *pain* is not normally contrasted with *happiness*. These differences between the opposites of *pain* and *douleur* are linked with three other differences between the two words.

First, *douleur* suggests a greater intensity of "bad feeling" than *pain*: one can of course speak in English of *a great pain*, as one can speak in French of *une grande douleur*, and one can speak of a *légère douleur*, as one can speak of *a slight pain*, but English expressions such as *a flickering pain, a pulsating pain*, or *a throbbing pain* could hardly be translated into French with the word *douleur*. The intensity of the prototypical French *douleur* is also reflected in common collocations with "extreme" adjectives, such as *une douleur atroce* ("atrocious"), *une douleur déchirante* ("tearing"), and *une douleur cruelle* ("cruel"). In English, comparable experiences would be more likely to be described with the word *agony* than with the word *pain*.

Second, *pain* is often spoken of as localized, so much so that expressions like *pain in the neck* have acquired a second, figurative meaning; and one can readily speak of *pain* in an infected finger or toe. By contrast, *douleur* is normally not localized. To speak of a localized "pain" in French, one would normally use the word *mal* (which, when used as a noun, can mean "illness" or "evil," and when used as an adverb means "badly"), not the word *douleur*. For example, to ask "Where does it hurt?" or "Where is the pain?" one would say *Où avez-vous mal?* ("where do you have *mal*?")

A third dimension of contrast between *douleur* and *pain* is that, prototypically, *douleur* is extended in time, whereas *pain* can be either prolonged or momentary. This extended nature of *douleur* is particularly salient in the case of the plural form: *les douleurs*, but the singular, too, suggests a certain duration. For example, in the case of an injection, the word *mal* rather than *douleur* would normally be used: *Ça fait mal!* Of course, in English, too, one would be more likely to say *It hurts!* in this situation than to use the word *pain*, but one could also speak, for example, of *the pain of an injection*, whereas *la douleur de la piqûre* is judged by many French speakers as somewhat marginal in French (see Goddard and Wierzbicka, In press; Wierzbicka, 2012f).

I am not suggesting that *douleur*, in contrast to *pain*, has two meanings, one emotional and one physical. On the contrary, I believe that such putative polysemy, posited by many French dictionaries, is untenable, as the following example from Balzac illustrates:

> *Louis Lambert souffrit donc par tous les points ou la douleur a prise sur l'âme et sur la chair.*
> "Louis Lambert suffered through all the points where *douleur* gets a hold on the soul and on the flesh."

Such indistinguishable uses of *douleur* show that in fact there is no polysemy here but that the meaning is unitary, with some components referring to the person, and some to this person's body. In this respect, *douleur* is similar to pain: both are unitary and both have a prototype based on the body. But while in the case of *pain* the main point of reference is an affected part of the body, in the case of *douleur* it is the whole body. A "bad feeling" engulfing the whole body is likely to be seen as "very bad," rather than merely "bad"; and it is more likely to be used as an image of a global "very bad" feeling affecting the whole person (i.e., roughly speaking, an "emotional pain") than a strictly localized "bad feeling" in a particular part of the body. *Pain* (in contrast to *it hurts*) does not need to be always localized, but evidence suggests that the conceptual prototype of *pain* (in contrast to that of *douleur*) is indeed localized.

The "localized" prototype of the English word *pain* is reflected in the official (English-based) definition of the International Association for the Study of Pain, which refers to "actual or potential tissue damage." But the French *douleur* does not bring to mind local "damage" (as in the case of torn tissue).

Thus, even in European languages the conceptualizations of human experience reflected in the English word *pain* do not have to match. A number of dimensions—such as intensity, duration, and localization, and also a focus on the body or on the person as a whole—can differ even between neighboring and genetically and culturally related languages such as English and French.

If pain, then, is a given of human life, so is *douleur,* and yet it is not quite the same "given." In each case, we are dealing with a given of human experience filtered through a language-specific conceptual filter. In particular, the IASP definition of "pain" reflects not simply a universal aspect of human life, but also a way of looking at this aspect through the looking glass of Anglophone psychology and medicine.

Sister in Kayardild

And what about the fact that people can have brothers and sisters? Is this a given of human life or a socio-biological fact seen through the prism of particular languages? Consider, for example, the Australian language Kayardild (of which very few speakers now remain). Like many other Australian languages, Kayardild doesn't have a word for "brother" or "sister" as such but requires its speakers to pay attention to the order in which the children of the same mother and father were born, and also, to the speaker's own gender.

For example, the Kayardild word *wakatha,* glossed in Evans's (1995) "Kayardild-English Dictionary" as "sister," is in fact (as Evans 1985 explains) a word that can only be used by a man to refer to a woman (if this man's mother and father are also this woman's mother and father). Thinking through English, one could say indeed that in a case like this, the woman is the man's sister. But in Kayardild a little boy could not call a little girl with whom he shares his parents, "wakatha," and neither could a woman or a girl call another daughter of the same parents "wakatha." Thus, the language has no word meaning "sister." The kind of abstraction involved in the English word *sister* (where neither age nor speaker's gender matter) reflects a particular perspective on biological and genealogical facts, and not simply a "given of human life." (In a diagram given in Evans's (1995) *Kayardild Grammar*, the word *wakatha* is portrayed as "male ego: EZ (elder sister) and YZ (younger sister).") This is more detailed than the dictionary gloss "sister," but it also involves looking at Kayardild through the prism of the abstract English concept "sister." (In anthropological and linguistic literature on kinship, "Z" is often used for "sister" because "S" is reserved for "son.")

A real-life example could be helpful at this point, so let's take a quick look at the British royal family from English- and Kayardild-speaking points of view. To speakers of English, it may seem incontrovertible that, for example, Princess Margaret was Queen Elizabeth's sister, and that Princess Anne is

Prince Charles's sister, too. To a speaker of Kayardild, however, the two cases are quite different. Anne is Charles's *wakatha* (and as such to be avoided), whereas Margaret was Elizabeth's *duujinda*, and to complicate the matter further, Elizabeth, who was born before Margaret, was not Margaret's *duujinda* but her *yakukathu*. (It might be added that Prince Edward and Prince Andrew are also Prince Charles's *duujinda*, whereas he, who was born before them, is their *thabuju*).

For English readers, these Kayardild distinctions can no doubt be confusing and it could be helpful for them if one said, "simply," that *duujinda* refer to "a younger sibling of the same sex." But Kayardild has no words for either "sibling" or "sex," so this would be an English, not a Kayardild, perspective on their family relationships. Furthermore, the word *yakukathu* could not be explained, along similar lines, as "older sibling, same sex," because a man's "older sibling, same sex" could not be called his *yakukathu* (he would be called his *thabuju*). Here, it would be more helpful for the English reader if one said that *yakukathu* refers to "a woman's or a girl's older sister" (and *thabuju*, to "a man's, or a boy's, older brother"). But again, this would be an English, not a Kayardild, perspective, and the very fact that the two words, *duujinda* and *yakukathu*, would require such vastly and improbably different glosses shows that the Kayardild categorization has its own logic, which doesn't depend on the concept of "sister," "brother," and "sibling" but on its own conceptual linchpins, different from English ones.

I will return to the meaning of kinship terms in Australian languages later. What matters here is that what is a "given" for a speaker of English is not a "given" for a speaker of Kayardild. For English speakers, it is a given that people can have brothers and sisters. For speakers of Kayardild, on the other hand, it is a given that people can have "*wakatha*-s," "*duujinda*-s," "*yakukathu*-s," and "*thabuju*-s" (as well as "*kularrinda*-s," a term that I have left out of this discussion for the sake of simplicity).

From a shared, pancultural point of view, the facts of the matter are that Charles and Anne have the same mother and father (Elizabeth and Philip), and also, that Elizabeth and Margaret had the same mother and father (Elizabeth senior and George). The rest is filtered, in each case differently, through language and culture.

The Human Story

Sixty years ago, anthropologist Clyde Kluckhohn (1953: 521) wrote:

> Valid cross-cultural comparison could best proceed from the invariant points of reference supplied by the biological, psycholinguistic and

sociosituational "givens" of human life. These and their interrelations determine the likenesses in the broad categories and general assumptions that pervade all cultures because the "givens" provide foci around which and within which the patterns of every culture crystalize. Hence comparison can escape from the bias of any distinct culture by taking as its frame of references natural limits, conditions, clues, and processes.

Kluckhohn wrote of the "givens of human life" as if assuming that they were directly accessible to the human mind and could be readily described through English. That was sixty years ago. Since then, we have had the "language turn" in human sciences and a massive expansion of knowledge about the diversity of ways of thinking embedded in words of different languages. Yet the assumption that there are psychological and social realities that can be accessed, directly and unproblematically, through English is still widespread in the human sciences, including anthropology, psychology, and linguistics.

I am not denying that *some* such realities can indeed be accessed through English. What I *am* denying is that English, with its global prestige and scientific glow, has a privileged access to the overall picture. If there are some fundamental human givens, then they should be accessible through all languages, not through *some,* and still less, through English alone.

So here is my story of these basic givens. People are born, live for some time, and then die (existential givens). People have bodies, with parts like heads, eyes, and hands (biological givens). People think, feel, and want; in particular, they want to do things, to know things, and to say things (psychological givens). People have mothers and fathers (socio-biological givens). People can do bad things and good things (moral givens).

Unlike other stories that scholars may tell about "the givens of human life," this story does not include words like, for example, "sex," "pain," or "brother" and "sister" (not to mention "cooperation," "a sense of right and wrong," or "emotion terms" like "anger," "grief," "frustration," and "disgust," which will be discussed later), that is, words that English has but many other languages don't. It is a story that can be told in any language, because, as empirical cross-linguistic investigations indicate, all languages have words for "live" and "die," "body" and "hands," "think" and "know," "mother" and "father," and all the other ones included in the sketch given above.

As I see it, then, it is not impossible to identify the main elements of the "human story" from a culture-independent perspective. But like any story, the "human story," too, has to be told with words. If we want to avoid a particular cultural slant in telling it, we need to choose our words carefully. As psychologist Merlin Donald remarked, words define reality for us (2001: 294). It is good to know, therefore, which words have emerged from empirical cross-linguistic studies as winners in the long search for lexical and semantic universals, that is, as words with meanings apparently shared by speakers of all languages. I believe that relying, as far as possible, on these words, we can get closer to the shared "human story" than if we use words that reflect a particular history, culture, and set of assumptions—as most (though not all) words of contemporary English necessarily do.

4

Universal Words, Semantic Atoms, and Semantic Molecules

More often than not, the meanings of words in different languages don't match. John Locke in his *Essay on Human Understanding* (1959[1690]) wrote:

> A moderate skill in different languages will easily satisfy one of the truth of this, it being so obvious to observe great store of words in one language which have not any that answer them in another. (...) Nay, if we look a little more nearly into this matter, and exactly compare different languages, we shall find that, though they have words which in translations and dictionaries are supposed to answer one another, yet there is scarce one of ten amongst the names of complex ideas (...) that stands for the same precise idea which the word does that in dictionaries it is rendered by.... These are too sensible proofs to be doubted.

A century later, Schopenhauer made a similar point, focusing on the need to learn many new concepts in learning a new language.

> [T]he difficulty in learning a language is mainly that of getting to know every concept for which it has a word, even if one's own language has no word which precisely corresponds to it—as is often the case. It follows that one must map out a number of completely new spheres of concepts in one's mind. Thus spheres of concepts arise where there were none before. One therefore does not learn words only: one acquires concepts. (Schopnehauer 1977 [1815] in Lefevere 1977: 98–99)

But if words of different languages don't match in meaning, and stand for different concepts, how can the speaker of one language ever understand the speakers of another? "They can't," it has often been asserted. This assertion, however, runs counter to the widely shared human experience of successful communication between native speakers of different languages. Of course, the experience of miscommunication is also widely shared, but one doesn't cancel out the other.

The testimonies of bilingual people who, like Eva Hoffman, have at some point moved from one language into another have particular weight here. Such testimonies show that, as Locke and Schopenhauer affirmed, many words in one language indeed have no semantic equivalent in the other and that for many others there are only very rough (and misleading) approximations. There are some, however, that do indeed match exactly.

My own bilingual experience as a "language migrant" alerted me early on to the fact that there are some important English words that have no semantic equivalents in Polish at all (for example, *privacy, fairness, frustration, deadline, babysitter,* and *lunch*), and others that have only very rough ones (for example, *blue, kindness, morning,* and *friend*). But reflecting on my experience, I have also been able to satisfy myself that there are many Polish words with perfectly matching equivalents in English. I have been able to learn hundreds of new (English) meanings, building on the old (Polish) meanings that, as it turned out, do have exact English equivalents.

Through this experience, I have come to appreciate how much words matter for "human understanding," and what an important role "shared words" (i.e., words with matching meanings) play in building bridges between speakers of different languages. I have also come to appreciate the scale of distortion that can be involved in claims that some English words and phrases (for example, *color, blue, anger, brother, politeness, cooperation, the sense of right and wrong*) capture universal human realities.

Polish does have words that correspond in meaning, for example, to *color* and *brother,* but it doesn't have words matching *blue, cooperation, frustration,* or *right* and *wrong.* Describing languages that don't have words for "color" or "brother" in terms of these English words distorts facts as much as describing the Polish color concept "niebieski" through the English word *blue,* or analyzing Polish moral concepts through the English words *right* and *wrong* does (cf. Wierzbicka 2012a). It prevents understanding and imposes conceptual categories of English (whether uniquely English or shared with other European languages) on humankind at large. For example, an account of "how people see the world" based on the English word *color* amounts to looking at the world through the prism of English. It distorts the picture of how speakers of other languages see the world and it prevents the discovery of what it is that speakers of all languages share.

Asifa Majid of the Nijmegen Language and Cognition Group writes (2010: 61):

> Wierzbicka and colleagues have argued that rather than looking for universals of colour, we should look for universals of the higher order concept of 'seeing' (because all languages have a word for seeing). But why stop there? If there is a named higher-order superordinate to 'seeing' (such as 'perceiving'), should we take perception as our domain instead?

But it is the **shared** words that provide the bedrock of genuine human understanding. "Color" is not a shared word, and neither is "perceive" (many languages don't have such words), whereas all languages have a word for "seeing." This means that an unbiased, conceptually neutral investigation of "how people see the world" must start from "seeing," not from "color" or "perception."

"See" is a good example of what can be called a "universal word" (strictly speaking, it is, of course, the meaning, not the word as such that is universally shared, but the phrase "universal words" is a handy abbreviation). In a sense, this is what the "NSM" approach on which this book is based is all about: the main idea is to approach any field of study in human sciences bearing in mind the distinction between "universal words" and words that are culture-specific.

To put it this way is inevitably to simplify, because what matters is not just words, but also grammatical patterns in which these words appear. According to the NSM theory (e.g., Wierzbicka 1996; Goddard and Wierzbicka eds. 2002), all languages share not only a lexical core but also a grammatical one, so that at the heart of all languages there lies a mini-language, with as many realizations as there are languages. Thus, there is a mini-English that can be called "NSM English," a matching mini-Russian ("NSM Russian"), and so on. Each of these mini-languages can serve as a culture-free metalanguage for analyzing meanings and ideas, for comparing languages and cultures, and for elucidating ideas in any domain of social science and in the Wittgensteinian "stream of life." This is where the acronym "NSM" comes from: the shared core of all languages provides a "natural semantic metalanguage" for explaining meanings and ideas across languages and cultures, places and times, in scholarship and in the classroom.

Abbreviating a complex body of theory and practice, however, we can say that the key to the NSM approach lies in the notion of "universal words." According to wide-ranging cross-linguistic investigations carried out in the NSM framework, there are two kinds of "universal words." One kind includes words with meanings that are very simple and cannot be defined in terms of any other words. These elementary, indefinable meanings can be called "atoms of meanings," although in NSM research they have been traditionally called "semantic primes" (or "semantic primitives"). Universal words of the other kind belong to the category of words known in NSM research as "semantic molecules."

As the name suggests, semantic molecules are more complex than "semantic atoms" (i.e., primes) and in contrast to primes, they can be defined. For example, SEE and HEAR, which are primes, cannot be defined, whereas "color" and "sound" can and have been defined—in terms of SEE and HEAR. (By convention, semantic primes, and they alone, are represented in writing in CAPS).

SEE, which is a semantic prime, cannot be defined, and all attempts to do so lead to vicious circles. For example, the *Longman Dictionary of the English Language* (1987) defines *see* via "eye" ("to see—to perceive by the eye"), then defines *perceive* via *see* ("to perceive—to become aware of through the senses, especially to see"), and *eye* via *sight* ("eye—any of various usually paired organs of sight"), and then defines *sight* as "something seen." By contrast, semantic molecules **can** be defined, because they can be decomposed (either directly or in stages) into primes.

Words belonging to many more or less abstract semantic domains (for example, emotions, values, speech acts) can be explicated directly in terms of primes, whereas words belonging to the concrete lexicon often require a level of analysis relying on "intermediate words" that can themselves be explicated via primes and that can function as integrated conceptual "chunks" in the construction of many other, more complex concepts. Such intermediate words are often language-specific, with no exact semantic equivalents in other languages. For example, "color" (which is part of the meaning of English words like *red*, *blue*, and *purple*) is an important molecule of languages like English, but is absent from many others. The same is true of the words *tree* (part of the meaning of words like *willow*, *pine*, *palm*, and *maple*) and *paper* (part of the meaning of *book*, *document*, *journal*, or *card*). Evidence suggests, however, that there are also many semantic molecules that are universal.

Extensive semantic investigations conducted over many years, by many scholars, in the NSM framework, have led to the conclusion that there are sixty-five primes, the same in all languages. This set of primes includes elements such as SOMEONE and SOMETHING, PEOPLE, THINK, KNOW, FEEL and WANT, BEFORE and AFTER, LIVE and DIE, SEE and HEAR, IF and BECAUSE, and fifty or so others (for a complete list, see **Table 4.1**). These sixty-five concepts, manifested as words or distinct meanings of words in all sampled languages, have their own inherent "grammar," that is, their own specifiable combinatorial properties, again, the same in all the languages sampled.

As for semantic molecules, cross-linguistic investigations carried out in the NSM framework suggest that all languages have words (or distinct word meanings) for "mother" and "father," "man," "woman," and "child," as well as "fire," "water," "ground," "hands," and a score or so others. Taken together, universal semantic primes and universal semantic molecules give us a neutral, non-Eurocentric and non-Anglocentric metalanguage for comparing ways of thinking embedded in different languages across all different domains. More generally, they provide a culture-neutral conceptual framework on which any area of human science can draw.

As mentioned earlier, being based on "universal words," this metalanguage can have as many versions as there are languages. Given the realities of today's world, in many contexts, the English version will be the most serviceable, because it can enable effective understanding among the largest number of interested people. There is a crucial similarity between the "mini-English" and the "maxi-English" here: because of the current position of English in the world, they can both have a vast outreach. At the same time, however, there is also a crucial difference between the two: whereas the "maxi-English" carries

TABLE 4.1:

Semantic Primes (English Exponents) in Comparable Categories

I, YOU, SOMEONE, SOMETHING~THING, PEOPLE, BODY	Substantives
KIND, PART	Relational substantives
THIS, THE SAME, OTHER~ELSE	Determiners
ONE, TWO, MUCH~MANY, LITTLE~FEW, SOME, ALL	Quantifiers
GOOD, BAD	Evaluators
BIG, SMALL	Descriptors
THINK, KNOW, WANT, DON'T WANT, FEEL, SEE, HEAR	Mental predicates
SAY, WORDS, TRUE	Speech
DO, HAPPEN, MOVE, TOUCH	Actions, events, movement, contact
BE (SOMEWHERE), THERE IS, BE (SOMEONE/SOMETHING), BE (SOMEONE'S)	Location, existence, specification, possession
LIVE, DIE	Life and death
WHEN~TIME, NOW, BEFORE, AFTER, A LONG TIME, A SHORT TIME, FOR SOME TIME, MOMENT	Time
WHERE~PLACE, HERE, ABOVE, BELOW, FAR, NEAR, SIDE, INSIDE	Space
NOT, MAYBE, CAN, BECAUSE, IF	Logical concepts
VERY, MORE	Augmentor, intensifier
LIKE	Similarity

■ Primes exist as the meanings of lexical units (not at the level of lexemes) ■ Exponents of primes may be words, bound morphemes, or phrasemes ■ They can be formally, i.e., morphologically, complex ■ They can have combinatorial variants or allolexes (indicated with ~) ■ Each prime has well-specified syntactic (combinatorial) properties.

with it a huge baggage of history and culture, the mini-English allows its users to enjoy the freedom of an unbiased conceptual and communicative framework.

To illustrate the liberating potential of NSM-based mini-English let us examine a set of words from a domain widely acknowledged as extremely important and yet notorious for its deep-seated ethnocentrism: kinship terminologies.

A conversation with a linguist working on a language that has no word for "brother" (e.g., the Australian language Pitjantjatjara) may go like this:

–Does this language have a word for brother?
–Sure.
–What is it?
–Well, actually there are two: one for older brother (*kuṯa*) and one for younger brother (*maḻanypa*). And actually, this second word is for younger siblings in general, not just brothers.
–So there is no word for brother as such?
–Well, not as such, no, but I'm sure they have the concept of "brother."
–Why are you so sure?
–Well, because the absence of a word doesn't prove the absence of a concept.
–So do you think that speakers of English have a concept of "maḻanypa"?
–What are you on about?

What I am on about is the double standard implicit here. It is widely assumed that English words that have no counterparts in other languages stand, nonetheless, for shared human concepts, but it is not similarly assumed that words from other languages that have no counterpart in English also stand for shared concepts.

It is a human given that people have mothers and fathers. Is it also a given that they can have brothers and sisters? Seemingly, yes, but actually no: as discussed in relation to Kayardild, this is a pseudo-given mediated by English and other European languages. While all (or almost all) languages have words meaning "mother" and "father," many languages don't have words meaning "brother" and "sister."

For example, we have seen that Pitjantjatjara has the word *kuṯa*, sometimes translated into English as "elder brother," and the word *maḻanypa*, sometimes translated into English as "younger sibling," but that it doesn't have a word meaning "brother." This means that from a Pitjantjatjara speaker's point of view, *kuṯa* cannot mean "elder" plus "brother"—for example, a Pitjantjatjara teacher could not explain its meaning to a language learner as "elder" + "brother" (because there is no word meaning "brother"). This point is often very hard to grasp for English speakers, including some linguists and anthropologists, to whom the fact that people can have brothers seems to be reality itself—a "brute fact," rather than a fact filtered through language.

But if *kuṯa* doesn't mean "elder brother," what does it mean? The answer that could be given both by a Pitjantjatjara teacher and an English-speaking teacher might take the shape of the formula below. (It is important to note that this formula portrays the primary sense of the word *kuṯa*, not its extended "classificatory" use.)

kuṯa ("older brother")

someone can say about a man: "this is my *kuṯa*"
    if this someone can think about him like this:
        "his mother is my mother, his father is my father
        he was born before I was born"
a child can say the same about another child
    if after some time this other child can be a man

The Pitjantjatjara word *maḻanypa* can also be explained in this framework without using the English words *brother* and *sibling*. (Again, the formula is meant to portray the primary meaning of the word *maḻanypa*, not its extended, "classificatory" use.)

maḻanypa ("younger sibling")

someone can say about someone else: "this is my *maḻanypa*"
    if it is like this:
        "this someone's mother is my mother,

this someone's father is my father
this someone was born after I was born"

Let us now try to turn the tables and to imagine what it could be like for a Pitjantjatjara teacher to explain in Pitjantjatjara what the English word *brother* means. First she could try something like "it can mean *kuṯa*, but it can also mean *maḻanypa*, except that it cannot be used about a woman or a girl." In order to explain, however, that for English speakers, "brother" is a unitary concept, not one structured in terms of "either…or…and except," she could use the same framework of shared and cross-translatable words that can also be used to explain to English speakers what *kuṯa* and *maḻanypa* mean. To do so, she could rely on the Pitjantjatjara words *ngunytju* and *mama,* which are polysemous but whose primary senses are "mother" and "father" because if a man is my brother, he has the same mother and father as I do:

brother

someone can say about a man: "this is my brother"
    if this someone can think about him like this:
        "his mother is my mother, his father is my father"
someone can say the same about a child
    if after some time this child can be a man

This explication of *brother,* carried out through the universal conceptual primes "this," "someone," "can," "say," "the same," "other," "after," "some time," "if," and "like" and the universal molecules "mother," "father," "man," and "child" will no doubt seem very strange to readers who all their lives have taken the word *brother* for granted. This is the effect of looking at one's own language from the perspective of other languages, as different as English is from Pitjantjatjara—the effect of "de-familiarization," or *ostranienie* (an important concept introduced into the human sciences by Russian literary scholars of the 1920s known as "the formalists"). Some English readers will no doubt baulk at such a strange representation of a familiar concept. Others, however, may feel a liberating and mind-stretching effect: looking at one's own conceptual home from a distance can bring a sense of heightened self-understanding, as well as of a better understanding of strangers who don't have a "basic" word like *brother* and think instead in terms of "*kuṯa*-s" and "*maḻanypa*-s."

Trying to practice social science without ethnocentrism requires an effort of de-familiarization. Otherwise, one's thinking about "people in general," or people living in other places, or at other times, can remain locked in one's own cultural perspective, and especially, in one's own language. To achieve such de-familiarization, it is helpful to do some exercises in cross-cultural imagination.

Anthropologist Richard Shweder gave his 1991 book a good title: *Thinking Through Cultures*. For Shweder, who is a cultural pluralist acutely aware of many different perspectives and languages, this includes thinking through one's own culture, as well as others. But thinking in what language? If we think through cultures, including our own, in English, we will carry with us everywhere our own culture-bound perspective. We will think about "kinship" ("kinship across languages and cultures") through the prism of the English words *brother* and *sister*, about "friendship" through the English word *friend*, about "human emotions" through the English words *anger* and *sadness,* about "morality" through the English words *right* and *wrong,* and so on.

I am not suggesting, needless to say, that book titles such as "Patterns of Friendship in Different Societies," "Human Perception of Colour," "How the Mind Works," or "The Philosophy of Mind" should be banished from sociology, psychology, cognitive science, and philosophy. Titles need to be brief, so culture-specific conceptual shortcuts are often necessary and harmless—provided the cultural and linguistic perspective reflected in them is acknowledged in the book's introduction and taken into account in the author's analysis and discussion. But even a modest effort of de-familiarization and de-anglicization can provide a rich payoff in virtually any area of study in present-day Anglophone human sciences, and having a set of universal words in one's tool kit always helps.

A Coda about the Royal Family

I imagine that for some readers, finding their way through the explications of the unfamiliar words *kuta* and *maḻanypa* and the de-familiarizing explication of *brother* might be as much kinship analysis as they can stomach. For those, however, who may feel curious about how to conceptualize the British royal family in a culture-independent framework, I am adding a coda with some more explications that outline who is who for whom among the royals without any conceptual intrusions from English such as "brother" and "sister."

To begin with the simplest concept, *wakatha*, the following explication makes clear why Princess Anne is a *wakatha* for Prince Charles, whereas Princess Margaret was not a *wakatha* for Queen Elizabeth:

wakatha ("a man's sister")

a man (e.g. Charles) can say about a woman (e.g. Anne): "this is my *wakatha*"

   if he can think about her like this:

      "her mother is my mother, her father is my father"

To understand why Queen Elizabeth was Princess Margaret's *yakukathu* but not the other way around, it is sufficient to read the following explication:

yakukathu ("older sibling, same sex, female ego")

a woman (e.g. Margaret) can say about another woman (e.g. Elizabeth): "this is my *yakukathu*"

    if she can think about her like this:

        "her mother is my mother, her father is my father

        she was born before I was born"

a child can say the same about another child

    if after some time both these children can be women

As for Princess Margaret being Queen Elizabeth's *duujinda,* and also, the Princes Andrew and Edward being Prince Charles's *duujinda*, this requires a longer explication, made up, however, of two simple and symmetrical halves:

duujinda ("younger sibling of same sex")

a woman (e.g. Elizabeth) can say about another woman (e.g. Margaret): "this is my *duujinda*"

    if she can think about her like this:

        "her mother is my mother, her father is my father

        she was born after I was born"

a child can say the same about another child

    if after some time both these children can be women

a man (e.g. Charles) can say about another man (e.g. Edward): "this is my *duujinda*"

    if he can think about him like this:

        "his mother is my mother, his father is my father

        he was born after I was born"

a child can say the same about another child

    if after some time both these children can be men

thabuju ("older sibling, same sex, male ego")

a man (e.g. Edward) can say about another man (e.g. Charles): "this is my *thabuju*"

    if he can think about him like this:

        "his mother is my mother, his father is my father

        he was born before I was born"

a child can say the same about another child

    if after some time both these children can be men

5

Human Bodies and Human Minds: What is Visible and What is Invisible

"Language [is] a symbolic guide to culture," Sapir (1949: 162) famously said, and (perhaps a little less famously), "vocabulary is a very sensitive index of the culture of a people" (1949: 27). Words shared by people speaking a given language are both reflections of, and guides to, these people's shared ways of thinking. That is, of course, not words as such, but the meanings of words.

For example, if we want to know how people in a particular language community think about the structure of the human body, we need to find out what words they use to refer to different parts of the body, and what exactly these words mean (that is, how these body parts are construed by these speakers). We also need to determine whether a word has one meaning or more, and if more, to sort out the different meanings before we can identify any of them. I will start with an example.

According to Asifa Majid and other researchers from the Nijmegen Language and Cognition Group, many Southeast Asian languages (of the Aslian group) lack a word for "head," among them Jahai, spoken in Malaysia. This is so despite the fact that there *is* a word that can be used for a person's disembodied head, after beheading: "Jahai *kuy* (and its cognates in the languages above) is the closest equivalent to head because if someone is beheaded this would be the term that would be used to refer to the disembodied head" (Majid 2010: 64).

But if the disembodied head after beheading is referred to by Jahai speakers as *kuy,* what are the grounds for affirming that Jahai has no word meaning "head"? Here is the answer: "When speakers of Jahai, Semelai, and the other Aslian languages are asked to colour in the head on a line drawing of a body they colour only that part of the head that is covered with hair." (Majid 2010: 64) Apparently, the Nijmegen researchers see the coloring-in exercise as more important than the talk about beheading because they rely, as a matter of principle, on a "stimulus methodology," which prefers visual stimuli to verbal explanations.

What could the word *kuy* mean, one wonders, from the perspective of a Jahai speaker, if it doesn't mean "head"? Majid doesn't say, but she insists that "this word has a much narrower sense than HEAD" (2010: 64). Apparently, the claim is that *kuy* means not "head" but "the top of the head," and it is based on the observation that "in everyday discourse, [*kuy*] refers to the top part of the head, not the whole generalized cone" [the "generalized cone" being the head].

So from the English-speaking investigator's point of view, *kuy* means "the top of the head." This explanation, however, could not be translated into Jahai itself, because if Jahai has no word meaning "head," then there is no way to render the phrase "the top of the head" in Jahai. Thus, according to the proposed story, the Jahai speakers don't have a word for "head" (in the sense of the English word *head,* as part of the body) even though they do talk about people being "beheaded," and while they do have a word "to refer to the disembodied head," the meaning of this word can only be explained in English, by an English speaker, not in Jahai, by a speaker of Jahai.

This is clearly an Anglocentric position. If, instead, we try to put ourselves in the shoes of a Jahai speaker, the situation can be described quite simply: The word *kuy* has two meanings, and both these meanings can be stated in Jahai itself. One of these meanings corresponds to the meaning of the English word *head,* and the other, to the meaning of the English phrase "the top of the head." The first meaning (kuy_1) can be explained (both in English and in Jahai) as, roughly, "that part of the body which is above all the other parts of the body, it is round," whereas the second one (kuy_2) can be stated as "that part of kuy_1 which is above all the other parts."[1]

As for the reason why the Jahai consultants in the coloring-in experiments were coloring the hair and not the face, the explanation may be very simple: the consultants may simply assume that they are being asked to color in the top of the head (i.e., kuy_2) rather than the whole head (including the face), that is kuy_1. In fact, Majid herself mentions that in the cognate language Mah Meri, the phrase *tɔc koy* glossed by her as "cut head" "means to cut someone's hair, **not** to behead someone" (p. 64). But if this phrase means "cut hair," why not recognize the polysemy and gloss it as "cut hair" rather than "cut head"?

Essentially, what applies to the alleged absence of a word meaning "head" in Jahai, applies also to the alleged absence of a word meaning "hands" in languages like my native Polish. From a native speaker's point of view, the Polish word *ręce* (an old dual form, singular *ręka*) has two distinct meanings, one of which matches the meaning of the English word *hands* and the other is similar to (though not identical with) the English word *arms.*

The evidence for this polysemy is extensive and cannot be fully presented here, but let me mention three facts. First, the form *w ręku* ("in hand(s)") can normally refer only to hands, not to arms. Thus, it can refer to something held in someone's hands, but never, for example, to someone held in someone's arms. Second, the two meanings underlie different derivates: the word *rękawiczka* ("glove") is derived from $ręka_1$ whereas *rękaw* ("sleeve") is derived from $ręka_2$. Third, the diminutive *rączki* (as in the polite phrase *rączki całuję,* "I kiss your dear-little-hands") can only refer to a woman's hands (*ręce₁*), not to her arms (*ręce₂*).

This last fact is particularly revealing given that the diminutive *nóżki* "dear-little-legs" can easily be used about a woman's legs, as well as her feet. (And in Russian, where the situation is similar to Polish, the poet Alexander Pushkin, a great admirer of women's legs, often wrote in his poems about their *nožki*, a diminutive from *nogi*, "legs"). Thus, the Polish word *nogi* ("legs"), which is used to refer to both legs and feet, is indeed vague, not polysemous. But the case of *ręce* is different: here, two meanings, "hands" and "arms," do need to be distinguished, on language-internal grounds. (I should add that when used in relation to children, the diminutive *rączki* can refer to the arms, as well as to the hands, because in Polish, all children's body parts are regularly referred to by the diminutive.)

Thus, I do not agree that my native language, Polish, doesn't have a word meaning "hands," and (on the evidence before us) I cannot accept that Jahai doesn't have a word meaning "head." On the other hand, I would readily agree that Polish doesn't have a (colloquial) word meaning "feet."[2]

I fully agree with Majid that "body part categories are [not] 'given' by visual perceptual discontinuities" and that "words are [not] merely labels for these predetermined parts" (Majid 2010: 59). Linguistic evidence indicates that the human body is indeed thought of in different ways by speakers of different languages. There are, nonetheless, some constants. What these constants are cannot be established by getting native speaker consultants to color in pictures, because to find out what the habitual ways of thinking are, we need to reveal what the indigenous meanings are, and this requires uncovering, in each case, language-specific patterns of polysemy. As the case of the Jahai "head" illustrates, this cannot be achieved through pictures (or other visual "stimuli").

Given the stimulus-based methodology, it is not surprising that Majid and her colleagues focus—like Kay and colleagues do in the case of visual semantics—on "naming," rather than on trying to discover indigenous meanings. For example, summarizing the results of her and her colleagues' studies, Majid (2010: 69) writes: "Regularities in body part naming come not from which geons are selected for reference. Instead, granularity and depth of naming of body parts differ across languages, with perception helping to provide constraints on the precise reference of the terms." "Geons" are discontinuous parts of the body in a schematic model used by another researcher. The Nijmegen researchers prefer to use a picture of the human body without artificial breaks between different predetermined parts. This is to their credit. But getting the consultants to color in certain areas does not reveal the construal of the body reflected in the words of a particular language, either.

The question of polysemy is of fundamental importance in this debate and Majid is right to present this issue as central to the NSM methodology. Thus, she writes:

Wierzbicka and Goddard argue that a polysemous interpretation is necessary unless a unitary definition—which can account for the range of the
word's usages—can be provided. Critically, they require that the unitary
definition should be a paraphrase in natural language.... This insistence
on a single definition in natural language **comes only from practitioners
of NSM**; it is not a generally accepted requirement. (Majid 2010: 63-64;
emphasis added)

Majid is right here: the insistence that if we posit a unitary meaning we must
support it with a unitary definition (substitutable in context for the definien-
dum) comes only from practitioners of NSM. What she does not say is that
NSM is the only approach to semantics that has actually proposed a large body
of definitions (many hundreds) for English and many other languages. These
definitions may not be perfect but they are in the public domain, open to testing and amenable to improvements. By contrast, other approaches to semantics tend to content themselves with meta-discussions without producing many
actual definitions, and the statements about the meaning of individual words
or expressions that they put forward are often unverifiable.

For example, when Evans and Wilkins (2001: 502, quoted by Majid
2010: 63) say that the word *tyerrtye* in the Australian language Arrernte means
"person/body" and that "the distinction between the 'body' sense and the 'person' sense (...) becomes blurred," this is a statement that cannot be tested. We
could equally well say that the English word *body* used in phrases like "body
and mind" and "the head and the body" has only one meaning because the
two senses evident in these two phrases "are blurred." In fact, Henderson and
Dobson's *Eastern and Central Arrernte to English Dictionary* (1994) does not
hesitate to posit two separate meanings for the word *tyerrtye*: 1. body, 2. person. The first meaning is illustrated, inter alia, with a sentence referring to "the
child's body" (*tyerrtye ampe*) onto which medicine fat is rubbed. Clearly, the
intended meaning is, "the child's body," not "the child's person."

Majid does not present any substantive arguments against the NSM
requirement that statements of meaning should be verifiable (through para-
phrases in ordinary language, which can be tested through substitution in context, in consultation with native speakers), but only emphasizes that this is not
a generally accepted condition. The lack of general acceptance, however, can
hardly be a key argument in a scientific debate.

Referring to the NSM view that all languages have a word, or distinct
word-meaning, for the body, Majid writes:

within NSM no distinction is drawn between semantic and conceptual representations. The BODY is viewed as a conceptual universal and to deny
that a language has a word meaning 'body' is to deny that the language
community has the concept BODY. But this conclusion follows only if we
conflate linguistic meaning with nonlinguistic representations; we can deny

that there is a specific word with the semantics 'body' without denying that a person could entertain that concept. (2010: 64)

What is at issue here, however, is not whether a person could entertain a concept without having a word for it, but whether it is justified to posit an **indigenous** concept—that is, a concept supposedly shared by the indigenous community— if this alleged concept is named in English but not in the indigenous language itself. What Majid calls "conflating linguistic meaning with nonlingusitic representations" is in fact a refusal to posit conceptual representations that have no support in the indigenous meanings and that are unverifiable and based on English. For example, to claim that the Arrernte have a concept of "the body" without having a word (polysemous or not) meaning "body," or that the Jahai have a concept of "the head" without having a word meaning "head," makes the talk of "conceptual representations" unverifiable and opens the floodgates to the large-scale Anglocentrism that pervades contemporary cognitive science and related disciplines.

Once these gates are open, one can easily claim that speakers of all languages have the concepts of "color," "mountain," "sibling," "brother," "fairness," "evidence," "cooperation," and anything else that happens to be named in English—because accountability for such claims is not required if conceptual analysis is allowed to be dissociated from semantic analysis and from language-specific semantic evidence. When Majid says that NSM conflates "linguistic meaning with nonlinguistic representations," she doesn't address the argument that in order to talk about "nonlinguistic representations" we still need some words, and that if these words—our analytical tools— come straight from the English lexicon, the resulting analysis is bound to be Anglocentric.

I will further illustrate this dependence on English in the analyses based on pictures, diagrams, and other "nonlinguistic representations" (especially, videoclips) with N. J. Enfield's (2011) study of "reciprocal events" in the Southeast Asian language Lao. Examples of such "reciprocal events" offered by Enfield include "they saw each other" and "they celebrated together."

The methodology used for studying "reciprocal events" is, as Enfield put it, "eliciting descriptions of a set of focused etic stimuli," complemented "by focused consultation with native speakers." The phrase "focused etic stimuli" refers to a set of video clips. The native consultants can be shown some video clips and then be asked what the events depicted in them are, and their responses can be re-coded by the researcher into his own analytical framework. This leads to statements in academic English with phrases such as "asymmetrical alignment" and sentences like "multiple participants map onto multiple roles of a single predicate" (p. 130), which presumably are not run past the native-speaker consultants. In Enfield's opinion (2011: 131), the combination of such methods, which are the trademark of the Nijmegen Language and Cognition Group, "is the ideal approach to semantic typology" and supplies "both an anchor for comparative work and a route to language-specific facts." As the paper illustrates, however, this approach does not lead the researcher to hypotheses about the indigenous meanings that could be discussed with native-speaker consultants. The facts referred to in the quote above appear to be analyzed exclusively from the researcher's own perspective and seem to have little to do with how Lao speakers themselves speak and, presumably, think.

As I discussed in detail in my article "Reciprocity: an NSM approach to linguistic typology and social universals" (Wierzbicka 2009b), the problem with a semantics based on video-clipping human behavior is that in human life the most important things are—as St. Exupery's Little Prince pointed out— invisible. One cannot capture on a video human values, moral categories, emotions, intentions, relationships, or understandings. And even human *physical* actions (for example, cutting and chopping) have a meaning construed in terms of motivation and projected outcome, inaccessible to any video camera (cf. Goddard and Wierzbicka 2008). One cannot capture on a video clip how Lao speakers think, but one can find out a good deal about it by framing one's hypotheses in simple words cross-translatable into Lao and by discussing them with Lao consultants—as in fact Enfield himself did in his earlier, NSM-based work (e.g., Enfield 2002).[3]

In my view, it was the emphasis on what is visible, and reliance on photographs, diagrams, drawings, and video clips (to the exclusion of in-depth conceptual analysis) that defeated the search for commonalities in the Nijmegen group's project on the human body, a project that concluded, inter alia, that there are languages without a word for "hands," without a word for "head," and without a word for "body" (cf. Wierzbicka 2007). The polysemy of such words cannot be established visually, so the reliance on visual data without in-depth conceptual analysis has led the researchers to conclude that not even the concepts of "hands," "head," and "body" are shared, and that, more generally, there appear to be no universals in the human conceptualization of the body across languages and cultures. I believe that these conclusions are mistaken.

Semantic analysis that recognizes polysemy and is based on conceptual analysis carried out in consultation with native speakers (in words that they can understand) suggests that all languages have distinct words, or word-meanings, for "body," "hands," and "head." To be sure, these words can be polysemous (as the Polish word *ręce/*"hands/arms" is), but usually this doesn't seem to confuse native speakers, although it can sometimes confuse linguists. But if one can get confused analyzing the domain of the human body on the basis of "stimulus methodology" and (for example) come to deny that speakers of all languages recognize (through their language) that people have heads, how can one hope to reveal, through video-clipping and diagrams, what goes on *inside* human heads?

In her defense of the video-clipping and the stimulus-based approach to semantics more generally, Majid writes:

> In principle there is no restriction on what domains can be handled using a stimulus-based approach. Recently, with the Language and Cognition group at the Max Planck Institute for Psycholinguistics, we have begun to investigate smells, tastes, and tactile texture using a non-linguistic stimulus-based approach (.... There is also no restriction on lexical categories. (Majid 2012: 62)

This would seem to include not only body parts and bodily perception but also people's minds, hearts, and souls—and indeed, Majid spells this implication out, confronting my scepticism head on:

> Wierzbicka (2009b: 165) critiques the stimulus methodology on the ground that 'the most important things are invisible.' She argues that video clips and other such depictions cannot capture 'human values, moral categories, emotions, intentions, relationships or understandings,' that what really matters for some sorts of concepts are motivations and projected outcomes rather than the physical acts themselves. No doubt there are serious challenges in depicting complex psychosocial states, but nevertheless there is reason to be optimistic about using a stimulus-based approach. (Majid 2012: 62-63)

As grounds for such optimism, Majid cites a 1944 study by Heider and Simmel, who "showed American undergraduates very simple cartoons featuring geometrical shapes, such as triangles and circles." When these shapes were shown as moving ("using a trick film method"), the participants described "the movements depicted not in terms of physical motions, but instead ascribing psychological intentions to the shapes." (Majid 2012: 63) The personality traits attributed to the moving shapes by the American undergraduates in the study are "aggressive, villainous, heroic, defiant, etc." Majid concludes:

> The Heider and Simmel studies demonstrate that even from the simplest of cues people infer complex social and psychological states, *contra* Wierzbicka. Moving from 2D black-and-white animations with geometric figures to naturalistic video would only increase the possible scenarios that could be depicted. (Majid 2012: 63)

I agree that we often infer complex psychological states from simple-looking physical states and I don't doubt that by using modern video technologies a researcher could elicit more detailed behavioral scenarios than those presented in a 1944 study. But there is still the question of the language in which those scenarios would be interpreted. If this is done in English, through English psychological categories like "aggressive" and "defiant," then the conclusions will reflect the conceptual world of the investigators, and not that of the native speakers whose behavior is being videotaped.

Majid does not address the question of the language of the interpretation, apparently assuming that in the psychological domain as in other areas, English categories are adequate. Thus, again, the researchers can see the videos, but their own reliance on their language of description and interpretation—English—is invisible to them. As I see it, therefore, they remain prisoners of English.

I have quoted Majid's paper on body parts here not for its own sake but as an example of extensionalist semantics, which is really a semantics without meaning, focusing on "how things are named" rather than on "what words mean." But, generally speaking, things are not named at all: obviously, even concrete nouns like *cup* or *bird* are not names of particular things but of certain categories, and as John Locke saw with particular clarity, it is the mind that makes categories (he said: "sorts"), not "nature." Having discussed various kinds of birds common in England and commonly distinguished in English, Locke concluded: "From what has been said, 'tis evident that **men** make sorts of things" (III,VI, 35).

> This, then, in short, is the case: nature makes many particular things, which do agree one with another, in many sensible qualities (...); but (...) 'tis men who, taking occasion from the qualities they find united in them (...) range them into sorts, in order to their naming, for the convenience of comprehensive signs; (...) and in this, I think, consists the whole business of genres and species. (III, VI, 36).

Thus, words do not stand for things, but for categories ("sorts") of things, and these categories are "made" by people, for the convenience of communication. Furthermore, as Locke was well aware, the categories distinguished by different languages do not match—a fact which, in the case of natural kinds, is the cornerstone of modern ethnozoology and ethnobotany (cf. e.g., Berlin 1992). The fact that the names of artifacts (cultural kinds) in different languages don't match either is well known in linguistics and linguistic anthropology, too (cf. e.g. Kronenfeld 1996; Malt et al. 2003).Yet many practitioners of contemporary extensionalist semantics keep returning to the idea that at least certain categories of objects are universal (independent of language) and can therefore be studied without any reference to the meaning of their names, on the basis of pictorial representations of various kinds.

For example, psycholinguists Dedre Gentner and Lera Boroditsky (2001) say that "concrete nouns are in many cases simply names for pre-existing natural referents" (p. 241). They also speak (quoting from an earlier paper by

Gentner) of the possibility that children are born with a set of "conceptual conflations" (p. 215) and that these conflations correspond to certain "natural partitions" in the world (p. 217):

> Natural partitions: "there are in the experiential flow certain highly cohesive collections of precepts that are universally conceptualised as objects, and...these tend to be lexicalized as nouns across languages. Children learning language have already isolated these cohesive packages—the concrete objects and individuals—from their surroundings" (Gentner 1982: 324).

The authors don't give any examples of such concrete nouns that may be simply "names for pre-existing natural referents" in the text of their article. In an accompanying diagram, however, they place "dog" and "spoon" at the end of a cline extending from "cognitive" (i.e., nonarbitrary and universal) to "linguistic" (i.e., arbitrary and dependent on a particular language). But even if most languages do indeed have a word largely matching the English *dog* in meaning, this is not the case with many other names of kinds of living creatures (suffice it to mention the well-known example of the Japanese word *nezumi*/"mouse/rat," cf. Eco 2003, Goddard 2011a).

Nearly two hundred years ago, Humboldt wrote:

> When, for example, in Sanskrit the elephant is sometimes called the twice-drinker, otherwise the double-toothed one, otherwise still the one-provided-with-a-hand, many different concepts are designated, even though the same object is meant. For language does not represent objects but rather the concepts which, in the process of speech, have been formed in the mind independent of those objects. (1903–36, v.7: 89-90)

The notion of "conceptual conflations" and "cohesive packages" lexicalized as nouns across languages corresponds to some extent to the NSM concept of universal semantic molecules such as "men," "women," "children," "hands," and "water," identified in NSM research. But first, evidence suggests that there are very few such cohesive conceptual packages showing up in all languages, and second, the categories in question cannot be identified through pictures or video clips. For example, to establish that all languages have a word meaning "hands" (though not necessarily a word meaning "feet") one needs methodological tools for determining polysemy (as in the case of the Polish word *ręce*: 1. hands, 2. arms). If we assume that categories like *spoons*, *cups*, and *mugs*, or *mice*, *rats*, and *butterflies* correspond to "natural partitions" and to "pre-existing natural referents," we are, once again, absolutizing lexical categories of English.

In her study "(Re-)naming the World: Word-to-Referent Mapping in Second Language Speakers" Aneta Pavlenko (2011b: 233) shows very nicely how the English names for "drinking vessels" such as *cup*, *mug*, and *glass* don't match their Russian "dictionary equivalents" *čaška, kružka,* and *stakan.* She seems to conclude, however, that no "bounded" (i.e., explicit) statements of meaning can or should be sought (at least in relation to the mental lexicon of bilingual people):

> The metaphor of bounded and holistic 'concepts' or 'mental representations,' commonly invoked in models of bilingual processing and the bilingual lexicon, fails to capture this context-dependence and the complexity of word-to-referent mapping in the real world. These phenomena are much better incorporated in approaches that view internal representations as distributed and emergent phenomena that function in a context-dependent manner, so that the same container may be named *cup* if it contained coffee and *bowl* if it contained mashed potatoes. (Barsalou 2003; Labov 1973; Malt et al 2003)

It is true that the same container may be called by someone *cup* if it contains coffee and *bowl* if it contains mashed potatoes. This doesn't mean, however, that the words *cup* and *bowl* have no stable and statable meanings. On the contrary, it confirms that the meaning of *cup* contains a component referring to "drinking," whereas the meaning of *bowl* contains a component referring to "things that people can eat." (Cf. Wierzbicka 1985a, 1984)

Lexical semantics is a guide to human cognition: it shows us how speakers of a language construe the world they live in. At the same time, it is a field essential to practical societal concerns such as dictionary-making, language teaching, translation, and so on. If one were to view the meanings of words only as "distributed and emergent phenomena that function in a context-dependent manner" and if one didn't try to state semantic invariants brought by particular words **to** the context, then one could hardly ever offer any constructive suggestions for improving dictionaries (whether monolingual or bilingual) or for second-language teaching.

Pavlenko refers in her discussion to a related study by herself and Barbara Malt (Pavlenko and Malt 2011), to some earlier studies by Malt and coauthors, and to a theoretical article by psychologist Barsalou, who argues that the content of conceptual categories is unstatable and who sees "simulations" as superior to verbal explications of meanings:

> a concept is a dynamical system. A given simulator can construct an indefinitely large number of specific simulations to represent the respective category. Rather than a concept being a fixed representation, it is a skill for tailoring representations to the constraints of situated actions. (Barsalou 2003)

One can't, however, put a "skill" into a dictionary or into any language-teaching materials. Whichever area of applied semantics one looks at—lexicography, language teaching, intercultural communication, endangered languages, historical and philological commentaries, and so on—the idea that meanings cannot be stated because they are "dynamic" and "context-dependent" is unhelpful. As the very extensive body of semantic descriptions developed in NSM-based research shows, it is also unfounded.

The insistence that the meanings of words such as the names of artifacts (e.g., *cups*, *mugs*, and *glasses*) are context-dependent can be seen as a healthy reaction against earlier assumptions that such categories are based on a list of necessary conditions or that their criterial characteristics can be formulated in purely perceptual terms (such as size, material, and shape; cf. e.g., Labov 1973, Malt et al. 2003). As NSM researchers have been arguing for decades (Wierzbicka 1984, 1985a; Goddard 1998), such assumptions are mistaken and lead nowhere.

To formulate adequate semantic descriptions of words like *cup*, *mug*, *čaška*, and *kružka*, we need to capture the "idea" of each such category: what are these objects made **for**, and what is envisaged as their prototypical use (including the prototypical situation of use) in the makers' minds. The "idea" of a *cup* is different, in some respects, from that of a *čaška*, and that of a *mug*, from that of a *kružka*. Each of these ideas can be articulated in simple everyday words (cross-translatable into other languages), usually according to a certain template. Such templates include prototypical settings as envisaged by the "producers," in accordance with local traditions and expectations.

Conceptual semantics formulates detailed hypotheses about what the "idea" in each case is, and what the template is that makes a complex conceptual category learnable. It sees its main task not in linking words with their referents but with language-specific ideas in the speakers' minds.

This is not to suggest that studies focused on patterns of naming cannot be valuable and revealing. They can. But if they are to be constructive, they need to work hand in hand with conceptual semantics, focused on concepts, not on referents. Concepts may be context-dependent, but equally, contexts are **concept-dependent**: if words had no "fixed" (though obviously changeable) meaning, contexts wouldn't have any recoverable meanings, either. Ultimately, if we want to understand "word-to-referent mapping" across languages and times, we have to formulate explicit and testable hypotheses about what words mean. This requires a methodology that enables researchers to "get into the speakers' heads" and that is equally applicable to words for psychological attributes, emotions, values, and social relations as it is to names of dishes, utensils, furniture, vehicles, and anything else. In all domains meanings are invisible. They cannot be pictured or videotaped—they can only be identified through words.

We cannot identify conceptual categories without using language. If we want to identify them through English, then we need to recognize that most English words are not cross-translatable into other languages and carry with them a particular culturally shaped perspective. To reach a neutral, language-independent perspective, we need not pictures, but cross-translatable words.

In his essay "Anthropology's Disenchantment with the Cognitive Revolution" anthropologist and cultural psychologist Richard Shweder writes:

> A major premise of behaviorism was the view that anything that could not in principle be observed (such as human mental states and processes) was unreal, or (...) at the very least the study of such things was methodologically beyond the scope of empirical/objective science...(Shweder 2012a: 360)

It is hard not to think that stimulus-based methodologies in linguistics, which substitute observable objects and pictures for meanings in the speakers' minds, harken back to the era of behaviorism, even if they appear to acknowledge the importance of the "Cognitive Revolution" and retain the label "cognitive." Shweder asks, rhetorically:

> If by definition the aim of any empirical science is to provide us with knowledge based exclusively on observation via some reliable sensing device together with whatever purely logical deductions follow from these observations, can empirical science provide us with a complete account of human mental life, including (for example) the study of meaning? (Ibid.)

Speaking of the new behaviorism, which seeks to marginalize, once again, the study of what is invisible, Shweder defines the subject matter of cultural anthropology as "the study of mental things (what people know, think, feel, want and value as good and bad) as one way of understanding what people and peoples habitually or customarily do within and across cultural groups." (Shweder 2012a: 361)

In spelling out these goals, Shweder is virtually speaking in NSM: "know," "think," "feel," "want," "good," and "bad" are all semantic primes that have emerged from decades of NSM-based research as universal human concepts. Thus, his remarks suggest a perspective that can not only take cultural anthropology and cultural psychology (including the study of meaning) beyond behaviorism but also free them from the Anglocentrism that threatens human sciences in today's English-dominated world even more than it did in the era before the "Cognitive Revolution."

PART TWO

Emotions and Values

6

Anglo Values vs. Human Values: Talking about Values in a Global World

From Violence to Cooperation: Steven Pinker's View of Moral Evolution

Steven Pinker opens his book *The Better Angels of Our Nature* (2012) with the following statement: "This book is about what may be the most important thing that has ever happened in human history. (...) Violence has declined over a long stretch of time." (p. xxi). Pinker doesn't explain exactly what he means by "violence," but he elaborates: "The mind is a complex system of cognitive and emotional faculties, which owe their basic design to some processes of evolution. Some of these faculties incline us towards various kinds of violence. (...) Others incline us towards cooperation and peace." (p. xxiii).

Viewing human evolution in terms of a decline in "violence" and the growth of "cooperation" is a very Anglo way of looking at it, given that most languages don't have words matching in meaning either of these words. For example, it would be a real challenge to translate the sentences quoted above into Russian. *The Oxford English-Russian Dictionary* (1980) offers *nasilie* for *violence*, and *sotrudničestvo* for *cooperation,* but neither of these words would make sense in the context of Pinker's statements.

Nasilie, sometimes translated into English with the phrase *by force* or with the word *coercion,* does not imply any uncontrolled impulses or emotions, and *sotrudničestvo* is (as already mentioned) closer to *collaboration* ("working together") than to *cooperation.* (Both *sotrudničestvo* and *collaborate* have, in addition to a neutral meaning, a pejorative one, but that is another story.) Pinker links *violence* with a lack of self-control: "Ever since Adam and Eve ate the apple (...) individuals have struggled with self-control (...). Violence too is largely a problem of self-control." (p. 592) He may be right as far as the English word *violence* is concerned—but this only highlights the differences between *violence* and words like *nasilie*, which have nothing to do with any self-control. English sentences like "Violence erupted in the streets" could not be translated into Russian with the word *nasilie* because *nasilie*—which is one-sided—can be carried out in cold blood (and with a good deal of "self-control"), whereas *violence* cannot.

Thus, *nasilie* is closer in meaning to the older meaning of *violence* in English, described by the OED as "the exercise of physical force so as to inflict injury on, or cause damage to, persons or property (...); treatment or usage tending to cause bodily injury or forcibly interfering with personal freedom." In this older meaning there was no implication that the actions of people "exercising physical force" in this way were due to uncontrolled emotions. For example, the 1718 quote "Almost all the Governments...had their commencement in violence" does not attribute to governments uncontrollable emotions, and neither does the 1651 quote from Hobbes's Leviathan: "Promises proceeding from (...) violence, are no covenants."

With time, however, *violence* did acquire a component suggesting actions due to uncontrolled or uncontrollable emotions, which is absent from the meaning of the Russian word *nasilie* (or from the German word *Gewalt*, offered by dictionaries as the German counterpart of *violence*). It is also absent from the Polish dictionary-equivalent of *violence,* which is *przemoc*—a word that occurs in the Polish national anthem in relation to the eighteenth-century partitions of Poland between the three neighboring powers Russia, Prussia, and Austria ("what foreign *przemoc* took away from us we will take back with sabers").

Evidently, the cultural concern with "control over one's emotions," which is very prominent in modern Anglo culture, has had its effect on the meaning of the word *violence.*

Pinker is not the only Anglophone scholar who has projected the modern Anglo value of "self-control" onto humanity as a whole and who is inclined to interpret human evolution through the prism of this value. For example, philosopher Kim Sterelny affirms that "we" (i.e., humans) "are far superior [to chimps] at inhibiting our immediate emotional response. Emotions and their expression are under much more voluntary control. So the early evolution of human **co-operation** set up an environment that selected for increased tolerance and improved inhibition; for bringing the expressions of emotion (...) under increasing top down control." (p. 22, emphasis added).

The great emphasis on keeping one's emotions under control and on "improved inhibition" is in keeping with some of the central cultural scripts of modern Anglo culture. To mention one other example, William von Hippel and Sally Dunlop (2005) link what they see as old people's tendency "to blurt out personal questions" with the deterioration of the frontal lobes of the brain, due to age. "It doesn't lead to a person becoming less intelligent but it gives them less control over thought suppression." (For discussion, see Wierzbicka 2008c).

Thus, terms like "suppression," "inhibition," "control," and "self-control" are very prominent in present-day Anglophone psychology, philosophy, and cognitive science as a yardstick with which to evaluate human development (or regress). Pinker's choice of "violence" and "self-control" as his twin measures for assessing the progress of humanity is strikingly consonant with modern Anglo cultural scripts, as is also his deep reverence for "cooperation."

Using NSM, we could dramatize the differences between *violence* and *nasilie* by means of the following explications:

violence (Modern English)

a. it can be like this:
b.   something happens in a place for some time because some people do some bad things to some other people in this place at that time
c.   these people do these things at that time because they feel something very bad at that time
d.   they can know that something very bad can happen to these other people's bodies because of this
e. it is very bad when it is like this

Component (b) presents the scenario in a social perspective, phrased in terms of "some people" and "some other people" (in a place). Component (c) says that the actors do what they do because they "feel something very bad at that time" (such as *anger, rage, fury, hatred*). The bad feeling doesn't necessarily have to be directed toward the victims, though it often is. Component (d) says that there can be a "very bad" effect on the bodies of the undergoers. This scenario is regarded as "very bad" (e).

nasilie (Russian)

a. it can be like this:
b.   something happens in a place at some time because some people do some bad things to some other people in this place for some time
c.   these other people don't want these people to do these things
d.   these other people want to do something because of this, they can't do anything
e. it is very bad when it is like this

Roughly speaking, *violence* (in contrast to *nasilie*) implies uncontrolled emotions and bodily injuries. In *nasilie*, on the other hand, there is no reference to emotions, and no reference to bodily injuries, but there is a reference to something like helpless resistance. These are quite different concepts, which reflect different cultural preoccupations.

Daniel Everett's View of Moral Universals: "Lying," "Greed," and "the Golden Rule"

Daniel Everett is well known for his extreme view about linguistic diversity and in particular, for his claims that the language of his special expertise, Pirahã (spoken in Amazonia) goes far beyond what has hitherto been regarded as possible in human languages. Languages differ profoundly from one another, because they are shaped (or even "created") by different cultures, he affirms. (See Everett 2012; for discussion, see Wierzbicka 2013a).

But though focused on diversity and opposed, generally speaking, to any search for universals, Everett makes strong claims about universal human values. "All cultures have values similar to 'It is good to treat others as you would have them treat you,' or 'Avoid lying' and 'Take only what you need,'" he asserts (p. 290). These assertions are not supported by any references and they are contrary to known facts.

Take, for example, "lie." It is true that most, if not all, European languages have a word comparable in meaning to "lying." Even in Europe, however, there are some differences. For example, Russian has two words, not one, corresponding, roughly speaking, to the English verb *lie* (*vrat'* and *lgat'*), and these two words don't mean the same thing.

But even leaving such differences aside, it is clear that outside Europe, many languages don't have words corresponding in meaning to the English word *lie*, although evidence suggests that they all have a word (or a distinct word meaning) for "true."

It is worth recalling in this context that the Ten Commandments of the Hebrew Bible do not include one proscribing lying. They do, on the other hand, include one condemning, roughly speaking, something like "slander": "You shall not bear false witness against your neighbour" (Ex. 20:16). In simple words, the sense of this proscription can be set out as follows:

[God says:]
it is bad if someone says something very bad about someone else to other people
    if it is not true
I want you not to do it

Comparing the ethical prescriptions of the Hebrew Bible, Hastings's (1908-1927) *Encyclopaedia of Religions and Ethics* emphasizes, for example, the lack of any strong norm prohibiting "lying" in ancient Greece:

> Early Hellenic sentiment viewed lying without horror; virtually, as craft, it had in Hermes a patron-god. Perjury, however, was deemed perilous, incurring the wrath of Zeus. Subsequently, as witness the gnomic poets, civic morality coupled veracity with justice as laudable (cf. Plato, *Rep.* i 331 B)

It is true that Greek philosophers often praised truthfulness, but they did not uniformly condemn "lying" in the modern English sense of the word. For example, of Plato's attitude to "falsehood," expressed in his *Republic* (ii.382 A, 389 B-D), Hastings's *Encyclopaedia* says that "while permitting his 'guardians' to use it, now and again, medicinally and officially, 'for the benefit of the State,'

[it] bids them punish it rigorously in private individuals as 'a practice pernicious and subversive of the commonwealth." At the same time, the *Encyclopaedia* emphasizes that what mattered most in Greek and Roman ethical thought was different from the modern condemnations of the "spoken lie" (p. 222):

> On the whole, the main difference between ancient and 'modern' views on inveracity is that in the latter censure is directed primarily on discrepance [sic] between statement and thought rather than on the divergence from reality of a spoken, or unuttered, proposition. 'Modern' morality tends to be severe upon misstatements, apparently wilful, of particular facts, but is strangely lenient wherever 'ignorance' can be pleaded—as if ignorance was not often wilful, or reckless, indifference to truth. Many persons will habitually declare as fact anything that they do not positively know to be untrue, and, when convicted of error, take no shame to themselves. They 'thought' it was so. To Plato such untrue 'thought' or 'lie in the soul' appeared more manifestly evil than any spoken lie.. .

As for the languages outside the sphere of Judeo-Christian and Greco-Roman civilization, many of them do not have a word corresponding, even approximately, to the English verb *lie*. For example, in the Australian language Pitjantjatjara (Goddard 1996), the closest counterpart of *lie* is the adverb *ngunti,* glossed in Goddard's dictionary as "1. (with verbs of saying and thinking) false, wrong, untrue, 2. pretend (to do), fake (doing)." The first of these meanings is illustrated with the sentence "I wrongly (*ngunti*) thought you were alone."

Thus, there is no word, or distinct word-meaning, corresponding to the idea of, roughly speaking, "saying (on purpose) something untrue, wanting someone else to think that it was true" (cf. Wierzbicka 2006a.) Empirical cross-linguistic investigations indicate that the distinction between thinking or saying something that is true and thinking or saying something that is not true is a universal human concern, because evidence suggests that all languages have a word meaning "true" and that in all languages this word can combine with the words meaning "say" and "think." It would be far more justified to say that, on the whole, truth is valued in all cultures, rather than to say that all cultures condemn, or even censure, lying.

Incidentally, from the point of view of many cultures that do strongly condemn "lying," Everett's formulation "avoid lying" may seem curiously lax, as if some forms of "lying" were being excused, perhaps even justified. This is in keeping with the English phrase *white lies*, which presents some forms of "lying" as harmless, perhaps even desirable. As I have discussed in *English: Meaning and Culture* (2006a), contemporary Anglo cultural scripts, reflected inter alia in the phrase *white lies,* contrast in this respect with the scripts of some other cultures (for example, Polish and Jewish).

In her memoir *New York* (2001), the Australian writer Lily Brett writes: "Some untruths are essential. For example, compliments that are not entirely accurate, and other forms of kindness or flattery. Sometimes it doesn't make sense to tell the truth. Sometimes it would be just plain stupid" (p. 82). Brett contrasts these cultural assumptions, which she accepts, with those of her father—a Polish Jewish Holocaust survivor, of whom she says ironically that "he is fond of the truth." Present at an interview given by his daughter, the father embarrasses her by interrupting and contradicting what she has said. Brett writes: "I couldn't believe it. 'It didn't happen the way you said it did,' my father said. I glared at my father. He deflected my glare. 'The truth is the truth,' he declared" (p. 84). This saying corresponds to the Polish expression "co prawda to prawda" (lit. "what truth that truth"), which may have been at the back of her father's mind; from a contemporary Anglo perspective, however, it seems too inflexible and too absolute. (Wierzbicka 2006a: 45)

What applies to the putative norm "avoid lying" applies also to the injunction against greed. Moses's tablets did not include a commandment "thou shall not be greedy," as they did not include "thou shall not lie." The idea that it is foolish to store up for oneself "treasures on earth where moth and rust consume and where thieves break in and steal" appears in Matthew's Gospel (Matt. 6: 19), and so does the commandment to feed the hungry (Matt. 25: 31–46), but these are both different from Everett's prescription, "Take only what you need."

Australian Aboriginal cultures include, roughly speaking, an obligation to share one's "good things" (like food, money) with one's relatives. This is evidenced, for example, in the meaning of words like *ngatini*, described in Goddard's (1996) dictionary of Pitjantjatjara/Yankunytjatjara as "ask, demand, request to be given something. Usually in connection with implied right to expect results, on account of kin obligations." The key word related to this norm in Pijtantjatjara/Yankunytjatjara is *walytja*, "one of the family, a relation, a kinsman" (ibid.). The norm for "sharing goods with one's walytja" can be formulated in simple words as follows (Wierzbicka 2013b):

THE "WALYTJA" NORM
many people think like this:
   "if someone is my 'kin' (*walytja*) it is good if I do something good for this someone
     when this someone says to me: "I want you to do something good for me"
       it will be good if I do it, it will be bad if I don't do it"

Clearly, this is quite different from Everett's "anti-greed" norm, which can be phrased (roughly) in the same simple words along the following lines:

THE "ANTI-GREED" NORM (cf. "take only what you need")

some people think like this about many things:

    "I want to have all these things"

if these people have many things they think like this:

    "I want to have more"

it is bad if people think like this

This rule, which Everett suggests as a moral universal, is likely to derive from his own culture-specific and perhaps even subculture-specific (anticapitalist?) set of values and beliefs.

As for the "Golden Rule" ("Do everything to others as you would have them do onto you," Matt. 7:12, Luke 6:13), this derives, one presumes, from Everett's training as a Christian missionary. The idea that this rule can be found in all cultures has no support in facts. (See Wierzbicka 2001: 191–202; Porpora 2001).

Generally speaking, it appears that Everett is eager to attribute to all cultures those values that he himself cherishes, partly because he takes them for granted and perhaps partly because to admit that they may not be found outside his own cultural sphere could smack of cultural superiority. "We cannot learn about the human condition by homogenizing it," writes Everett, urging other scholars to investigate "the connection between languages and human values" (p. 317). But there are many ways to homogenize the human condition, and interpreting it through the conceptual vocabulary of English is increasingly prominent among them.

Everett emphasizes the value of each and every language for humanity as a whole:

> A language is a repository of the riches of highly specialized cultural experiences. When a language is lost *all* of us lose the knowledge contained in that language's words and grammar—knowledge that can never be recovered if the language has not been studied or recorded. (. . .) this knowledge (. . .) [is] vital in providing us with different ways of thinking about life, of approaching day-to-day existence on planet earth. (p. 293)

I wholeheartedly agree that every language is a repository of unique ways of thinking about human existence and a unique cultural "take" on human existence, and in particular, on human values. But we will not recover these unique cultural perspectives on values by interpreting them through the prism of English value words and Anglo cultural scripts. To find out what speakers of other languages value we must listen attentively to their own words and to decipher the meanings inscribed in them. To do this without Anglocentric distortions, we need to do it through shared human concepts, not through value concepts embedded in English—whether specific ones like "lying," "greed," "tolerance," "integrity," and "fairness" (cf. e.g., Wierzbicka 2006a,

Gladkova 2008) or very general ones, like "right" and "wrong," to which I will now turn.

Marc Hauser's "Universal Sense of Right and Wrong"

Marc Hauser is a Harvard psychologist and evolutionary biologist, best known for his website called "the moral sense test (MST)." He is also the author of a book titled *Moral Minds: How Nature Designed Our Universal Sense of Right and Wrong* (2006). Even aside from the uniquely English word *mind* (cf. Wierzbicka 1989), it would be hard to devise a more concentrated dose of Anglo culture in just a few words than that contained in this title.

The English words *right* and *wrong*, which can be applied to answers to arithmetical questions as well as human conduct, represent the quintessence of rationalist ethics embedded in modern English. Roughly speaking, these words—which have no semantic equivalents in most other European languages—tend to present a person's moral misconduct as a matter of bad thinking, just as a "wrong answer" to an arithmetical question is a result of a faulty calculation or "bad thinking."

The word *sense*, on the other hand, represents the quintessence of "British empiricism," in which modern English as a whole is steeped. The expression "sense of right and wrong" is untranslatable into other languages for two reasons: the rationalist perspective on human morality encoded in the meanings of the English adjectives of *right* and *wrong*, and the empiricist take on epistemology embedded in the English word *sense*.

I have studied the semantics of *right* and *wrong*, in a historical perspective, in *English: Meaning and Culture* (2006a), and that of various *sense* expressions (including *moral sense* and *the sense of right and wrong*) in its sequel, *Experience, Evidence and Sense: The hidden cultural legacy of English* (2010a). What is particularly striking about the title of Hauser's book is the combination of those quintessentially English concepts with the pronoun "our," the adjective "universal," and the noun "nature." Evidently, when Hauser says "our," he doesn't mean "us Anglos," but "us humans."

To speakers of English, the concepts "right" and "wrong" often appear to be fundamental, rooted in nature itself. According to some scholars, even animals have a sense of "right" and "wrong." For example, Frans de Waal (1996, p. 2), the author of *Good Natured: The Origins of Right and Wrong in Humans and Other Animals*, states: "A society lacking notions of right and wrong is about the worst thing we can imagine—if we can imagine it at all." But sometimes our imagination needs to be stretched on the basis of cross-linguistic evidence; in this case, cross-linguistic evidence shows us that *most* societies don't have the notions of "right" and "wrong" and that in fact these notions are peculiar to Anglo culture.

The distinction between "right" and "wrong" occupies a central place in the English moral lexicon and indeed in Anglo moral discourse generally—so much so that many Anglophone scholars, including even anthropologists, regard it as fundamental to human nature. (The very first example of the use of *right* offered by the *Shorter Oxford English Dictionary*, dated from 1737, reads: "You must acknowledge a Distinction betwixt Right and Wrong, founded in Nature.")

As I have discussed in detail in *English: Meaning and Culture*, the ascendancy of "right" and "wrong" over "good" and "bad" reflects a more rational, more procedural, more reason-based approach to human life, and a retreat from a pure distinction between GOOD and BAD unsupported by any appeal to reason, procedures, methods, or intersubjectively available evidence. An ethics of right and wrong is an ethics in which the choice between good and bad is seen as something that can be decided by reason, by good thinking, and something that can be interpersonally validated—like science. It is a *rationalist* ethics, an ethics that doesn't need to be grounded in metaphysics (in particular, in God) but can be grounded in reason.

Turning now to the word *sense* (as in "moral sense" and "a sense of right and wrong"), I will note, first, that it is one of the most common abstract nouns in the English language, and second, that it lies at the center of an extremely rich family of collocations, including *a sense of humor, a sense of reality, a sense of freedom, a sense of responsibility, a sense of self, common sense, practical sense,* and *to make sense*—most of which, like *sense* itself, have no equivalents in other languages and yet are seemingly indispensable in Anglophone societies. British empiricism, which now permeates contemporary English language (in all its varieties, American as well as British or Australian), is grounded in the basic trust in the "five senses"; and "common sense" lies at the center of Anglo-English folk philosophy and folk ethics (cf. Wierzbicka 2010a).

The phrases "moral sense" and "a sense of right and wrong" are part and parcel of this tradition. The concept of moral sense plays an important role in books on philosophy, psychology, and popular science authored by those who write in English and take the English language for granted. For example, in his atheist tract, *The God Delusion*, the evolutionary biologist and public intellectual Richard Dawkins asks (in a chapter title): "Does our moral sense have a Darwinian origin?" (Dawkins 2006: 245). He then replies, "Our moral sense, like our sexual desire, is indeed rooted deep in our Darwinian past"; he also affirms that "we have a moral sense which is built into our brains, like our sexual instinct or our fear of heights." (p. 246) Like Hauser, Dawkins uses the phrase *moral sense* interchangeably with the phrase *a sense of right and wrong*.

The phrase *moral sense* plays a significant role in contemporary philosophy, science, and popular science, and it is an important tool in the conceptual kit with which the English language equips its speakers, writers, and thinkers. Anglophone scientists often take this phrase for granted and assume that it corresponds neatly to something "built into our brains" (Dawkins 2006). Yet this phrase has no exact equivalents in other European languages, let alone non-European ones: it is part of the Anglo cultural heritage going back not only to eighteenth-century British moral philosophers like Shaftesbury, Hutcheson, and Hume, but even further—to Locke's influential tenet that all knowledge ultimately derives from the senses.

While the meaning of the phrase *moral sense* has changed in the course of the last three centuries, there is also a continuity here. Scientists and popular science writers who today write in English about "moral sense" generally do not seem to be aware that they are part of a particular linguistic and conceptual tradition and that by equating "human morality" with "moral sense" they are interpreting it through the prism of that tradition. Hauser's "moral sense test" and "the universal sense of right and wrong" are both examples of the same phenomenon.

Conclusion

In a globalized world in which English has become, effectively, the first ever global lingua franca, it is increasingly easy to forget that the whole world doesn't think in English. If humankind does (e.g., as Shweder 2012c suggests) share some deep moral intuitions on which a global ethic could build, then these intuitions must relate to particular speakers' conceptual worlds. The diversity of languages that people across the world speak means that there is a diversity of conceptual worlds. If these different conceptual worlds didn't share a common core then there would be no possibility of genuine cross-cultural understanding and no way to articulate any moral values that could provide a common frame of reference for comparing, and explaining, values.

However, as decades of empirical cross-linguistic investigations in the NSM framework have shown (Goddard and Wierzbicka, eds 2002), such a common frame can be found in words for "good" and "bad," which can be used in "canonical" sentences like the following ones:

> People can do good things.
> People can do bad things.
> It is good if people want good things to happen to other people.
> It is bad if people want bad things to happen to other people.

Shweder suggests that "variations in concrete moral judgments of the many peoples of the world can be viewed, in part, as expressions of the many answers that are possible to (...) universal questions":

> Those in the social sciences who have over the decades engaged in descriptive research in the cultural psychology of morality investigate local answers to those unavoidable and hence universal existential and

metaphysical questions. (…) What they have discovered is that moral judgments around the world are ubiquitous, passionate, motivating, truth asserting and divergent; and that in all cultures there is some sense of natural moral law and the development of some kind of normative language of rights, duties, obligations or values for regulating and justifying action. (Shweder, 2012c: 98)

All this is very persuasive. I would add, however, that next to "local answers" to "universal questions" there are also "local questions," and among them, questions formulated in the culture-specific conceptual language of the investigator. (For example: is there in a given society a norm to avoid lying?) If we want to find out what many people around the world may share, it would clearly be more fruitful to ask questions in a conceptual language that people around the world can understand. Such language would have to be based on the universal concepts "good" and "bad," and not on culturally shaped concepts like "right" and "wrong," "lying" and "honesty," "violence" and "cooperation": to compare various local answers to universal questions we need a common conceptual measure independent of conceptual moral languages developed within particular cultures, including Anglo culture.

Shweder offers, as examples of moral absolutes, "benevolence" and "malevolence," no doubt meaning by this that "benevolence is good" and "malevolence is bad." The words *benevolence* and *malevolence* are quite close to the conceptual core of all languages, because they are obviously built on the universal concepts "good," "bad," and "want." I would propose, as a starting point for discussion, statements [A], [B], [C], and [D], phrased in universal concepts and according to universal conceptual grammar:

[A] It is good if someone wants to do something good for someone else.
[B] It is bad if someone wants to do something bad to someone else.
[C] It is good if people want to do good things for other people.
[D] It is bad if people want to do bad things to other people.

The words *benevolence* and *malevolence* could also be understood as referring to "good will" and "ill will" alone, without any reference to actions. Relying on the universal conceptual language, we could articulate such intuitions as in [E], [F], [G], and [H]:

[E] It is good if someone wants something good to happen to someone else.
[F] It is bad if someone wants something bad to happen to someone else.
[G] It is good if people want good things to happen to other people.
[H] It is bad if people want bad things to happen to other people.

These statements, too, could be useful reference points for a culture-independent, non-Anglocentric comparison of values across languages and cultures.

In the contemporary globalized world, where the tempo and intensity of international and intercultural contacts are continuously strengthening, communication about values has become increasingly crucial. In multicultural and multiethnic societies, the question of common understanding about values is also urgent, as many world leaders are more and more aware.

To illustrate: In a chapter entitled "Values" in his book "The Audacity of Hope," Barack Obama (2006) presents shared values as one of the central questions facing America. Referring to the "constant cross-pollination" occurring within America, "a not entirely orderly but generally peaceful collision among people and cultures," Obama asks insistently: "What are the core values that we, as Americans, hold in common?" He sees debates about values as vitally important. "It is the language of values that people use to map their world. It is what can inspire them to take action, and move them beyond their isolation (. . .) the broader questions of shared values—the standards and principles that the majority of Americans deem important in their lives, and in the life of the country—should be the heart of our politics, the cornerstone of any meaningful debate about budgets and projects, regulations and policies." (pp. 51–52)

But discussions and debates about values require a language. If shared values are to be the cornerstone of any meaningful political or economic debate, the prior question of a shared language is crucial, whether in America, Australia, or anywhere else in today's shrinking and globalizing world. To work toward peace and harmony in the world, individuals and groups have to be able to achieve some understanding of how their values differ. Emphasizing shared values may be rhetorically effective, but if it is done at the cost of a clear recognition of differences in values, in the end, it may not contribute a great deal to nationwide, let alone worldwide, understanding.

At a party conference in November 2010, German Chancellor Angela Merkel said that "any migrant who learns German and respects our laws and values [*Werte*] is welcome" (Garton Ash 2011: 24). One wonders, however, where Turkish migrants in Germany can read a clear and intelligible explanation of what exactly those "German values" are. Garton Ash identifies as a key German value "everything that is summed up in the untranslatable German word *Bildung*" (ibid). In what conceptual lingua franca can the meaning of such an untranslatable and yet crucial value word be explained to immigrants who are expected to respect this value?

In a speech on February 5, 2011, British Conservative Prime Minister David Cameron told the Munich Security Conference that "A passively tolerant society (. . .) stands neutral between different values. (. . .) A genuinely liberal country does much more. It believes in certain values and actively promotes them." (*The Australian*, Feb. 7, 2011, p.11). Once again, whichever stand one is inclined to favor, it is clear that discussions about values are unavoidable in modern multicultural and multiethnic societies. It is not clear, however, how such discussions can lead to greater mutual understanding if they cannot draw on a common conceptual lingua franca. As this chapter illustrates, such a lingua franca can be found in a mini-English based on shared human concepts.

7

Human Emotions and English Words: Are Anger and Disgust Universal?

Are there "Basic Human Emotions," Independent of Languages and Cultures?

How many different kinds of emotions are human beings capable of? Philosopher and psychologist William James observed more than a hundred years ago that there was no definite answer to this question, because—as introspection tells us—we are capable of a great variety of feelings and these feelings are not clearly separated from one another and cannot be counted. Upon this largely nebulous world of feelings every language imposes its own interpretive grid.

> If one should seek to name each particular one [of the emotions] of which the human heart is the seat, it is plain that the limit to their number would lie in the introspective vocabulary of the seeker, each race of men having found names for some shade of feeling which other races have left undiscriminated. If we should seek to break the emotions, thus enumerated, into groups, according to their affinities, it is again plain that all sorts of groupings would be possible, according as we chose this character or that as a basis, and that all groupings would be equally real and true. (1890: 485)

The way of looking at human emotions that came to dominate psychology toward the end of the twentieth century couldn't be more different: emotions were now viewed by many psychologists as clearly discriminable categories of experience, enumerable and discrete. As the recent special issue on "basic emotions" of the journal *Emotion Review* (2011) illustrates, this view of human emotions is still strongly represented in contemporary psychology. To understand the contemporary scene, however, we need first to go some decades back.

A keen interest in emotions emerged in modern psychology rather suddenly, in the late 1960s and early 1970s. As noted by anthropologist Ben Blount in 1984, this sudden "efflorescence of interest in emotions" was related to the new theory of "basic emotions," put forward at that time by psychologists Paul

Ekman (e.g., 1972), Carroll Izard (e.g. 1971), and others. The main idea of this theory was summed up in the following statement by two of its adherents, psychologists Philip Johnson-Laird and Keith Oatley (1989: 90):

> According to our theory, there is a set of basic emotion modes that correspond to internal signals that can impinge on consciousness. These modes—happiness, sadness, anger, fear, disgust—should be universally accepted as discriminable categories of direct experience.

In the special issue of *Emotion Review*, the editors sum up the idea of "basic emotions" as follows:

> The various emotions we witness or experience can be divided into classes. All languages include words for such classes; English lists *joy, grief, fear, love,* and on and on. Some theorists—called here *basic emotion theorists*—propose that these are classes that cut nature at the joints, that capture hardwired centrally organized syndromes of coordinated emotional responses (. . .). (Russell et al. 2011: 363)

The theory of "basic emotions" has been vigorously critiqued by many scholars for over thirty years, and remains the subject of strong disagreements. In particular, anthropologists have often pointed out that in non-Western cultures emotions can be conceptualized and categorized differently than they are in English and that the emotion types named in English were not any more "natural" and well-founded than those named in other languages. This point was highlighted by the ironic title of Catherine Lutz's (1988) book *Unnatural Emotions*, and also the title of her well-known article "Ethnopsychology compared to what?" (1983) From Lutz's perspective, the emotion types singled out in the Ifaluk language spoken on an atoll in Micronesia were just as "natural" as those singled out by English, and the psychology of emotions embedded in the English lexicon was one "ethnopsychology" among others, not a scientifically valid analysis of the human mind.

From the point of view of such critics, focusing on the English-based emotion concepts to the exclusion of those singled out by other languages leads not only to an Anglocentric perspective on human emotions but also to a very narrow vision of what human emotional lives can be. Different "ethnopsychologies" carry with them different insights, and these insights are lost in approaches to psychology based on one cultural tradition that either refuse to look at any other traditions or are determined to always view them through the prism of one's own.

Nonetheless, within psychology, the theory of "basic emotions," corresponding, at least roughly, to English emotion terms, continues to be very strong. In fact, according to the editors of the special issue of *Emotion Review*, "Basic emotions theory has been and remains *the* major program for scientific research on emotion" (p. 363). The foremost proponent of "basic emotions" was, from the outset, Paul Ekman. Since I cannot undertake a comprehensive review of the work and ideas of all the leading "basic emotion" theorists, I will treat Ekman here as a representative of the entire paradigm. Ekman's early lists of such emotions included the following English terms: happiness, sadness, anger, fear, disgust, and surprise. More than anybody else, Ekman linked "basic emotions" with what he saw as universal facial expressions of emotion. These facial expressions, too, could be identified, in his view, through English words like *happiness*, *sadness*, and so on.

Ekman was not unaware that other languages may not have equivalents for these English terms. Indeed, reporting on his research with the Dani people of the New Guinea Highlands, he noted himself that they "don't even have words for the six emotions" (Ekman 1975: 29). But this didn't stop him from regarding his six chosen English words as fitting labels for universal human emotions or their facial expressions: "Regardless of the language, of whether the culture is Western or Eastern, industrialized or preliterate, these facial expressions are labelled with the same emotion terms: happiness, sadness, anger, fear, disgust and surprise" (Ekman 1980: 137-8).

Regardless of language…as if the words *happiness*, *sadness*, and so on did not belong to any particular language—or, as if the language to which they belong fitted reality so well that it could name, with perfect adequacy, the emotions of people anywhere in the world, whether or not they had words for them in their own languages.

A decade later, "surprise" was removed from Ekman's list of "basic emotions," and "happiness" was replaced with "enjoyment," but the overall strong claims about universal emotions and universal facial expressions (identifiable through English emotion terms) were maintained. For example, Ekman (1992: 175) wrote: "The strongest evidence for distinguishing one emotion from another comes from research on facial expressions. There is robust, consistent evidence of a universal facial expression for anger, fear, enjoyment, sadness and disgust."

Belgian philosopher Jaap van Brakel, an incisive critic of both the theory of basic colors (identifiable through English color terms) and the theory of "basic emotions" (identifiable through English emotion terms) commented wryly (1993: 188): "Why should 20th century English name these universal emotions correctly? It can only be because Ekman believes that English is at the pinnacle of the evolution of naming of the structure of the experiential world."[1]

Emotion Wars

Van Brakel's question, "Why should 20th century English name universal emotions correctly?" lies at the heart of the "emotion wars" that have been going on for a few decades and to which there is yet no clear end in view. As one who was involved in these wars almost from the start, let me adduce here a quote from an article of mine entitled "Human emotions: Universal or culture-specific?," which was published in *American Anthropologist* in 1986:

> English terms of emotion constitute a folk taxonomy, not an objective, culture-free analytical framework, so obviously we cannot assume that English words such as *disgust, fear* or *shame* are clues to universal human concepts, or to basic psychological realities. (p. 584)

As a solution to the problem, I proposed then, as I do now, giving up the use of English-bound emotion labels as analytical tools, and exploring human emotions through simpler and cross-translatable words:

> Different systems of emotion terms are likely to reflect different ways of conceptualizing emotions (cf. Geertz 1973, Levy 1983, Rosaldo 1980, and Lutz 1983), and conversely, any possible universals in the way different societies conceptualize emotions are likely to be reflected in the ways those different societies converge in the labelling of emotions. But whether emotion terms available in different languages truly converge (...) is a problem that cannot be resolved without rigorous semantic analysis, and without a language-independent semantic metalanguage. (p. 593)

Around the same time, philosopher Rom Harré (1986: 3) spoke of "the overwhelming evidence of cultural diversity and cognitive differentiation of the emotions of mankind."

Some psychologists and psychiatrists came to concur with the view that English emotion terms represent cultural constructs. For example, medical scholar Christopher Dowrick in his book *Beyond Depression* (2004) paid a great deal of attention to the English word *depression* and to the impact that it had on modern psychiatry, medicine, and pharmacology, stressing that "words that we take for granted, like depression, do not translate readily into other languages and cultures" (p.122). Referring in particular to my 1999 book *Emotions Across Languages and Cultures*, Dowrick writes: "It is not that specific words like depression do not exist in certain languages. It is more that different cultures and languages are constructed in such different ways that there may be no room for a concept like depression, rendering it virtually meaningless." (p.23)

On the other side of the barricade, numerous psychologists have argued for many years (and some still do) that "the problem of language" should not be exaggerated. For example, the distinguished psychologist and emotionologist Richard Lazarus (1995: 250), whom I had criticized for his reliance on English emotion terms in Wierzbicka (1995), wrote:

Wierzbicka suggests that I underestimate the depth of cultural variation in emotion concepts as well as the problem of language. (p. 255)
Words have power to influence, yet—as in the Whorfian hypotheses writ large—they cannot override the life conditions that make people sad or angry, which they can sense to some extent without words. (...) I am suggesting, in effect, that all people experience anger, sadness, and so forth, regardless of what they call it... Words are important, but we must not deify them. (p. 250)

When I responded to Lazarus in my book *Emotions Across Languages and Cultures* (1999), I pointed out that by refusing to pay attention to differences between different languages, scholars who take this position end up doing precisely what they wish to avoid, that is, "deifying" some words from their own native language and reifying the concepts encapsulated in them. I also pointed out that we need to take some interest in words (in this case, emotion words), in order to be able to go beyond words, and that Sapir's warning that "the philosopher needs to understand language if only to protect himself against his own language habits" (1949[1929]: 165) applies to psychologists as much as to philosophers.

An important benchmark in the debate surrounding the theory of "basic emotions" was a volume entitled *The Nature of Emotions: Some Fundamental Questions*, which appeared in 1994 and which was edited by two proponents of the theory, Ekman and Davidson (Ekman and Davidson (eds) 1994). Ekman argued in this volume that "there is evidence (...) for distinctive patterns of autonomic nervous system (ANS) activity for anger, fear and disgust, and (...) there may also be a distinctive pattern for sadness" (p. 17). In their joint epilogue to the volume, Ekman and Davidson vigorously defended Ekman's earlier claims about the existence of universal facial expressions of at least five basic emotions, about lexical convergence between different languages with regard to these emotions, and about the presence of distinctive patterns of "autonomic nervous system (ANS) activity" characterizing each of them: "There is consistent evidence for pan-cultural facial expressions for five emotions: anger, fear, sadness, enjoyment, and disgust (...). Study of the emotion lexicon suggests roughly the same emotions." (Ekman and Davidson 1994: 413)

Despite the statement about emotion lexicons (implying their convergence across languages), Ekman and Davidson do note reports such as Levy's (1984) about the absence of a word comparable to *sadness* in Tahitian, and Signe Howell's observation about the absence of a word comparable to *anger* in languages like Chewong, but they feel confident that they "can deal" with them, one way or another:

If there truly is no trace of anger, no pattern of behaviour when provoked, insulted, or frustrated, no evidence of anger displaced onto other targets, it would directly contradict the position of those who presume emotions to be universal. (...)

> The universalists can deal with reports from anthropology about "absent" emotions by presuming that the anthropologist must have missed subtle signs of the emotion, or that the emotion occurs but is not named, or that its manifestations were discouraged early in life. (p. 415)

Thus, Ekman and Davidson seem to be dismissing empirical evidence inconsistent with their claims. They also appear to derive comfort from the fact that the emotional behavior of people lacking a word for one of the supposedly universal "basic emotions" (e.g., "sadness") can nonetheless be *interpreted* through the English emotion terms (e.g., *sadness*):

> Such a view is buttressed by Levy's (1984) observations that while Tahitians do not either label or recognize sadness, sadness nevertheless was apparent in the behaviour of Tahitians. Tahitians, Levy said, show sad expressions and behaviour when experiencing a rejection by a loved one, but they interpret their behaviour as sickness, not sadness, and do not relate it to the rejection.

This is in fact consistent with Shweder's view of emotion concepts such as "sadness" as interpretive schemes: no doubt, speakers of English *can* interpret Tahitians' behavior through the prism of the Anglo interpretive scheme associated with the English word *sadness*. Where "social constructionists" like Shweder and "universalists" like Ekman and Davidson disagree is the special significance attached by the former but not the latter scholars to the English interpretive scheme: from the "universalist" perspective, no matter how the Tahitians may interpret their own emotional experience, the English interpretive scheme associated with the word *sadness* fits their (and everybody else's) emotions better.

Shweder's response to Ekman and Davidson, expressed in the same volume, refers to my own long battle against Anglocentrism in emotion research:

> With regard to the distribution of the emotions, for every Johnson-Laird and Oatley (1989; pp. 90) who claim that there exists "a set of basic emotion modes" (viz., happiness, sadness, anger, fear, and disgust) that "should be universally accepted as discriminable categories of direct experience" or for every Paul Ekman (1973; pp. 219-220) who claims that regardless of language, culture, and history "these facial expressions are labelled with the same emotion terms: happiness, sadness, anger, fear, disgust and surprise" there is an Anna Wierzbicka (n.d., also see 1990) who points out (with those assertions by Johnson-Laird & Oatley and Ekman explicitly in mind) that the whole world does not speak English; that English words such as happiness, sadness, anger, fear, and disgust encode concepts that are "different from those encoded in the emotion terms of different languages"; that "in fact, there are NO emotion terms which can be matched neatly across language and culture boundaries"; that "there are NO universal

emotion concepts, lexicalized in all the languages of the world"; and that it is all too easy in the translation process to unwittingly assimilate other people's linguistic meanings to an ethnocentric set of analytic categories— the abstract "emotional" states favoured by the English-speaking world. (Shweder 1994: 33)

In the same volume, a leading European emotion researcher, Klaus Scherer, lent support to calls for a cross-linguistic approach to the study of emotions, endorsing the view that verbal labels provided by different languages construe and categorize people's emotional experience in different ways:

> Given the prominence and frequency of occurrence of these episodes of highly similar emotional experiences, it is not surprising that they have been labelled with a short verbal expression, mostly a single word, in most languages. (...) Thus, discreteness is—at least in part—bestowed by linguistic categorization and the cultural prototypes these categories reflect (...). Linguistic categories conceptually order the world for us in many domains, and they do so for emotion. (Scherer 1994: 30)

Responding to Shweder (and, indirectly, to Scherer) in the same volume, Ekman and Davidson (1994: 46) rejected the suggestions that the cross-linguistic variability of emotional concepts presented a problem for the theory of "basic emotions" (labeled with English words such as *happiness*, *sadness*, and *disgust*):

> In challenging Ekman and also Johnson-Laird and Oatley, Shweder cites Wierzbicka's arguments about language differences. Even Scherer would not accept Wierzbicka's position about the total variability in the lexicon of emotion. Shweder fails to note that the evidence for universality is not limited to words, but includes studies of expression that did not involve words as well as studies of physiology, antecedents, and so on.

Ekman was not totally unmoved, however, by the critique that his theory met with, and in the last decade or so modified it in some respects. Whether these modifications allowed him to overcome the Anglocentrism of his earlier position will be considered in the next section.

"Basic Emotion Theory" Now: Ekman and Cordaro 2011

In the 2011 special issue on "basic emotions," the paper by Ekman and Cordaro summarizes, by and large, Ekman's chapter on basic emotions in *Nature of Emotions* (1994), although the answers to two of the editors' questions are drawn primarily from Ekman's 2003 book *Emotions Revealed*. Although he now speaks of "emotion families," Ekman still maintains (contra James) that emotions are "discrete automatic responses to (...) events" (Abstract) and that they can be identified by means of English emotion terms such as *anger* and *fear*. In answer to the editors' question "What is your list of basic emotions?," Ekman and Cordaro list seven: anger, fear, surprise, sadness, disgust, contempt, and happiness.

Taking account of the charge of Anglocentrism leveled in the past at the "basic emotion" theorists (such as Ekman), the editors of the special issue ask: "If your list of basic emotions is a set of English terms, how do you respond to the claim that some languages lack equivalent terms for those emotions but include emotion terms that differ in meaning from English terms?" (p. 369) To this key question, Ekman and Cordaro reply:

> Language and emotion are independent of each other; both can evolve independently without the presence of the other. (....) Language is socially constructed, basic emotions are not. Individual societies create what is and is not directly expressed with words, and this does not necessarily negate the shared experiences of our basic emotions. (p. 369)

In fact, a vast body of evidence has now been amassed showing that language and emotions are *not* mutually independent—a fact recognized in a remarkable early paper by the psychologist James Russell (now one of the two editors-in-chief of *Emotion Review*) and increasingly acknowledged by many other psychologists. This doesn't mean that there are no shared experiences or no universal emotions, but it does mean that the categories of emotions that have been singled out for naming by a particular language depend, conceptually, on that language, and on the culture associated with it. Accordingly, categories of emotions that have been singled out for naming in contemporary English depend, conceptually, on modern English and Anglo culture. I will illustrate this with the "basic emotion of disgust," drawing on a recent study of this theme by Cliff Goddard (In press).

As noted by Goddard, Charles Darwin (1872) observed that "the expression of disgust can be simulated by a person posing as though he is refusing or rejecting from the mouth something which tastes bad." Ekman and Cordaro follow in Darwin's footsteps when they describe "disgust" as "repulsion by the sight, smell or taste of something" (p. 365) and observe: "Disgust triggers the gag reflex and restricts airflow to our olfactory receptors. That which has been taken in comes out." (p. 308) They do not note that, for example, German doesn't have a word corresponding in meaning to the English *disgust*, and that its closest colloquial counterpart, *Ekel*, is associated with an impulse to recoil rather than with the gag reflex.

German dictionaries usually describe *Ekel* as *Abscheu* or *Abneigung*, that is, something like "aversion" rather than "disgust," and link it, prototypically, with spiders, snakes, and worms rather than nausea or vomit. For example, *Langenscheidt's Grosswörterbuch* (1997) describes *Ekel* as "eine sehr starke Abneigung gegen jemanden/etwas, die sich oft in einer physischen Reaktion zeigt" ("a very strong aversion to someone or something which often shows itself in a physical reaction"). As examples of *Ekel* and *ekelhaft* (adjective), the dictionary offers the sentence, "Ich empfinde Ekel vor/gegenüber Schlangen und Spinnen" ("I experience *Ekel* towards snakes and spiders") and "Ich finde Regenswürmer ekelhaft" ("I find earthworms *ekelhaft*"). Bilingual German-English dictionaries give similar examples. For example, *Harrap's Standard German and English Dictionary* (1963) cites the sentence "Spinnen sind mir ein Ekel," glossing it, interestingly, as "spiders give me the creeps."

Both "aversion" to spiders and snakes and "disgust" associated with gagging and vomiting are no doubt widespread human behaviors, independent of language. Indeed, many speakers of English have an aversion to spiders and snakes, and equally many speakers of German at times show facial and body expressions that in English would be described as "disgust." Nonetheless, the fact is that colloquial German doesn't have a word corresponding in meaning to the English *disgust*, and that in colloquial English, *disgust* is far more salient than words like *revulsion, repugnance,* or *aversion,* which are closer to the German *Ekel.* Thus, by choosing the English word *disgust* (rather than, for example, *revulsion*) to identify one of the supposedly basic human emotions, Anglophone theorists are being guided by their native language. Conversely, when a philosopher writing in German (such as Aurel Kolnai 1929) devotes a lengthy study to *Ekel,* in choosing this particular category of experience for detailed exploration he is guided, to some extent, by the German language.

In this context, it is worth noting that while *disgust* played a role in Darwin's writings (as well as those of Ekman and other "basic emotions" theorists), *Ekel* played a considerable role in the writings of Freud. In particular, as noted by William Miller in his book titled *The Anatomy of Disgust, Ekel* was often presented by Freud as an inhibitor of libido. Miller comments: "The German *Ekel,* for instance, bears no easily discernible connection to taste. Did that make it easier for Freud to link disgust as readily with the anal and genital as with the oral zone?" (Miller 1997: 1, quoted in Goddard, In press). Strictly speaking, it was of course *Ekel,* not *disgust,* that Freud linked with the anal and genital zones, and the fact that in the English translation of Freud's works, *Ekel* is regularly translated as *disgust* obscures Freud's thought on this point. For example, the statement, "Disgust appears earlier in little girls than in boys," which we find in the English version of Freud's writings (e.g., Freud 1954: 233), seems to distort the original idea phrased in terms of *Ekel* and discussed in the context of sexual repression. Darwin talked about "disgust," but Freud talked about "Ekel," and clearly, they were not talking about the same thing.

Of course, Ekman and Cordaro could say that it is the meaning of the English word *disgust* that is socially (culturally) constructed, not the "basic emotion of disgust," which is (they would say) independent of language and identifiable in physiological terms through a certain distinctive pattern of autonomic nervous system activity. But if the choice of the English word *disgust* as a label for the putative basic emotion in question is arbitrary, then this emotion might just as well be labeled "emotion X." To understand human beings we need to know something about their feelings, and not only about the patterns of autonomic nervous system activity. In fact, the only thing about the patterns of autonomic nervous system activity that is of broader interest is whether they can be correlated with the types of emotions that ordinary people identify, in themselves and others, through ordinary language.

As psychologist (and Founding editor of *Emotion Review*) Lisa Barrett (2006: 24) points out, "if we want to know whether a person is experiencing an emotion, we have to ask them," and their answer will of course depend on the language that they speak and on which they rely for self-understanding. As Barrett (2006: 37) further notes, "Language not only enters into the categorization process, but it also directs the development of emotional category knowledge."

It is certainly a matter of general human interest whether or not there are some common foci in people's emotional experience (as they interpret it themselves), across languages and cultures. I will explore this question in the next section, taking as my examples Ekman's "basic emotions" of "fear" and "anger."

"Fear" and "Anger": English vs. German

As mentioned, according to Ekman and Cordaro (2011: 365), there is evidence for the universality of seven emotions: fear, anger, surprise, sadness, disgust, contempt, happiness. Since labels like "anger" and "fear" are language-specific and are known not to have exact equivalents in many other languages, how can we pin down the seven emotions that Ekman and Cordaro posit as universal?

To begin with "fear," Ekman and Cordaro describe it as follows: "Fear: the response to the threat of harm, physical or psychological. Fear activates impulses to freeze or flee." This suggests that the type of emotion linked by Ekman and Cordaro with the label "fear" is based on the following scenario:

"Fear" as a Universal Emotion Type Posited by Ekman and Cordaro

"Fear" as a universal emotion type posited by Ekman and Cordaro – Version 1

it can be like this:

  someone thinks like this:

    "something bad can happen to me now, I don't want this"

> when this someone thinks like this, this someone feels something bad because of this,
> > like people often feel when they think like this

The "impulse to freeze" suggests an additional component, referring to an inability to move (or, more generally, to do anything): "I can't do anything because of this." On the other hand, the "impulse to flee" suggests a different and seemingly incompatible component: "I don't want to be here, I want to do something because of this (i.e., flee)." Since the putative components "I can't do anything now" and "I want to do something now" (in this order) don't fit together, it may appear that the prototype of "fear" proposed by Ekman and Cordaro is limited to the two components mentioned earlier: "something bad can happen to me now" and "I don't want this."

In fact, however, Ekman and Cordaro appear to give more weight to the putative "impulse to flee" than to the putative "impulse to freeze." Thus, contrasting "fear" with "anger" (which in their view causes an increased flow of blood to arms and hands), they affirm that "in fear, blood flow redirects from the hands and arms to the legs and feet, supporting the idea that evolution prepares us to flee (...)." The fact that "the impulse to freeze" is not mentioned in this context suggests that in Ekman and Cordaro's conception only the "impulse to flee" is essential to the "fear-like" emotion type that they posit as a universal outcome of evolution. If so, then the more complex scenario spelled out below may represent the emotion type that they have in mind better than the simple one presented in Version 1:

"Fear" as a universal emotion type posited by Ekman and Cordaro – Version 2

it can be like this:
> someone thinks like this:
> > "something bad can happen to me here now
> > I don't want this
> > I don't want to be here
> > I want to do something because of this"
> when this someone thinks like this, this someone feels something bad because of this,
> > like people often feel when they think like this

As the two scenarios presented here illustrate, it is possible to posit universal emotion types comparable to Ekman and Cordaro's "fear" without relying on English emotion terms. We might note that the need to choose between "an impulse to flee" and "an impulse to freeze" as the reference point of a universal human emotion is an artifact of the "basic emotion" theory rather than a fact about human beings. Presumably, both these things can happen to people at different times (as the English lexical distinction between *fear* and *terror* suggests); and different languages may emphasize one or the other in their emotion lexicon. Indeed, lexical differentiation in this area can be very rich. But no matter how many different scenarios may be distinguished by a particular language, all those scenarios can be formulated without relying on English emotion terms.

I have discussed folk psychology of the "fear-like" emotions distinguished by the English lexicon (such as *fear, terror, fright, dread,* and so on) in my book *Emotions Across Languages and Cultures* (Wierzbicka 1999). A very different range of conceptual distinctions in this field can be found, for example, in the Austronesian language Mangap-Mbula, of which Bugenhagen (1990: 208) writes:

> Life in an animistic society is very fragile. Dangers abound. Sickness, sorcery, malevolent spirits, jealous neighbours are all potential threats. It is hardly surprising, then, that out of all the different emotions, fear appears to have the broadest range of encodings. Key parameters in delineating the various encodings are:
>
> 1. Does the fear have a particular object?
> 2. Does one fear for himself or for someone else?
> 3. Does one fear physical harm to oneself?
> 4. Is the feared entity proximate?
> 5. Is the fear the result of one's having done something?
> 6. Is the fear a response to having "felt" some sensation?
> 7. Is the feared entity a spirit?
> 8. Is the fear a response to something having happened?

At the same time, while recognizing the diversity of construals embedded in different languages, we can also go along, at least part of the way, with Ekman and other "basic emotion" theorists, by recognizing the widespread occurrence, across languages, of words consistent with the "fear-like" emotion type articulated above in Version 2.

Thus, the methodology for analyzing emotions and emotion concepts provided by the NSM framework allows us to detach the key idea behind the "fear type" emotions posited by theorists such as Ekman, and in the process, to shed any English-specific extras suggested by the English lexicon.

In principle, the same applies to Ekman and Cordaro's emotion type linked by them with the word *anger,* which they characterize as follows: "Anger: the response to interference with our pursuit of a goal we care about. Anger can also be triggered by someone attempting to harm us (...). In addition to removing the obstacle or stopping the harm, anger often involves the wish to hurt the target" (p. 365). Since the second sentence in this characterization includes the qualifier "can," and the third one, the word "often," it appears that only the first of those three sentences is regarded by the authors as essential. Accordingly, a cognitive scenario corresponding to this invariant of Ekman and Cordaro's "anger" could look as follows:

"Anger" as a universal emotion type posited by Ekman and Cordaro

it can be like this:
 someone thinks like this about someone else:
  "this someone is doing some things now
  this is bad
  I want something to happen, it can't happen if this someone does things like this
  this someone knows this
  because of this, I want to do something (bad) to this someone"
 when this someone thinks like this, this someone feels something bad because of this,
  like people often do when they think like this

This scenario appears to be compatible with Ekman and Cordaro's comment that "in anger, blood flow to the arms and hands increases, which is consistent with the argument that we are prepared phylogenetically to fight when angry (...)" (p. 368).

It is not my purpose to debate here at length the plausibility of the emotion types described above as putative emotional universals. My main purpose is to show that human emotions *can* be discussed from a neutral perspective, without relying on English emotion terms. Nonetheless, some brief observations pertaining to the variability of emotion concepts encoded in different languages are in order. Rather than recalling in these observations much-discussed examples from out-of-the-way languages such as Ifaluk and Ilongot (cf. Lutz 1988, Rosaldo 1980, see also Wierzbicka 1992), I will focus again on examples from a language more generally accessible: German.

Briefly, the basic colloquial counterparts of *fear* and *anger* in German are *Angst* and *Wut* (and not *Furcht*, a little closer to *fear*, or *Zorn*, a little closer to *anger*). From a German cultural perspective, both *Angst* and *Wut* loom large as basic human emotions. To begin with *Angst*, which is, significantly, the source of the English loanword *angst*, it is a word glossed in German-English dictionaries not only as "fear" but also as "anxiety" (and used in English-German dictionaries as a gloss for *anxiety*). From a comparative perspective, its most striking feature is that it evokes neither "an impulse to freeze" ("I can't do anything now") nor "an impulse to flee" ("I don't want to be here, I want to do something because of this"). Rather, it implies something like indecision and uncertainty: "I don't know what I can do." A plausible cognitive scenario corresponding to *Angst* might look like this (cf. Wierzbicka 1998, 1999 Ch. 3):

Angst

it can be like this:
 someone thinks like this:

> "something bad can happen to me now
> I don't want this
> it can be good if I do something because of this
> I don't know what I can do"
> when this someone thinks like this, this someone feels something bad because of this,
> like people often do when they think like this

According to the Luther scholar Birgit Stolt (2012: 81), "in present-day spoken colloquial German only 'Angst' is used ("is nur 'Angst' gebräuchlich"). This doesn't mean, however, that *Angst* has come to mean the same as *fear*, but rather that the concept which is, so to speak, a cross between "fear,'" "anxiety," and "angst" looms large in contemporary German culture as one of the basic human emotions. In my 1998 study of this concept I traced its origins to Martin Luther and to his use of expressions such as *Höllenangst* (roughly, "anxieties about hell"), a hypothesis that Stolt does not find persuasive. But whatever the historical and cultural roots of the German concept "Angst," it is clearly different from the English concept "fear."

Turning now to *Wut*, arguably the cultural counterpart of *anger* for speakers of German, I will note first of all that *Wut* (often rendered in German-English dictionaries as "rage" as well as "anger"), is not the closest semantic counterpart of the English *anger* (*Zorn* is closer). It is *Wut*, not *Zorn*, however, which is the most basic colloquial word in the area of "anger-like" feelings. Durst (2001) cites frequencies of the adjectives *wütig* and *zornig* from three large German corpora, showing that the former is roughly three times more frequent than the latter. *Wut* implies that the person experiencing it feels something "*very* bad," rather than merely "bad," and also, that they are "out of control." For both these reasons (among others), *Wut* is not always translatable into English as "anger" (and vice versa). For example, the informal title of Beethoven's short piano piece "Wut über den verlorenen Groschen" is usually rendered in English as "Rage (rather than "anger") over a lost penny." *Wut* implies an impulse to hit someone or smash something—apparently an uncontrollable desire to do "something bad" to someone or something. The idea of an "interference with our pursuit of a goal we care about," which Ekman and Cordaro link with the putative universal emotion of "anger" is far less plausible as a reference point for *Wut* than it is for *anger*.

A cognitive scenario for *Wut* could look like this:

Wut

it can be like this:
> someone thinks like this:
> > "something bad is happening here now
> > I don't want this
> > I want to do something to something because of this now, I can't not do something

I want to do something bad to something now"
when this someone thinks like this, they feel something very bad because of this,
like people often feel when they think like this

From the point of view of the "basic emotions" theory, perhaps the most interesting aspect of *Wut* is its "destructive" rather than "aggressive" quality: the impulse implied by *Wut* is to do something "bad" to *something* rather than *someone*. In this respect, the German concept of "Wut" appears analogous to the Ilongot concept of "liget," investigated by Michelle Rosaldo, who glossed the word *liget* as "anger/passion/energy" and who insisted that it didn't mean the same as the English *anger*. According to Rosaldo, the Ilongots, who were traditionally headhunters, would take some other people's heads "with *liget*"— not in order to fight but to prove themselves as men; and they would similarly talk about "liget" in relation to women's "fierce" work in the garden (presumably, fighting the weeds and the like).

Returning to the German *Wut*, its apparent focus on "destructive" rather than aggressive impulses is highlighted by common compounds such as *Putzwut*, from *putzen* "to clean." Much has been written about the traditional German emphasis on cleaning, and the "hatred" of *Schmutz* and *Dreck* (dirt, filth). The compound *Putzwut*, "the passion for fierce cleaning," appears to be the focal point of a whole series of compounds based on *Wut*, such as *Arbeitswut* "fierce passion for work," *Zerstörungswut*, "fierce passion for destruction," and so on.

It seems obvious that the universal emotion types posited by Ekman and Cordaro under the labels "fear" and "anger" fit the English words *fear* and *anger* better than they do the German words *Angst* and *Wut*, just as the universal emotion type posited under the label "disgust" corresponds more closely to the English word *disgust* better than to the German word *Ekel*. This does not *prove* that the emotion types envisaged by Ekman and Cordaro are necessarily colored by the perspective suggested by the English lexicon, but it certainly does raise such a possibility.

Cross-linguistic evidence shows that many languages do have words comparable, to some extent, to English words like *fear* and *anger*, but also, that there is a good deal of variation in the precise semantics of these words. Presumably, the best way to pinpoint the convergences is to focus on semantic components that appear to be shared by many languages. Both "fear-like" emotions and "anger-like/*Wut*-like" emotions appear to be areas of such convergences. Thus, for "fear-like" emotions it seems reasonable to propose the following "lean" characterization:

"Fear-like" emotions

it can be like this:
someone thinks like this:

"something bad can happen to me now, I don't want this"
when this someone thinks like this, this someone feels something bad because of this

This formula does not privilege English over German because it doesn't include the component "I want to do something because of this"; and it is consistent with "fear-like" emotion terms documented in many other languages.

For "anger-like/*Wut*-like" emotions, a lean characterization consistent with both English and German key concepts in the relevant areas, and consistent with the data from many other languages, could look like this:

"Anger-like" and "*Wut*-like" emotions

it can be like this:
    someone thinks like this:
        "something bad is happening here now
        I don't want this
        I want to do something (to something) because of this"
    when this someone thinks like this, this someone feels something bad because of this

This scenario does not include references to "aggression" (wanting to do something bad to someone), and is compatible with a wide range of emotion concepts from many languages of the world, including those where there is no lexical evidence of "aggressive" emotions. As we have seen, Ekman and Davidson (1994) expressed a disbelief in the absence of "anger-like" concepts in such languages and cultures, apparently assuming that an impulse "to fight" (to do something bad with one's hands to someone who is "interfering with our goals") was part of human evolutionary heritage. But the question is still open to debate.

Emotion concepts like the Ifaluk "song," glossed by Lutz as "justified anger" (1988) or the Malay "marah," glossed by Goddard (2011a [1998]: 117-188) as "angry, offended," do not imply anything about "interference with our goals" or about an "impulse to fight." Could these emotion concepts, too, be interpreted as compatible with the tripartite construal "something bad is happening, I don't want this, I want to do something because of this"? The matter requires further investigation. On balance, lexical evidence available at this stage suggests that this tripartite construal constitutes an interpretive scheme that is widespread across languages and cultures, without being necessarily universal.

Studying Emotions without Words?

As we saw earlier, in their response to Shweder, Ekman and Davidson insist that "the evidence for universality is not limited to words but includes studies of expression that did not involve words, as well as studies of physiology, antecedents, and so on."

It is not my purpose to argue against emotional universals in general, or against universals of facial expression. On the contrary, I have argued for the presence of such universals myself (see Wierzbicka 1999, 2009a). The question is what exactly those universals are, and crucially, in what metalanguage they can best be articulated.

To begin with facial expressions, these have always played a central role in Ekman's theory. But to take the example of "anger," what facial expression do Ekman and his associates propose as one that can identify "anger-like emotions" and distinguish them from the other types? The "bared teeth, square mouth" expression, which according to Ekman (1975: 38) shows anger? Or rather the facial gesture of tightly pressing one's lips, interpreted in Ekman and Friesen (1975: 83) as a manifestation of anger? Clearly, these are different expressions, associated with different cognitive scenarios, only one of which includes the "aggressive" component "I want to do something bad to you now." Both the baring of teeth and the "determined" tightly pressed lips suggest the component "I want to do something now," but presumably this component alone would not be enough for Ekman and Cordaro's intended category of the "anger" family of emotions. Ekman could say, of course, that as there is a whole family of anger-like emotions, there is also a whole family of anger-like facial expressions. But this would mean that there is no facial invariant that could serve as a stable reference point for the whole "anger" family of emotions.

It is true that speakers of English often interpret people's expressions in global terms, for example, as an "angry" face, or a "sad" face, but clearly, in doing so, they are being guided by their native language.

It is worth recalling in this context Gergen's (1991: 9) comment quoted in Chapter 3 that, as speakers of English, we sort out human emotions into categories such as anger, disgust, fear, and so on, then "we treat these emotion terms as representing biological givens," and then "we literally see the expressions of these emotions in people's faces." Clearly, speakers of different languages will see different emotions in people's faces, depending on the categories provided by the language one speaks. As psychologists Roberson et al. (2010: 258) cautiously put it, the "development of a rich representational structure for facial expressions of emotion may require the integration of a verbal categorization system with a perceptual processing system that is category-agnostic." To put it differently, people interpret other people's facial expressions in accordance with the ways they interpret their own feelings, and this depends to some extent on the language they speak and think in.

What applies to facial expressions, applies also to physiological changes and situational antecedents associated with particular types of emotions. For example, according to widely shared experience reflected in language, people can be "red with anger," but they can also be "pale with anger," and the same applies to *Wut* (Durst 2001). Similarly, people can get "angry" when someone wants to prevent them from achieving their goal, but they can also get "angry" when they misplace some object, and again, the same applies to *Wut* (as in the case of "Wut über den verlorenen Groschen"). So none of these areas offers us a stable point of reference for identifying a particular type of emotion and distinguishing it from all others. On the other hand, minimal cognitive scenarios formulated in simple and universal words do provide a solution, since they give us a stable reference point for any emotion type that we may want to pinpoint.

English emotion terms embody certain interpretive schemes that are neither unchangeable through time nor constant across different cultures. The extent of convergence between interpretive schemes favored by various languages and cultures for making sense of human emotional experience remains an open question, and it is a question of great human interest. An evolutionary perspective on this question can be helpful and illuminating. There may indeed be certain universal human impulses linked with certain salient types of feelings as well as with certain physiological changes (such as, for example, an increased flow of blood to certain parts of the body): for example, impulses to hit, to flee, to freeze, to gag, to recoil, to laugh, to cry, to moan, to smile, to frown, to clench one's teeth, and so on. And there may be some adaptive value to them that could be clarified from an evolutionary point of view. But such impulses themselves make sense when they are linked with certain rudimentary cognitive scenarios, accompanied by certain types of feelings, good or bad, along the following lines:

> an impulse to hit –
> "I want to do something bad to this someone"
> an impulse to flee –
> "I don't want to be here, I want to do something because of this"
> an impulse to gag –
> "I don't want this to be inside my mouth"
> an impulse to recoil –
> "I don't want this to touch my body"
> an impulse to cry –
> "something bad is happening to me now"
> an impulse to laugh—
> "something is happening here now, not like at many other times
> people here can feel something good because of this"
> an impulse to open one's eyes widely –
> "I want to see more, I want to know more about this"

Ekman and Cordaro say that evolution has prepared us to fight, linking this claim with a universal emotion type that they call "anger." From a lay point of view, however, it is not clear just how adaptive aggressive feelings would have been for early humans. Given the current emphasis on the adaptive value of "cooperation" in human evolution (cf. e.g., Tomasello 2009), Ekman and Cordaro's focus on "fighting" seems one-sided.

The adaptive value of what Ekman and Cordaro call "sadness" and "happiness"—as emotions and facial expressions—is also far from clear. The English word *sadness* suggests, roughly speaking, that "something bad happened, I can't do anything about it," and *happiness*, that "something very good is happening to me." It is far from clear why facial expressions signaling a "resigned" feeling like "sadness" or a self-centered feeling like "happiness" should have been particularly valuable, in evolutionary terms. By contrast, the potential adaptive value of crying and laughing is easy to see: crying draws attention to the fact that "something bad is happening to me now" and thus may elicit help, whereas laughter signals to fellow humans that "something unusual is happening here now" and that "people here can feel something good because of this," and presumably it can lead to social bonding.

The minimal cognitive scenarios linked here with bodily impulses such as gagging, recoiling, wanting to do something with one's hands (e.g., hit someone or strike something) or with one's legs (flee), and opening one's eyes wide also seem to make a good deal of sense from an evolutionary point of view (Fabrega in press), and any cross-linguistic convergences in the emotion lexicons that can be linked with such scenarios are worth noting.

The extent of commonalities (and continuities) in human emotional lives cannot be established as long as English—one language among six thousand or so human languages—is treated as a privileged "scientific" metalanguage for describing what anthropologist Melvin Spiro (1994: 334) called "the generic human mind." It is heartening to see that the importance of a suitable metalanguage for the exploration of human emotions is increasingly appreciated by emotion researchers. I would like, therefore, to close this chapter with a quote from Ekman and Cordaro, which strikes a new note in this interdisciplinary debate. In the same passage that starts with the sentence "Language and emotion are independent of each other" (p. 369), the authors write: "That being said, it is an important and delicate job for emotion theorists to construct an accurate vocabulary of how to describe our feelings and emotional experiences" (p. 369). It is indeed.

PART THREE

"Politeness" and "Cooperation"

8

Talking to Other People: "Politeness" and Cultural Scripts

How to be polite - in Anglo English

Speech practices and tacit assumptions associated with them vary a great deal across languages and cultures. Yet in Anglophone social science, such diversity is often ignored and Anglo/English ways of speaking are mistaken for the human norm. For example, in an often cited article on "Indirect Speech Acts," John Searle (1975: 64) wrote:

> ordinary conversational requirements of politeness normally make it awkward to issue flat imperative sentences (e.g. *Leave the* room) or explicit performatives (e.g. *I order you to leave the* room), and we therefore seek to find indirect means to our illocutionary ends (e.g. *I wonder if you would mind leaving the* room). In directives, politeness is the chief motivation for indirectness.

Discussing this passage in my 1985b article "Different languages, different cultures, different speech acts: Polish vs. English," I pointed out that in Polish, there was no similar taboo on "flat imperative sentences" or explicit performatives (e.g., *I ask you, leave the room*), and that in fact both were widely used. I argued that both these taboos were highly language- and culture-specific. In a later study, "Anglo cultural scripts against 'putting pressure' on other people," I developed this theme further, taking as my point of departure a set of 25 postcards entitled "How to be British." Postcard 12 bore the heading "How to be polite."

> The card is divided into two halves. Each half shows a picture of a river in a city in which a man appears to be drowning and calling for help as a gentleman in a bowler hat is passing by, walking his dog. In the first picture, labelled "Wrong," the drowning man is screaming: HELP!, and the gentleman is walking away, clearly without any intention of coming to the rescue. In the second picture, labelled "Right," the speech bubble emanating from the mouth of the drowning man says instead: "Excuse me, Sir,

I'm terribly sorry to bother you, but I wondered if you would mind helping me a moment, as long as it's no trouble, of course." Phrased like this, the request for help is clearly effective: the gentleman with the dog is turning towards the drowning man and throwing him a lifebelt. (Wierzbicka 2006b: 31)

Some aspects of the two vignettes are indeed specifically "British," but the avoidance of an imperative and of any linguistic devices that could be perceived as putting pressure on the addressee to do something can be said to be not only British, but, more generally, Anglo. In a wide variety of situations and relationships, it is important for many English speakers to avoid giving people the impression that anyone is "telling them" to do something: if someone wants me to do something, it is important that I can feel that I can do it if I want to. If I do indeed do it, I want to feel that I'm doing it because I myself want to do it, not solely because this other someone wants it. As Searle rightly noted, and as the postcard "how to be polite" emphasizes, the locutions "I wonder if," "I was wondering if," and "would you mind" play an important role in this regard (cf. Wierzbicka 2006b).

Far from being exclusively British, this norm applies in North America, in Australia, and in other English-speaking countries of "the inner circle" (Kachru 1985; Kachru ed. 1992). It is also a norm that should be an essential part of teaching English in non-English-speaking countries.

Referring to her long experience of teaching English to Russian university students, Russian linguist Tatiana Larina (2009: 17) notes that Russian students are often resistant to accepting the English phrase *would you mind...?* She quotes one of her students as saying, "But surely only princesses speak like that? Why on earth should we?" Larina also comments that from a Russian cultural point of view, an English utterance like "Would you mind watching the phone while I go to the toilet?," addressed to an office mate, sounds odd, and that a plain imperative sentence (softened perhaps with a *požalujsta* "please," or with an endearment) sounds much more natural and appropriate. Thus, avoiding imperatives is not an "ordinary requirement of politeness," but a culture-specific norm "institutionalized" (and to some extent, grammaticalized) in English.

A particularly striking example of such an absolutization of Anglo norms is presented in the very influential article by the American philosopher H. P. Grice (1975), entitled "Logic and Conversation." In this famous article, Grice launched the cooperative principle (or "CP") and a set of "maxims" allegedly underlying all ordinary conversation in natural language. One or another of the maxims can sometimes be "flouted," but when this happens, "the hearer is entitled to assume that that maxim, or at least the overall Cooperative Principle, is observed at the level of what is implicated." (p. 52)

These celebrated "Gricean maxims," which were enthusiastically accepted by many linguists and which are still often appealed to by "neo-Griceans," included prescriptions like the following ones: "Do not say that for which you lack adequate evidence." (p. 46), "Be brief (avoid unnecessary prolixity)" (p. 46), "Be relevant." (p. 50)

According to Grice, "it is REASONABLE for us to follow" (p. 48) these and other similar maxims. Who are these "we," one might ask: speakers of English, who have words like *evidence, concise, relevant*, and *reasonable* at their disposal, or the rest of humanity, who don't have such words (Wierzbicka 2006a, 2010a) and who don't feel the need to be "concise," "relevant," or "reasonable"? The answer, seems clear: Grice did not say either "we Anglos" or "we humans" because he did not draw any distinction between Anglo cultural norms and the "logic of [human] conversation" in general.

"Universals of politeness" or "seven deadly sins"

Grice's ideas were transplanted onto the ground of linguistics in Penelope Brown and Stephen Levinson's "Universals in language usage: politeness phenomena" (first published as part of Goody 1978, reissued as a book entitled *Politeness: Some universals in language usage* in 1987). In this work, whose Anglocentrism I have criticized in a number of publications (see, e.g., Wierzbicka 1985b, 1991/2003), the authors accepted Grice's "Cooperative Principle" and built on it a theory of "universals of politeness," which, like Grice's maxims, became extremely influential in linguistics and related disciplines.

Calling Grice's theory "essentially correct," Brown and Levinson (1987: 3, 4) strongly endorsed "what is at the heart of Grice's proposal, namely that there is a working assumption by conversationalists of the rational and efficient nature of talk." From a cross-cultural point of view, however, it seems unlikely that all over the world, people talking to other people are making such an assumption. Both "rationality" and "efficiency" are Anglo values, and the words naming them are hard to translate into other languages, even in Europe, let alone further afield. (Neither Polish nor Russian, for example, have words that could translate "efficient" in a phrase like "efficient nature of talk.")

Brown and Levinson's further assumption that everywhere in the world speakers care a great deal about their personal "territories," "personal preserves," and "rights to non-distraction, i.e. to freedom of action and freedom from imposition" (1987: 61) has been questioned by a number of scholars, as inapplicable to, for example, Asian cultures such as Japanese and Chinese. Thus, Matsumoto (1988: 405) wrote:

> What is of paramount concern to a Japanese is not his/her own territory, but his/her position in relation to the others in the group and his/her acceptance by those others. Loss of face is associated with the perception by others that one has not comprehended and acknowledged the structure

and hierarchy of the group. The Japanese concepts of face, then, are qualitatively different from those defined as universals by Brown and Levinson. The difference transcends the variability of cultural elaboration acknowledged in Brown and Levinson's theory (e.g. what kinds of acts threaten face, what sorts of persons have special rights to face-protection, etc.) and calls into question the universality of a core concept: the notion of face as consisting of the desire for approval of wants and the desire for the preservation of one's territory.

Sachiko Ide (1989) similarly questioned the relevance of Brown and Levinson's "principles of politeness" to Japanese, pointing out that in Japanese, "discernment" (*wakimae*) was far more important than "freedom from imposition" or the right to act "unimpeded by others":

> Brown and Levinson (1978, 1987) proposed principles of language usage according to politeness, which they claim to be universal. (...) However, the universality of the principles is questionable from the perspective of languages with honorifics, in particular Japanese. Their framework neglects two aspects of language and usage which are distinctly relevant to linguistic politeness in Japanese. The neglected linguistic aspect is the choice of 'formal linguistic forms' among varieties with different degrees of formality. The neglected aspect of usage is 'discernment': the speaker's use of polite expressions according to social conventions rather than interactional strategy.

My own long battle against what I saw as the Anglocentrism of Brown and Levinson's theory started in 1983. I described how this battle started, and how skeptically my criticisms were at first received, in the introduction to the second edition (2003) of my book *Cross-Cultural Pragmatics*:

> When in 1983 I presented, at the monthly meeting of the Sydney Linguistic Circle, a paper entitled "Different cultures, different languages, different speech acts: English vs. Polish" (Wierzbicka 1985b), in which I argued that the supposedly universal maxims and principles of "politeness" were in fact rooted in Anglo culture, my ideas were regarded as heretical. When I argued, in particular, that the "freedom from imposition," which Brown and Levinson (1978: 66) saw as one of the most important guiding principles of human interaction, was in fact an Anglo cultural value, and that the avoidance of "flat imperative sentences," which Searle (1975: 69) attributed to the "ordinary (human, A.W.) conversational requirements of politeness," did not reflect "universal principles of politeness" but rather, expressed special concerns of modern Anglo culture, my claims were confidently dismissed. As a matter of fact, it was the hostile and dismissive reaction of that audience which was for me the initial stimulus for engaging in a long-term campaign against what I saw as the misguided orthodoxy of that time.

Brown and Levinson (1987: 15) acknowledged the existence of cultural variation, but they minimized its significance. Having mentioned, in passing, the charges of Anglocentrism such as those raised by myself (Wierzbicka 1985b) and by anthropologist Michelle Rosaldo (1982), they concluded (p. 15):

> Such cultural differences doubtless exist and work down into the linguistic details of the particular face-redressive strategies preferred in a given society or group. Nevertheless, for the purposes of cross-cultural comparison developed here, we consider that our framework provides a primary descriptive format within which, or in contrast to which, such differences can be described.

Thus, just as Kay proposed that Polish and Russian color terms should be described in relation to the English set, so Brown and Levinson suggested that Polish and Ilongot speech practices should be described in relation to the baseline of English cultural norms.

In my critique of the Anglocentrism of Brown and Levinson's "politeness theory," I have drawn, in particular, on the experience of immigrants to English-speaking countries. The assumption that "the principles of politeness" are essentially the same everywhere flies in the face of reality as experienced by people who had to build a new life for themselves in countries like the United States, Canada, Britain, and Australia (as, for example, the personal stories collected by Mary Besemeres and myself in our edited 2007 book *Translating Lives* testify). Both in my essay in *Translating Lives* and in *Cross-Cultural Pragmatics,* I have also drawn on my personal experiences and observations from "multicultural" Australia. For example, I cited the conversation with a well-meaning liberal Anglo-Australian who said to me about her Chinese neighbors: "they are very good neighbours—but they are so rude ... for example, they said to me: cut down that branch—we don't want it on our side of the fence" (Canberra 2002). As I have pointed out in the cited publications, if linguists tell well-meaning but cross-culturally inexperienced "Anglos" that the principles of politeness are essentially the same everywhere, we can only confirm them in their view that their non-Anglo neighbors are very rude (cf. Clyne 1994).

As such examples illustrate, the principle of "pan-cultural interpretability of politeness phenomena" (Brown and Levinson 1987: 283) is not only intellectually untenable, but misleading and potentially socially harmful.

In my view, the most effective critique of the "Universalist Pragmatics" advocated by Brown and Levinson and colleagues was formulated by Cliff Goddard in his list of what he called the "Seven Deadly Sins of Universalist Pragmatics":

(1) Universalist Pragmatics (UP) grossly underestimates the cultural shaping of speech practices.

(2) Being framed in terms which are alien to the speakers concerned, UP necessarily imposes an "outsider perspective."

(3) UP creates a gulf between pragmatics and the description of other cultural phenomena.

(4) UP describes, but it seldom explains.

(5) UP is terminologically "slippery": different authors use its technical descriptors with different meanings.

(6) UP is Anglocentric: it implicitly adopts Anglo norms and practices as baseline universals, and its English-based descriptors are replete with terminological ethnocentrism.

(7) Being locked into the vocabulary of a foreign language, UP closes off the description to the people concerned. (Goddard 2007: 18)

Goddard contrasts the "universalist pragmatics" based on putative universals of politeness, with the "cultural scripts" approach based on universal semantic primes and cross-translatable into Chinese, Spanish, or any other language. Here is Goddard's explanation of why it is so important that cultural scripts purporting to state tacit cultural norms should be translatable into the language of the speakers whose tacit norms are being articulated:

> First, it means that they are accessible to the people whose speech practices are being described. Native speaker consultants can discuss, assess, and comment on them. This makes for increased verifiability and opens up new avenues for evidence. Second, translatability is crucial to the practical value of cultural scripts in intercultural education and communication, i.e., in real-world situations of trying to bridge some kind of cultural gap, with immigrants, language-learners, in international negotiation, etc. (cf. Goddard & Wierzbicka 2004, 2007). Third, the fact that cultural scripts are expressible in the native language of speakers gives them a *prima facie* better claim to cognitive reality than technical formalisms which are altogether unrecognizable to native speakers. (Goddard 2007: 18)

To illustrate the use of the cultural scripts approach, I will take an example from Goddard's more recent paper "Cultural scripts: Applications to language teaching and intercultural communication," (2010) which has direct bearing on the avoidance of direct requests in English. Since this paper was intended for a Chinese readership and was published in China, it includes a Chinese version of the script, which I add here to illustrate the cross-translatability of cultural scripts into other languages.

[A1] *An Anglo English cultural script for "personal autonomy"*

many people think like this:

when someone does something, it is good if this someone can think like this:

"I am doing this because I want to do it"

[A2] 许多人这样想：

当有人做某件事情时，

如果这个人这样想"我做这件事是因为我想要做这件事"， 这是好的。

This "master script" explains, in simple, cross-translatable words, the Anglo values of, roughly speaking, "personal autonomy." Building on this general script, Goddard proceeds to offer a more specific one, describing how the learner of English can make requests in accordance with "Anglo" expectations (such as Searle's) without offending or annoying the addressee:

[B] *Anglo English cultural script for avoiding direct requests*

many people think like this:

at many times when I want someone to do something, it is not good if I say something like this:

"I want you to do something, I think that you will do it because of this"

if I say this, this someone can feel something bad because of it

Fallacies of "politeness"

In his 2005 article titled "Politeness: Is there an East-West divide?" Geoffrey Leech, a prominent supporter of Gricean maxims and Brown and Levinson's "theory of politeness" reaffirms his belief in the universal basis of "politeness" and defends Brown and Levinson's theory against criticisms such as Goddard's and mine. Speaking of "culture relativism," Leech (2005: 3) describes it as "a perspective most forcibly championed by Wierzbicka (2003) [1991/2003]." This is ironic, in view of the fact that I have also been often attacked for being a universalist (cf. e.g., Everett 2005). The fact of the matter is that my colleagues and I have always opposed the positing of a choice between "relativity" and "universalism" as simplistic and argued for a middle road, a position epitomized by the subtitle of my 1992 book *Semantics, Culture and Cognition: universal semantic concepts in culture-specific configurations.*

In the same article in which he presents me as a champion of "culture relativism," Leech points out that "politeness research" is now a thriving field of academic study, with its own journal (*Journal of Politeness Research,* founded in 2005) and a huge bibliography, "growing steadily week by week" (p. 2).

The fact is, however, that most languages have no word meaning "politeness" and reflect, in their lexicon, other concerns. For example, in my native Polish, the English word *polite* has two counterparts: *grzeczny,* used normally only about children (as *naughty* is in English), and *uprzejmy,* closer to the English word *courteous,* but more colloquial.

As I have discussed in other publications, the key Polish value to do with, roughly speaking, interpersonal communicative behavior, is not "uprzejmość" but "serdeczność" (from *serce*, "heart")—a value which is not lexically recognized in English, as "politeness" is not recognized in Polish. I will list three key differences between "serdeczność" and "politeness." First, "serdeczność" is normally shown to people one knows, and typically, knows well, whereas "politeness" is especially focused on strangers or people whom one doesn't know well. Second, "serdeczność" consists in showing "good feelings" toward someone, and "politeness," in not causing "bad feelings" (so that "politeness" can be "cold," whereas "serdeczność" cannot). Third, "serdeczność," which "flows from the heart," does not involve any knowledge about how to behave (what to say or do) in a given situation, whereas "politeness" does.

I should stress that the Polish cultural value of "serdeczność" does not correspond to what Brown and Levinson (1978, 1987) described as "positive politeness" and defined as "the individual's desire that her/his wants to be appreciated and approved of in social interaction." "Serdeczność" is not about anyone's wants to be appreciated and approved by others. It is about what the speaker feels toward the addressee. The closest counterpart of this value recognized in English is not "politeness" but "warmth"—except that in English "warmth" is a somewhat marginal value, whereas in Polish, "serdeczność" is central. (For a study of the Russian values comparable to both "serdeczność" and "warmth," see Wierzbicka 2009; for a comparison with the Colombian Spanish concept of "calor humano," see Travis 2006).

Of course, the value of "politeness" (in the ordinary sense of the word) does not occupy a particularly high position in the Anglo hierarchy of values, either—certainly not as high as what ordinary speakers of English refer to as "friendliness" (cf. Bellah et al. 1985; Hochschild 1983; Wierzbicka 1994). Bellah et al., in their *Habits of the Heart*, spoke of the rise of the value of "friendliness" in American life, taking as their point of departure Alexis de Tocqueville's observation (made in his monumental work *Democracy in America* (1966[1848])) that "Democracy does not create strong attachments between man and man, but it does put their ordinary relations on an easier footing," adding:

> in the mobile and egalitarian society of the United States, people could meet more easily and their intercourse was more open, but the ties between them were more likely to be casual and transient (...) "Friendliness" became almost compulsory as a means of assuaging the difficulties of these interactions, while friendship in the classical sense became more and more difficult. (Bellah et al. 1985: 117–118)

As these remarks indicate, "friendliness," unlike "serdeczność," is not focused on a particular person toward whom someone feels very good feelings. The fact that

Bellah and his colleagues anchored their observations in ordinary language, high-lighting the widespread use of the word *friendly* in modern English, gave their discussion both a clarity and a persuasiveness that the debates relying on tech-nical terms such as "positive politeness" and "negative politeness" usually lack.

But returning to the word *politeness* as it is used in ordinary English, it is worth noting that in the last decade or so the literature on language use has increasingly emphasized the lack of correspondence between the English term *politeness* and its closest counterparts in other languages. For example, Watts (2005) notes that even the German word *Höflichkeit* and the French word *poli-tesse* may not mean exactly the same as the English word *politeness*. (cf. also Ehlich 2005; Rathmayr 1999). Furthermore, several writers have pointed out that the meaning of *politeness* in English has changed in the last three centuries (Watts 2002).

Given the language-specific and time-specific character of the meaning of English *politeness*, it seems clear that scholars who use this word as their basic analytical tool in comparing communicative norms and practices across lan-guages and cultures are looking at humankind through the conceptual prism of present-day English and adopt a perspective that is not only culture-bound but also time-bound. Yet while the tide seems to have largely turned against Brown and Levinson's theory of "politeness," the term *politeness* continues to be used widely in linguistic literature as if it were a legitimate tool for analyzing human speech practices in all societies.

Increasingly, writers on "politeness" seek to meet the charge of ter-minological and conceptual ethnocentrism by distinguishing between two terms: "politeness$_1$" and "politeness$_2$" (cf. Eelen 2001), or "first-order polite-ness" and "second-order politeness"; but such a maneuver can hardly over-come the problem: the analysis remains locked in a perspective influenced by the meaning of the English word *politeness*.

For example, Richard Watts, in his 2003 book *Politeness*, writes:

> We can call the varied interpretations of politeness and impoliteness in ongoing verbal interaction 'folk interpretations' or 'lay interpretations.' They are clearly not of the same order as the terms 'politeness' and 'impoliteness' when these are used as technical concepts in sociolinguistic theorising about social interaction. (...) [T]hroughout this book I shall make a concerted effort to keep the two perspectives apart. I shall call 'folk' interpretations of (im)politeness 'first-order (im)politeness' (or fol-lowing Eelen 2001, (im)politeness$_1$), and (im)politeness as a concept in a sociolinguistic theory of (im)politeness, 'second-order (im)politeness' (or impoliteness$_2$). (p. 4)

Having said this, Watts seeks to introduce a cross-linguistic perspective into his discussion of language use in a chapter entitled "Politeness across languages and cultures." The chapter opens with the following sentence: "A theory of linguistic (im)politeness should take as its focus the ways in which the members of a social group conceptualize (im)politeness as they participate in socio-communicative verbal interaction" (p. 27). But the speakers of a language that has no word matching *politeness* do not "conceptualize politeness" (or "impoliteness") in any way at all. They may have ideas about how people should talk to others (depending on a variety of factors), but not about "politeness," which is an English concept, whether it is qualified as "politeness$_1$" or "politeness$_2$."

Watts is aware of the historical changes in the meaning of the word *politeness*, as the heading of one of the sections in his chapter 2 shows: "The historical relativity of first-order politeness: politeness in Western Europe from the sixteenth to the nineteenth century" (p. 34). This doesn't stop him, however, from using the term "politeness" as a tool for comparing languages and cultural traditions, both within Europe and in other parts of the world. For example, speaking of "Western societies," he observes (with reference to my article "Different languages, different speech acts: English vs. Polish"): "even within what would normally count as Western Europe there is a great deal of variation between social situations in which politeness is mandatory and those in which it is not—not to mention other parts of Europe (cf. Wierzbicka 1985)" (Watts 2003: 83). The point about variation within Europe is well taken, but speaking about it in terms of "politeness" and of how "mandatory" it is in different parts of Europe in different situations is misleading.

In my 1985 paper to which Watts is referring, I described a scene (that I had witnessed myself) when a Polish host at a public gathering in Australia urged an Anglo-Australian guest of honor to take a seat, saying: "Sit! Mrs. Frances, sit!" (a literal translation from Polish). Such a use of a bare imperative in a situation of this kind is obviously inappropriate (and even comical) in English, whereas it is quite appropriate in Polish. The reason, however, is not that "politeness" is not mandatory in Polish in this situation, but rather that the cultural scripts for appropriate behavior are different. (The host was not indifferent to what from an English-speaker's point of view could be described as "politeness," but above all, he was showing "serdeczność" to the guest).

No matter how much scholars can insist that they are using the word *politeness* (and *impoliteness*) in a scientific rather than ordinary sense, the fact remains that the former sounds like something good in English, and the latter, like something bad. To suggest that "politeness" is mandatory in a wider range of situations in English than in Polish is not a neutral way of describing the differences between the two cultural traditions. If complex English words must be used to describe such differences, then words like "appropriate," "desirable," and "valued" would be much more useful here than the word "polite." But to teach immigrants in an English-speaking country how to communicate appropriately in different situations, or to teach native speakers of Anglo English how not to interpret the use of the bare imperative by immigrants as "rude," simple words cross-translatable into their own languages are obviously more useful still.

A good illustration of the conceptual confusion and Anglocentric bias to which the theory of "politeness$_1$," and "politeness$_2$," can lead is provided by a recent paper by Marina Terkourafi (published in the *Journal of Politeness Research*), who writes:

> Increasing attention to the distinction between first- and second-order im/politeness has led to considerable soul-searching among theorists regarding which of the two should form the basis of a theory of im/politeness. In this article, I take an alternative path: I build on norms of Politeness$_1$, as attested in influential texts laying out Politeness norms in different parts of the world from antiquity to this day, to extract from them the core elements of a theory of Politeness$_1$. (2011: 159)

Having said this, the author goes on to "examine canonical understandings of politeness as captured in didactic and/or prescriptive words from different parts of the world and from antiquity to this day" (p. 163). Thus, not only does the author aim to examine social worlds across many different languages and epochs through the prism of the English word *politeness*, but she deliberately sets out to use as her yardstick the English folk concept of "politeness" as it is used in present-day English ("politeness$_1$"), rather than some more abstract and more technical concept such as "politeness$_2$."

As the quotes adduced here from Watts (2003) and Terkourafi (2011) illustrate, in the post-Brown & Levinson literature on language use many writers worry a great deal about how the term "politeness" should be used, how it should be defined, and what the "valid object of a theory of linguistic politeness" is.

My own suggestion would be to try to let go of this term as an analytical tool altogether, and to employ instead simple, neutral, and cross-translatable words such as *say* and *do*, *someone* and *something* or *good* and *bad*, as illustrated in the cultural script cited earlier from Goddard's paper in two versions, English and Chinese. (See also Waters 2012). Watts closes his book with the following words:

> the only valid object of a theory of linguistic politeness is (...) the ways in which interactants classify social, verbal acts as realising their own personal conceptualisations of what is 'polite' and what is 'impolite.' (Im)politeness is an area of discursive struggle in social practice in every society and in every language. It is what makes it interesting, and it is that which makes it universal. (p. 263)

The statement that politeness (in some complex and not defined sense) is universal may not be as evidently Anglocentric as the notion that everywhere in the world speakers are concerned a great deal about their "personal territory" and their "freedom from imposition." It is not clear, however, what exactly the purported meaning of this statement is, how it can be verified, or in what ways it can contribute to intercultural understanding. As I see it, here as elsewhere, real progress can be achieved if we stop relying in our analyses on complex words taken from the historically shaped conceptual vocabulary of English and use instead empirically established lexico-grammatical universals to investigate different cultural norms from a non-Anglocentric, culture-independent perspective, thus facilitating genuine cross-cultural understanding. Four hundred years ago Francis Bacon (1860[1620], Vol. 4, xliii) wrote:

> For men converse by means of language; but words are formed at the will of the generality; and there arises from a bad and unapt formation of words a wonderful obstruction to the mind. Nor can the definitions and explanations, with which learned men are wont to guard and protect themselves in some instances, afford a complete remedy: words still manifestly force the understanding, throw everything into confusion, and lead mankind into vain and innumerable controversies and fallacies.

I don't think Bacon's warning applies to simple and cross-translatable words such as *say*, *know*, *do*, and *happen*. It does apply, however, to the word *politeness*, and to *politeness₁* and *politeness₂* even more so.

9

Doing Things with Other People: "Cooperation," "Interaction," and "Obščenie"

The value of "Cooperation" in Anglo Culture and English Scholarly Discourse

While both the Gricean maxims and the "universals of politeness" based on them have lost much of their appeal for linguistics and related studies (e.g., Davis 1998, Watts et al. 2005), by contrast, Grice's "Cooperation Principle" is now back on the agenda and in fact is being used by "neo-Griceans" as a rallying cry for a new interdisciplinary field of studies envisaged by them: the field of "human sociality."

Thus, in a volume entitled *Roots of Human Sociality* (2006), in which linguists N. J. Enfield and Stephen Levinson discuss what they see as "distinctive properties of human sociality" and "the riddle of human cooperative behaviour," the notion of "cooperation" plays a key role and Grice's presence in the background is palpable. The authors do not say explicitly, however, what they mean by "cooperation" and "cooperative behavior," or how they reconcile their claims about "cooperation" as a uniquely human phenomenon with, for example, the evolutionary biologist Dugatkin's (1997) claim that "cooperation" is pervasive among fishes, birds, and insects.

Similarly, in his recent book *Why We Cooperate*, developmental psychologist Michael Tomasello (2009: 3) says: "One of the great debates in Western civilization is whether humans are born cooperative (e.g., Rousseau), or whether they are born selfish (e.g., Hobbes)." But strictly speaking, Rousseau never said that humans are born cooperative, and he couldn't have said so, because the English word *cooperative* has no equivalent in French—apart from a very recent loan from English described in French dictionaries as an anglicism.

The same evolutionary biologist Dugatkin says in his book *Cooperation Among Animals* that the most prominent advocate of the "cooperation" view of animal behavior was Petr Kropotkin, the Russian prince and anarchist. But again, Kropotkin didn't speak—and couldn't have spoken—of "cooperation" among animals, because there is no such word in Russian. He spoke instead of something that he called "vzaimopomošč'," which has been reasonably translated into English as "mutual aid." "Mutual aid" is not the same thing as "cooperation," however.

"Cooperation" is a highly culture-specific idea, which first emerged in the context of political economy, in nineteenth-century Britain. As the Oxford English Dictionary (OED online) notes, initially the word was used specifically for "economic cooperation." The OED offers a quote from Henry Fawcett's *Manual of Political Economy* (1863), which says that "The essential characteristic of cooperation is a union of capital and labour." Before the end of the nineteenth century, however, the term spread to other contexts, and in the twentieth century it rose to its present position as one of the central cultural values in Anglo societies (championed, for example, in children's television, as I will illustrate shortly). Such values are often absolutized by Anglophone scholars and even put forward as explanations for human behavior in general. Grice's celebrated "Cooperation Principle" is a good example here.[1]

The semantic history of the English word *cooperation* can throw a great deal of light on the emergence of modern Anglo cultural norms encouraging "cooperative behavior." But this is a topic for a separate study. Here, I propose to do three things: first, to unpack the meaning of the words *cooperate, cooperation*, and *cooperative* as these words are used in ordinary English; second, to show some examples of how these words are used in present-day scholarly discourse; and third, to illustrate by means of one extended example how the ideas linked with these words in contemporary cutting-edge psychological research can be made clearer through the use of semantically simpler and less English-bound words such as *do, happen, want*, and *the same*.

"Cooperate," "Cooperation," and "Cooperative" in Ordinary English

The *Collins Cobuild English Language Dictionary* distinguishes two meanings of the verb *cooperate*, which it defines as follows: 1. If people cooperate they work together for a purpose, 2. If you cooperate you help someone willingly when they ask you for your help. These definitions are far from precise but the recognition that there are two distinct meanings is important. For ease of reference, we can call these two meanings "symmetrical" and "asymmetrical." The "symmetrical" meaning can be illustrated with the following sentences from the Collins Wordbanks corpus of English:

> Women's groups and mixed groups will **cooperate** without
> compromising women-only groups...
> It should enable agencies to **cooperate** (...) to track potential
> terrorists.
> But we want to **cooperate** on the basis of equality, mutual
> understanding and reciprocity.

Those unable to **cooperate** relapsed into lonely helplessness.

The agreement called on the two bodies to **cooperate** and seek mutual benefits.

It should be a voluntary choice of the travel agents whether to **cooperate** or not.

The noun *cooperation* (in most of its uses) is derived from that first "symmetrical" meaning of the verb. There is, however, one important difference between the noun and the verb: the positive evaluation that is built into the meaning of the noun. As the last example above illustrates, such a positive evaluation is not an inherent feature of the meaning of the verb. The noun, however—which is used in many resounding names of organizations (such as, for example, Organization for Security and Cooperation in Europe (OSCE) and Asia-Pacific Economic Cooperation (APEC)) is inherently positive. Some examples from Wordbanks:

> The recent changes in Eastern Europe have prompted political leaders on both sides of the Iron Curtain to proclaim a new era of global **cooperation**.
> I think it's also an interesting sign that the democratisation of Eastern Europe is leading to a new **cooperation** which is making the whole of Europe a hostile area for terrorists and their support organisations.
> [the summit]...has ended in Kuala Lumpur, with a call for increased **cooperation** between ASEAN members.
> China's Minister of Public Security, Mr Wang Fang, has called for increased international **cooperation** to combat drug smuggling.

As these examples illustrate, *cooperation* is particularly prominent in the language of international relations. But *cooperation* is also promoted as a positive practice and value to children, as in, for example, the songs and skits on the children's television program *Sesame Street*. The following *Sesame Street* song "Cooperation" (played over footage of three children moving a piece of play equipment together) appeared in the 1970s, but successive generations of viewers have had their own cooperation-themed songs.

> One can do anything better than none (it's indisputable)/
> Two can do some things better than one, with **cooperation**/
> Three is often even better than two, ooo, ooo, ooo. The more help you get, the better for you.
> **Cooperation** can be lots of fun (co-op **cooperation**)/
> It's incredible what kinds of things can be done, with **cooperation**/
> When you make something that all of you share, here and there, you also make friends, friends who care, friends everywhere.

You'd be surprised what can be done, with two not one, with just a
little **cooperation**.
(http://www.youtube.com/watch?v=aofjMGfZ53M, accessed 03/30/12)

The positive sense of *cooperation*, which embeds one of the key values of
modern Anglo culture, can be articulated in the following explication:

[A] *cooperation*

a. it can be like this:
b.   someone does some things with some other people
          because this someone thinks like this about these other people:
c.   "these people want something to happen
d.   I want the same
e.   if it happens, it will be good for these people
f.   at the same time, it will be good for me
g.   because of this. I want to do some things with these people"
h. it is good if it is like this

The key aspects of this concept are, roughly speaking, a willingness to participate in a joint activity (components b and g), a shared purpose (d), an expectation of benefits for all the participants (e and f), and a positive evaluation (h).

Turning now to the "asymmetrical" sense of the verb *to cooperate,* we can
illustrate it with the following sentences from Wordbanks:

He said: "I will fully **cooperate** in any way I can with the investigation
staff of the Ombudsman's department."
The best thing for them to do is **cooperate** with the independent review.
The effort marks a new willingness to **cooperate** with U.S. forces.
Cullen has agreed to **cooperate** with authorities.
But even though she was nervous, she **cooperated** by answering the
questions and even smiled once or twice.
He has always refused to **cooperate** with police inquiries.

This asymmetrical usage (*cooperate₂*) does not require any joint activities or a
common purpose. Rather, it is a question of a willingness to do something that
someone else wants me to do, in order to assist them to reach *their* goal, in an
expectation of a definite benefit for them and a potential benefit for me. As the
last example above illustrates, a positive evaluation of such a conduct is not
required. More precisely, the meaning of the asymmetrical *cooperate₂* can be
articulated as follows:

[B] *she cooperated with the authorities (with the investigators, etc.)*

a. she did something because she thought like this about some people:
b.   "these people want something to happen

c.   they want to do some things because of this

d.   at the same time, they want me to do something because of this

e.   I can think about it like this:

f.   'if I do it, it will be good for these people

g.   at the same time, it can be good for me'

h.   because of this, I want to do it"

As the *Collins Cobuild Dictionary of English* recognizes, the adjective *cooperative* (in most of its uses) builds on the asymmetrical meaning of the verb *to cooperate*. The *Dictionary* defines "cooperative behaviour" as "behaviour in which someone helps you willingly when you ask them for their help," and it offers the following examples:

> The Swiss authorities have been very **cooperative**.
>
> Most **cooperative** of you, Doctor!
>
> Parents hope to raise children who are considerate and **cooperative**.

The definition of the adjective *cooperative* offered by the *Dictionary* is virtually identical with that assigned to the verb *to cooperate* in its asymmetrical sense. In fact, however, there is an important difference here: both the adjective *cooperative* and the noun *cooperativeness* derived from it imply a positive evaluation ("it is good if someone is like this"), whereas the verb does not.

Thus, the lexico-semantic field including the verb *cooperate*, the nouns *cooperation* and *cooperativeness*, and the adjective *cooperative* is quite complex. When these words are used in scholarly literature, where writers sometimes feel that they don't have to comply with ordinary English usage because, after all, they are writing scientific prose and not ordinary English sentences, the complexity can turn into utter confusion.

This would not be the case, of course, if the writers announced at the outset that they were going to use these words in special technical senses, and if they defined those technical senses. But more often than not the scholarly discourse about "cooperation" and "cooperativeness" glides imperceptibly from one meaning to another, or floats on the waves of familiar-sounding words, without ever being solidly anchored. Since the words are familiar, and since they all seem to have positive connotations, the readers may go with the flow and not even notice that they have no clear idea of what the author is trying to say.

"Cooperate," "Cooperation," and "Cooperative" in English Scholarly Discourse

For example, in the already-mentioned book *Why We Cooperate* written by the psychologist Michael Tomasello with contributions from four other scholars, philosopher Brian Skyrms writes:

> Humans may well be more cooperative than chimpanzees—I leave it to the
> experts to judge—but we are far from the most cooperative species on the
> planet. Meerkats, mole rats, many types of social insect, and even bacteria
> achieve high levels of cooperation. (p. 145)

What does Skyrms means by "cooperative" and "cooperation," one wonders.
Clearly, the meanings he has in mind—which apply to insects and even bacteria, as well as to chimpanzees and humans—must be different from those
that the words have in ordinary English, but what exactly are they? There is no
explanation in the text.

It is also not clear how Skyrms's intended use of these words relates to the
book's title. Presumably, Tomasello's question "why [do] we cooperate?" refers
to humans. One of the many clues that Tomasello offers to his own intended
use of the word *cooperate* is the phrase "shared intentionality." This is not
clearly defined, either, but evidently has to do with thinking and wanting, and
thus seems to exclude bacteria, at least inasmuch as thinking is concerned. Yet
Skyrms's piece is a commentary on Tomasello's essay and there is no mention
of any intentional differentiation in the meaning of the key words. As a result,
the reader may well feel disoriented.

What I propose to do now is set out what appear to be Tomasello's own
main ideas arising from his and his associates' recent research linked with the
words *cooperate*, *cooperation*, and *cooperative*. I will not attempt to define these
words as used by Tomasello himself, because as far as I can see his use of them
is also in flux. Sometimes, these words appear to be used interchangeably with
the words *altruism* and *altruistic*, sometimes with *collaboration* and *collaborative*, at other times with *help* and *helping*, and so on.

In the introductory chapter of *Why We Cooperate*, Tomasello characterizes *cooperation* in the sense in which he is using this term as a combination of
"altruism" and "collaboration." To quote:

> Our empirical research on cooperation in children and chimpanzees
> focusses on two basic phenomena:
>
> (1) Altruism: one individual sacrificing in some way for another; and
> (2) Collaboration: multiple individuals working together for mutual ben-
>   efit. (Tomasello 2009: XVII)

This notion of "cooperation" as a combination of "altruism" and "collaboration" is reinforced in the concluding chapter, "Where biology and culture meet":

> most, if not all, of the highly complex forms of cooperation in modern
> industrial societies—from the United Nations to credit card purchases
> over the Internet—are built primarily on cooperative skills and motiva-
> tions biologically evolved for small-group interactions: the kinds of altru-
> istic and collaborative activities that we have seen here in our simple studies
> of great apes and young children. (Tomasello 2009: 104)

The key semantic component of *altruism* (as the word is usually used in English) is, roughly speaking, "wanting to do good things for other people, even if it is bad for me." This fits in with Tomasello's characterization, which focuses on "sacrifices" and presumably takes the "doing good things for others" for granted. Thus, the cognitive scenario of "altruism" (both in the ordinary sense and in Tomasello's sense) can be portrayed along the following lines:

[C] The cognitive scenario of "altruism"

someone can think like this about some other people:

    "I want to do something good for these people

    I know that if I do it, it can be bad for me

    I don't want not to do it because of this"

The key semantic component of *collaboration* (as the word is normally used in present-day English) has to do with "doing something *with* someone else" (not *for* someone else). In addition, the word implies "common goals" (the "collaborators" want the same outcome), and also, a good deal of thinking focused on those goals. This last aspect of *collaboration* may not be immediately obvious, but when one asks native speakers of English, "Can bees collaborate?," they usually laugh.

Two people working together in the garden, picking fruit together, or hunting together, would normally not be described as "collaborating," either. As several dictionaries of present-day English note, (apart from helping occupying forces) the word is now normally used in relation to intellectual endeavors (such as writing an academic paper or doing a research project), not to physical labor. For this reason alone, when Tomasello talks, for example, about "mutualistic collaboration as the evolutionary source of human skills and motives for shared intentionality" (2009: 47), he cannot be using the word *collaboration* in its ordinary English sense.

The component of "doing something with someone else" does seem to be part of his intended sense, and his key phrase "shared intentionality" appears to imply that the "collaborators" want the same outcome. In addition, Tomasello's characterization of "collaboration" quoted earlier suggests that he sees some calculation of "mutual benefits" as also being part of the notion. In ordinary language, some such calculation appears to be included in the meaning of *cooperation* rather than *collaboration* (as the historical link between *cooperation* and "cooperative societies," formed to pursue "mutual benefits," indicates). Of course, when two people "collaborate" on a joint project, it is likely that they do so because they see that "collaboration" as beneficial for them both, but this expectation of mutual benefit is not part of the word's meaning as such.

Thus, the two meanings of *collaboration*—the ordinary English one and Tomasello's technical one—appear to share two components (roughly speaking, "doing something with someone else" and "wanting the same outcomes") and to differ in the third component: in ordinary language, "an intellectual endeavor," in Tomasello's technical term, "a calculation of mutual benefits." Using NSM, we can make this comparison more precisely, as follows:

[D] "collaboration" in ordinary English

a. it can be like this:

b.   someone is doing something for some time
             because this someone wants some things to happen

c.   someone else is doing it with this someone during this time
             because this other someone wants the same things to happen

d.   these people know that if they don't think about these things well, these things
        can't happen

[E] "collaboration" as characterized by Tomasello (2009) in his Introduction

a. it can be like this:

b.   some people are doing something for some time
             because they want some things to happen

c.   some other people are doing it with these people during this time
             because they want the same things to happen

d.   all these people think about it like this:
             "if I do this with these other people, it will be good for these people
             at the same time, it will be good for me"

It does not seem, however, that Tomasello intended his characterization of *collaboration* offered in the Introduction to *Why We Cooperate* as a definition in a strict sense or that he intended to use the word *collaboration* in some specific technical sense. Accordingly, rather than studying how complex English words like *cooperation, altruism,* and *collaboration* are being used throughout the *Why We Cooperate* volume and in Tomasello's other publications, I will try to reformulate, in simpler and I believe clearer words, the main ideas that he appears to be putting forward.

Tomasello's Theory of Young Children's "Natural Cooperativeness"

I have already (partially) quoted Tomasello's arresting remark that "one of the greatest debates in Western civilization is whether humans are born cooperative and helpful and society later corrupts them (e.g., Rousseau), or whether they are born selfish and unhelpful and society teaches them better (e.g., Hobbes)." Essentially, Tomasello sides with Rousseau, and he posits a naturally cooperative stage (superimposed on an equally natural selfish streak that all "viable organisms" (pp. 4-5) must have). Comparing children with chimpanzees, he argues that "from around their first birthday—when they first begin to walk and talk and become truly cultural beings—human children are already cooperative and helpful in many, though obviously not all, situations. And they do not learn this from adults; it comes naturally." (p.4)

This early human cooperativeness is not a single trait: Tomasello distinguishes three different types of it, which he discusses under the headings "helping," "informing," and "sharing" (e.g., fetching an out-of-the-way object, pointing at the keys that an adult has dropped, or giving objects to people). Alternating in his discussion between the terms "cooperativeness" and "altruism," Tomasello writes: "It is important to distinguish among these three types of altruism because the costs and benefits of each are different, and they may have different evolutionary histories" (pp. 5-6).

Tomasello emphasizes that young children's willingness to "help," "inform," and "share" is not a result of acculturation, although "socialization does play a critical role, obviously, as children mature" (p. 28). Alternating again between the terms "altruism" (and "altruistic") and "cooperation" (and "cooperative"), he elaborates:

> So the development of **altruistic** tendencies in young children is clearly shaped by socialization. They arrive at the process with a predisposition for helpfulness and **cooperation**. (p. 43)
>
> Children are **altruistic** by nature, and this is a predisposition (...) adults attempt to nurture. (p. 47)
>
> In the second chapter we turn to the question of how human beings might have become so **cooperative** evolutionarily. (p. 47)

I will now try to rephrase Tomasello's three hypotheses about young children's natural tendency to "help," "inform," and "share" (as I understand them) in terms of simple, clear, and semantically stable words like *do* and *happen, think, know*, and *want*, and *someone* and *something*.

Tomasello's Conception of Young Children's "Natural Cooperativeness"

[F] "helping" (e.g., fetching an out-of-the-way object, as requested)

a.   for some time after they are born, children are like this:

b.   they often do something because they think like this about someone else:

c.   "this someone wants something to happen

d.   it will be good for this someone if it happens

e.   it can happen if I do something now

f.   I want to do it because of this"

g.   other living creatures are not like this

[G] "informing" (e.g., pointing to the keys that an adult has dropped)

a.   for some time after they are born, children are like this:

b.   they often do something because they think like this about someone else:

c.   "I know something, this someone doesn't know it

d.   it will be good for this someone if this someone knows it

e.   this someone can know it if I do something now

f.   I want to do it because of this"

g.   other living creatures are not like this

[H] "sharing" (giving objects to people)

a.   for some time after they are born, children are like this:

b.   they often do something with something because they think like this about someone:

c.   "I can do something with this thing now, this

                someone can't do the same with this thing

d.   it will be good for this someone if this someone can do the same with this thing

e.   because of this, I want to do something with this thing now

f.   if I do it, after this, this someone can do the same with this thing"

These three cognitive scenarios correspond, as far as I can see, to Tomasello's three hypotheses about an early "altruistic human cooperativeness," which jointly constitute one part of his answer to the question of why we cooperate. The other part of the unique human tendency to "cooperate" is linked for him with the term "collaboration" (in his sense of the word): "multiple individuals working together for mutual benefit" (p. XVII).

In his discussion of these two sides of "cooperation," the early one linked with "altruism" and the later one linked with "collaboration," Tomasello uses the phrase "human cooperation in the large sense." A fuller quote is in order here:

> I do not believe altruism is the process primarily responsible for human cooperation in the larger sense of humans' tendency and ability to live and operate together in institution-based cultural groups. In this story, altruism is only a bit player. The star is mutualism, in which we all benefit from our cooperation but only if we work together, what we may call collaboration. (p. 52)

So at this later stage, "mutualism" is the star, which is introduced with reference to both "cooperation" and "collaboration," though not really defined. Yet in order to follow Tomasello's argument it is important to understand what exactly he has in mind when he says "mutualism," and what exactly it is that distinguishes, in his conception, human "mutualism" from a situation when animals "work together," for example, in a group hunt. It seems to me that on the basis of the clues provided, we can reconstruct Tomasello's idea of human "mutualism" as follows:

[I] "mutualistic (human) collaboration" (in Tomasello's conception)

a. people often do some things with other people

   because they think like this about some other people:

b.   "these people want something to happen, I want the same

c.   if it happens, it will be good for these people, at the same time, it will be good

       for me

d.   it can't happen if some people don't do some things with other people

e.   because of this, I want to do some things with these people"

f. animals don't think like this

Animals, too, engage sometimes in "joint activities" with other animals, but according to Tomasello and his co-researchers, there are some crucial differences between human and animal joint activities. Above all, as Joan Silk in her contribution to *Why We Cooperate* puts it, animals don't seem to share "our concern for the welfare of others" (p. 111). In simple terms, this would mean that animals do not seem to think in terms of "what is good for those other fellows," only in terms of "what is good for me." Thus, one key difference lies in component (c) of the two cognitive scenarios, [I] and [J]. (This is not *my* proposal, but an attempt to express in simple words the proposals formulated by psychologists in complex terms.)

[J] joint activities of some animals, such as a group hunt (in Joan Silk's conception)

a. animals sometimes do something with other animals of the same kind

   because they think like this about another animal:

b.   "this someone wants something to happen, I want the same

c.   if it happens, it will be good for me"

Attributions of such thoughts to animals may cause some incredulity, because the use of simple words and phrases like "think," "good for me," or "because of this" lays bare something that in most conventional scholarly discourse is somewhat hidden behind words such as "decide," "motivate," and "intend," which are intuitively less clear and therefore less arresting. To quote Joan Silk herself:

> Even in the best-case scenario for mutualism [among animals], the stag hunt, individuals are motivated by the benefits that they will obtain themselves, not by their concern for the welfare of others. Both players decide to participate in the stag hunt because this is the best strategy for each of them, and they do not need to give any consideration to the benefits that their partners will derive in order to decide whether to participate.

They need to know what their partners intend to do but they do not need to place a positive value on the benefits that their partners will receive. (pp. 117-118)

Tomasello, who appears to share Silk's view on the stag hunt, presents a number of specific evolutionary hypotheses about the development of "cooperation" in that broader sense, including development of "collaborative activities" (p. 981), hypotheses framed in terms such as "joint goal" (p. 99), "distinct roles" (p. 99), "joint intentions" (2006: Notes), and "coordinated plans" (2006: Notes). All these hypotheses can, it seems to me, be sharpened and made clearer by translating them from the language of semantically complex words with shifting and undefined meanings into a mini-English of simple, clear, and semantically stable words along the same lines as has been done in the scenarios presented above.

In her commentary on "Why We Cooperate," developmental psychologist Carol Dweck writes: "I am extremely excited by the ideas and the research that Tomasello presents. It is of inestimable importance that someone has had the courage and insight to stake out this domain and to ask those big, big questions." I share Dweck's appreciation for Tomasello's ideas and research. I would suggest, however, that the pursuit of very big questions is not always best served by the use of very complex words. In particular, words like "cooperation," "altruism," and "collaboration" may create unnecessary obstacles in our search for understanding of how young children think about other people and what they want to do—for other people, with other people, and in accordance with what other people want.

I would also venture to suggest that the experimental work by many different researchers on which Tomasello reports could, perhaps, often be more fruitful and more focused if the questions addressed in it were framed in terms of simpler words (which are self-explanatory and not English-bound) rather than those "big" and complex ones, which can be obscure and variably used, and which are not cross-translatable into other languages.

In her commentary on Tomasello's ideas, another contributor to the volume *Why We Cooperate*, developmental psychologist Elizabeth Spelke, writes: "The fundamental questions of human nature and human knowledge, questions that have been outstanding for millennia, are beginning to yield answers" (p. 172). Hopefully, this is true—but for this very reason it is important for scholars tackling these fundamental questions to try to formulate their hypotheses clearly. NSM techniques make such clarity achievable, while at the same time freeing the analysis from an unwitting imposition of Anglo conceptual categories on all humans, as well as our remote biological ancestors.

English "Interaction" and Russian "Obshchenie"

To a large extent, what applies to the term "cooperation" applies also to the term "interaction," which frequently co-occurs with it and which also occupies a very prominent position in current discussions of languages, human evolution, and "human sociality," as well as discourse studies, pragmatics, and the literature on "politeness." For example, Enfield and Levinson (2006), in the introduction to their book *The Roots of Human Sociality*, write (under the heading "Human Interaction as the Focus of a New Interdisciplinary Field"):

> One aim of this book is to define and consolidate a new field of research, a multidisciplinary approach to human interaction, its organization, and its constitutive role in social life. The project asserts the centrality of social interaction in the organization of human societies. (...) Underlying all this is a specialized cognition, crucially involving intention attribution or "mind reading" and the accumulation of shared understandings that makes historical culture possible. (p. 9)

"Interaction is shot through and through with culture," Levinson (2006: 55) states, but he doesn't seem to be aware that his key analytical tool—the word *interaction*—is also shot through and through with culture—Anglo culture. (It is not an accident that there is no word for "interaction" in Russian, as there is none for "turn-taking," called in Enfield and Levinson (p. 53) "an apparent universal of interaction.") (cf. Wierzbicka 1991/2003, Tannen 1981).

Thus, the theory of "human sociality" proposed by these authors is framed in concepts derived from English and is highly culture-specific. If Russian scholars wanted to come up with a comparable theory (based on a central Russian word for how people can be with other people, talk to other people, do things with other people, and "read other people's minds"), they would probably base it on the Russian key concept of "obščenie"—an everyday word in Russian, for which English has no equivalent. The word *obščenie* (which derives from the adjective *obščij* "common" and is cognate with the noun *obščestvo* "society") plays a key role in Mikhail Bakhtin's theory of what it is to be human.

According to Bakhtin, "one can 'open' another person—or rather, make him or her open themselves—only by means of *obščenie* with him/her, dialogically" (Bakhtin 1963: 338). Only in *obščenie* "a human being can be opened [revealed] within a human being, for others and for him/herself" (p. 338). Anthropologist Dale Pesmen, in her book *Russia and Soul*, translates Bakhtin's key word *obščenie* as "communion" and ingeniously renders his "dialogičeskoe obščenie" by alternating the word *dialogue* with the word *communion*. She also rightly introduces into her discussion of Bakhtin's key notion of the "dialogical principle" the word *soul* (as the nearest English analogue of the Russian *duša*). To quote:

> Communion, dialogue, is, ideally, life-changing (...) Bakhtin's work is inspired by the premise of the life-changing and life-giving power of dialogue. (...) Bakhtin was committed to describing soul as emerging between people, the depths as "outside [oneself], in the soul of others." (Pesmen 2000: 272)

Pesmen rightly links Bakhtin's focus on "dialogical communion" and on its importance for a person's "soul" or "self" (*duša*) with certain important aspects of Russian culture, which she calls a "dusha culture" (for discussion, see Wierzbicka 2002a).

The English word *interaction* evokes the image of free-standing individuals, doing things with one another but remaining separate. The Russian word *obščenie* (closer to a "communion of selves that can be achieved through talk" than to "cooperative interaction") evokes a very different image and reveals very different cultural traditions, values, and assumptions.

I am not suggesting that there is no possibility of mutual understanding between someone who thinks about people in terms of "interaction" and "cooperation," and someone who thinks in terms of "obščenie." Rather, I am suggesting that genuine understanding cannot be reached through culture-specific English concepts but only through shared ones (as in "wanting to say something to someone else," "wanting to know what someone else wants," "wanting to do something with other people," and so on).

John Locke on the "Abuse of Words"

It is hard not to think in this context of John Locke's *Essay Concerning Human Understanding* and his reflections on the various forms of what he called "the abuse of words" and the obstacles to understanding that they create. One such form is, according to Locke, using words that have no clear meanings attached to them. Another is using the same word in different senses, without explaining what sense one has in mind. To quote (with modernized spelling):

> Another great abuse of words is, *inconstancy* in the use of them. It is hard to find a discourse written of any subject, especially of controversy, wherein one shall not observe, if he read with attention, the same words (and those commonly the most material in the discourse, and upon which the argument turns) used sometimes for one collection of simple *ideas,* and sometimes for another, which is a perfect abuse of language, words being intended for signs of my *ideas,* to make them known to others, not by any natural signification, but by a voluntary imposition, 'tis

plain cheat and abuse, when I make them stand sometimes for one thing, and sometimes for another...(p. 492)

Locke also deplores the use of familiar words in unfamiliar senses without a definition: "Another abuse of language is, an *affected obscurity,* by either applying old words to new and unusual significations; or introducing new and ambiguous terms without defining either; or else putting them so together as may confound their ordinary meaning" (p. 493). Another serious problem for "human understanding" is, according to Locke, the reification of terms frequently used within one's own speech community or one's own scholarly or philosophical community of discourse:

> Another great *abuse of words is, the taking them for things.* This, though it, in some degree, concerns all names in general, yet more particularly affects those of substances. To this abuse, those men are most subject, who confine their thoughts to any one system, and give themselves up into a firm belief of the perfection of any received hypothesis: whereby they come to be persuaded, that the terms of that sect, are so suited to the nature of things, that they perfectly correspond with their real existence. (p. 497)

At the risk of annoying those readers who don't like lengthy quotes from the classics and prefer to engage only with their own contemporaries, I will adduce one more quote from Locke, which seems particularly apposite to some contemporary uses of words like *cooperation* and *interaction*:

> There remains yet another more general, though, perhaps, less observed *abuse of words;* and that is, that men having by a long and familiar use annexed to them certain *ideas,* they are apt *to imagine so near and necessary a connection between the names and the signification* they use them in, that they forwardly suppose one cannot but understand what their meaning is; and therefore one ought to acquiesce in the words delivered, as if it were past doubt, that in the use of those common received sounds, the speaker and the hearer had necessarily the same precise *ideas.* Whence presuming, that when they have in discourse used any term, they have thereby, as it were, set before others the very thing they talk of. (p. 503)

More than three centuries later, Locke's analysis of the "abuse of words" has lost none of its relevance. In the globalized world of the twenty-first century, however, and in the era of global English, one point can be added to these Locke makes so aptly: the terminological Anglocentrism of much of present-day scholarly discourse, as invisible to those who succumb to it as the forms discussed by Locke were invisible to the seventeenth-century targets of *his* critique. On this last point, let me quote a contemporary critique by my colleague Cliff Goddard.

A more general problem with formulating putative human universals in English-specific terminology (terms such as "information," "communication," "interaction," and the like) is that the concepts behind these words are complex and deeply culture-specific. To frame a theory or model in such terms is to shackle it from the beginning with an Anglo bias, not only linguistically, but also conceptually (…). To my mind, there is a fundamental epistemological problem here which is not yet widely understood in the discourse of modern social science. This is not the place to pursue this issue at length but perhaps I can dramatize it as follows: Would it not be a cause for concern if the results of scientific work were to be irrevocably locked into the vocabulary of one language (English)? In view of this danger, why not try formulating hypotheses about human universals from the beginning in terms which are as clear and as non culture-bound as possible? (Goddard 2007: 533)

PART FOUR

Entering Other Minds

10

Grammar and Social Cognition: The Hawaiians, the Dalabons, and the Anglos

Different languages reflect different ways of speaking and thinking. As many linguists studying endangered languages have often emphasized, every language contains, in its lexicon and grammar, a distinct conceptual universe that is going to disappear forever when the last remaining speakers of that language die out. Forty years ago, anthropologist Clifford Geertz published a famous paper titled "From the native's point of view" (1974), in which he presented capturing "the native's" ways of thinking as a major goal of cognitive anthropology. Since then, however, doubts have been often expressed as to whether this is ever achievable. Can speakers of one language ever understand the conceptual universe contained in another, especially if this other language is very different from one's own?

Geertz's title echoed, deliberately, that of the English translation of a famous book written half a century earlier by another anthropologist, Lucien Levy-Brühl: *How Natives Think* (1926). Geertz's use of the term "the native" was ironic, but the goal of understanding the thinking of insiders of another language and culture very different from one's own was in his view legitimate and compelling. When Geertz took up the question a few decades later, not long before he died, the context and the intellectual climate had changed considerably:

> Over the past twenty-five years or so, the post-everything era (post-modernism, structuralism, colonialism, positivism), the attempt to portray "how the 'natives' think" (or thought), or even what they are doing when they do what they do, has come in for a good deal of moral, political, and philosophical attack. (Geertz 2000: 102)

Although Geertz evidently wanted to distance himself from the spirit of the "post-everything" era, he did seem to have come, at that stage, to be sincerely skeptical about any attempts to portray "how the 'natives' think." In my view, such skepticism is misplaced. How could we possibly seek to understand others if we didn't try to grasp "how they think"? And how could the humanities and social sciences give up their aspiration to try to understand others? "The days of simple 'the Dangs believe, the Dangs don't believe' anthropology seem truly over," Geertz came to think (2000: 102). But without some further comment, this statement can be misleading. As I see it, questions like "how do the Dangs think?," and "what do the Dangs believe?" are, in principle, legitimate, and indeed necessary, if we wish to come close to "understanding others." But they are only legitimate on two conditions.

The first condition is that we ask such questions not only about indigenous people in various parts of the world, but also about our own speech communities, and in particular, about "Anglos." As I have discussed in many publications (see, e.g., Wierzbicka 2006a and b, 2010a), while there are many "Englishes" in the world and many cultural worlds associated with them, there is also a cultural world associated with what Braj Kachru (1985) calls "the English of the Inner Circle" and what I (2006a) have called "Anglo English." Denying this usually leads to taking cultural norms and assumptions associated with "Anglo English" for the human norm. The NSM perspective seeks to free us from the inadvertent Anglocentrism of such a position and allows us to recognize that, alongside Dangs, Hawaiians, Russians, and all the other human cultural groups (changeable, of course, and fluid, but nonetheless recognizable), there are also "Anglos."

The second condition is that when we attribute shared understandings and cultural knowledge to a group of people, we try to posit only beliefs that they could, in principle, express in their own language. The language of the investigator can be used for convenience as a shorthand for provisionally recording indigenous ideas but it cannot be the only medium in which those ideas **could** be expressed.

Geertz (2000: 102) writes:

> The mere claim "to know better" which it would seem any anthropologist would have at least implicitly to make, seems at least faintly illegitimate. To say something about the forms of life of Hawaiians (or anybody else) that Hawaiians do not themselves say opens one to the charge that one is writing out other peoples' consciousness for them, scripting their souls.

As I see it, there is nothing inherently wrong with the claim "to know better," because someone who has studied a subject deeply may indeed "know better" than someone who has never studied it at all. This applies not only to "knowing others" but also to knowing one's own community. For example, most "Anglos" are not aware of the existence or the exact nature of Anglo cultural key concepts and simply take them for granted. This can prevent them from cultural self-understanding and can distort their understanding of others.

In principle, then, I don't see anything wrong with saying something about Hawaiians (or anybody else) that they themselves do not say. But to say something about Hawaiians (or anybody else) that they **could not themselves say** (in their own words, because they have no such words), does indeed open one to the charge that one is "writing out other peoples' consciousness for them, scripting their souls."

Consider for example, Nicholas Evans's attempt (in his splendid book *Dying Words,* 2010a: 77–79) to offer English readers a glimpse of the social world of the speakers of the Australian language Dalabon. The cognitive category that Evans is trying to explain is usually referred as to "disharmonic." Evans glosses the meaning in question as "the two of them, who are in odd-numbered generations with respect to one another." Pointing out that Dalabon, which is a polysynthetic language, can condense into a single word a content that would take an entire sentence in English, he puts this gloss in the first person, as if it represented the speaker's perspective. To quote:

Wekemarnûmolkkûndokan.

> I'm afraid that the two of them, **who are in odd-numbered generations with respect to one another**, might go, with consequences for someone else, and without a key person knowing about it; by choosing the form of words I do, I hereby indicate that one of those carrying out the action is a mother-in-law of mine or equivalently respected relative.

Strictly speaking, of course, this cannot be how the native speakers of Australian languages think, because their culture has no concept of "odd number" and their languages have no words for it (not even for "number," let alone "odd number"). As I wrote two decades ago in my *Semantics, Culture and Cognition*, "terms such as (...) "odd-numbered generations" (...), useful as they are as an analyst's shorthand, cannot represent native speakers' meaning." (1992:358).

Evans comments: "Intricate as it is, this one-word example only scratches the surface of how languages use their grammars to construct and update their speakers' ever-unfolding dossier of the social universe they move in." However, terms like "odd-numbered generations" cannot capture the speakers' way of thinking, or, in Evans's words, the "socially relevant categories of experience" (as seen from the experiencer's point of view). It could be said, of course, that the characterization of the "disharmonic" category phrased in terms of "odd-numbered generation" in Evans's gloss is only a place-holder for the speakers' meaning. But if so, then the question must be asked: what *is* the speaker's meaning that this phrase is a place-holder for?

The term "odd-numbered generations" is a traditional technical term in Australian linguistics, which can be found, inter alia, in Ken Hale's classic paper "Kinship reflections in syntax: some Australian languages" (1966). What is novel about Evans's use of this term is that he puts it in the mouth of a Dalabon speaker (in the translation), in an attempt to enter the Dalabon speakers' mental world and to present their social cognition from an insider point of view.

This is a bold move for which I believe Evans should be applauded. If in this "post-everything" era one still wants to try to understand "how the natives think," one must make that move and try to speak, sometimes, in the first person. By explicating the Dalabon speaker's meaning in a first-person mode, Evans is, of course, not implying that the Dalabon speakers carry the knowledge of their social categories in their heads in a propositional form and could easily articulate it themselves. He is evidently trying to explicate the *tacit* knowledge of a Dalabon speaker—knowledge which is unconscious but which, in Sapir's words, could in principle be "dragged to the light" of one's consciousness.

Articulating one's tacit knowledge in propositional form may not be a traditional cultural practice in an Aboriginal society. This does not mean, however, that if it is articulated, empathetically, by a linguist or anthropologist it cannot be assessed by a native speaker as something that "rings true," or not—provided, of course, that it is articulated "in their own words"—or in the words of their second language (such as Aboriginal English) which match "their own words."

As I have sought to demonstrate in detail elsewhere (Wierzbicka, 2013b), we can try to enter the mental world of speakers of a language like Dalabon by relying on indigenous conceptual categories such as "father" and "mother," but not on technical terms such as "harmonic" and "disharmonic," "odd-numbered" and "even-numbered."

An interpretive formulation like "odd-numbered generations" distorts the indigenous perspective, by relying on the culturally alien concept of "odd number." Moreover, it oversimplifies and distorts the social model implicit in the indigenous perspective—a model evidently based on prototypes and on provisions for extensions.

What lies at the heart of the "disharmonic" category is clearly the contrast between parents and their children, whereas the "harmonic" one is modeled on the relationship between two people who have the same father and mother (i.e., from an English speaker's point of view, siblings). In fact, this is how anthropologist A. R. Radcliffe-Brown in his classic work *The Social Organization of Australian Tribes* first described the feature of Australian kinship systems, which later came to be linked with technical terms like "harmonic" and "disharmonic" or "even-" and "odd-numbered" generations:

Another important principle of Australian system is connected with the relations between persons of different generations. The relationship of generation has its origin in the family in the relation of parents to children. It becomes of importance in general social life because social continuity requires that the body of tradition possessed by the society shall be handed on by one generation to the next, and this handing on of tradition entails a relation of superiority and subordination as between one generation and the next. The generation of parents must have authority over the generation of children (....) As between persons who are separated by an intervening generation a new situation arises. If we call the generations 1, 2 and 3, then those of generation 1 exercise authority over those of 2 and those of 2 over those of 3, but...persons of 1 and 3 are brought together into a different kind of relationship which, in spite of the difference in age, links them together on terms of familiarity and almost of equality. (Radcliffe-Brown 1973[1930-31]: 432–433)

Thus, as Radcliffe-Brown envisaged eighty years ago, it is the relationship between parents and children that provides a conceptual anchor for the distinction in question—or, more precisely, the relationship between children and their mothers and fathers.

In his 1982 study of the "alternating generations" phenomenon in Dalabon, another researcher, Barry Alpher, records a revealing comment on the "disharmonic" category offered by a native Dalabon speaker, Don Bununhoa: "like mother and father" (Alpher 1982: 21). As this comment plainly shows, "mother" and "father" are the focal categories, and this is what is lost in the "odd-numbered generation" approach. Since for speakers of a language like Dalabon the social universe is divided into two categories, based on those focal relationships, the prototypical "harmonic" and "disharmonic" categories can be extended to many other interpersonal configurations, both "vertical" and "horizontal." But a characterization that obliterates the key role of those focal points—"mother" and "father"—distorts the structure of the indigenous socio-cognitive model.

To do justice to the indigenous perspective, we need to account for both the prototypes and the extensions. By proceeding in this way, we can ensure both the predictive power of our analysis and its psychological reality; and at the same time, we can avoid putting our own words into other people's mouths and our own concepts into their heads.

Trying to provide a characterization of the cognitive categories in question that would be closer to the indigenous perspective, I have proposed (Wierzbicka, 2013b), first, two explications based on the prototypes indicated above, and second, several "cultural scripts" for extending these prototypes to other relationships. Thus, for the "disharmonic" aspect of the Dalabon word cited by Evans, I have proposed an explication based on the contrast between parents and their children:

disharmonic

I think about these people like this:
    "they are not people of the same kind
    they are like two people are if one of them is the father of the other one,
    they are like two people are if one of them is the mother of the other one"

This explication does not claim that only parents and children are treated as "disharmonic." On the contrary, the use of the word "like" indicates that these two categories are regarded as prototypes for a much wider range of relationships.

The same kind of conceptual structure based on a prototype can be posited for the "harmonic" category, as the phrasing of the formula below shows:

harmonic

I think about these people like this:
  "they are people of the same kind
  they are like two people are if the father of one of them is the father of the
    other one,
  they are like two people are if the mother of one of them is the mother of the
    other one"

These explications have been formulated in words that are known to have exact equivalents in many Australian Aboriginal languages (see, e.g., Goddard 1994, Harkins and Wilkins 1994, Knight 2008), and so they have a claim to psychological reality that formulations like "odd-numbered generations" cannot have. By themselves, however, they do not have sufficient explanatory power to predict that, for example, a person's grandparents will be placed in the "harmonic" category, and great-grandparents in the "disharmonic" one. To account for this, we need to combine the explications with "cultural scripts" that would show who is to be treated as someone of the same kind as the speaker or the person spoken of. (See Wierzbicka, 2013b).

The identification of children not only with their siblings but also with their grandparents may at first sight also seem strange to many English readers, but on reflection they can probably perceive a certain logic in this: if the children are contrasted with the parents, and parents with their own parents, then it is not beyond comprehension that the children and the grandparents may fall into one category and the parents into another. But this can make sense in terms of a contrast between children and their parents, not in terms of some magic of even and odd numbers.

Evans says that "until you have the concept of 'harmonic' vs. 'disharmonic' generations you cannot make even (...) the unavoidable move of using Dalabon subject correctly" (2010a: 159). But while he highlights the importance of this concept, he doesn't explain in what this concept consists. He notes, poignantly, that when a language like Dalabon dies, "no one's mind will again have the thought-paths that its ancestral speakers once blazed" (p. xviii). But this being so, it is all the more important to try to understand those thought-paths from the speakers' point of view; and that should rule out presenting them in academic English.

In trying to understand what the shared modes of thinking and shared cultural scripts of Aboriginal people are, we do not have to accept the sterile and self-defeating intellectual fashions of which Geertz (2000:102) wrote:

> Postmodernists have questioned whether ordered accounts of other ways of being in the world—accounts that offer monological, comprehensive, and all-too-coherent explanations—are credible at all, and whether we are not so imprisoned in our own modes of thought and perception as to be incapable of grasping, much less crediting, those of others.

As I hope the explications presented here illustrate, we are not imprisoned in our own modes of thinking and perception if we can rely on a shared, universal set of concepts that provide us with a common intellectual currency for "understanding others," and indeed, for understanding ourselves.

I do not claim that the explications presented here are perfect just as they are and that there is no room for improvement. Neither do I believe, however, that they can be improved by shifting back from indigenous categories like "father" and "mother" to nonindigenous ones like "odd numbers" and "even numbers."

There can, of course, be no objection to using terms like "odd-numbered generations" or "disharmonic generations" as scholarly shorthand—part of convenient scientific terminology. To serve its purpose, however, such terms need to be defined, and if the definition is to be intelligible, it should be formulated in simple, intelligible, and cross-translatable words (not through other technical and English-bound terms).

As Geertz pointed out, in recent decades the attempts to portray how speakers of languages in remote communities think has come under a good deal of moral, political, and philosophical attack. On the other hand, the term "social cognition" is very much in vogue in present-day anthropology, linguistics, and other related fields. But what exactly is this "social cognition" if not how people in a given society think about themselves and other people? Clearly, the subject-matter of studies in "social cognition" involves the assumptions and understandings concerning people, which are shared by many people within a particular society or country (Goddard, Forthcoming).

Using simple words we could say, roughly, that geography is about different places, linguistics is about how people in different places speak to other people, and social cognition is about how people in different places think about people. People's thoughts can be illuminated from within, by their subjective understanding of what it is that they think, and of the words that they can use in their thinking. Our knowledge of geography (geology, astronomy, botany, zoology, etc.) can never be illuminated by this kind of subjective understanding with which we can comprehend our own thoughts (and also, the words of our native language).

Psychologist Lisa Barrett (2006) rightly says that to find out what another person feels we need to ask them, and in principle, the same applies to what another person thinks. We can find out what other people feel and think if they tell us—in their own words. Up to a point at least, the same applies to whole speech communities: to find out how people in these communities think, we can't dispense with understanding their own words.

In the era of English as the main international language of science, the global discourse of geography is largely Anglocentric, with words like *river*, *lake*, *mountain*, and *hill* playing a prominent role. Is this a problem for geography as a science? To some extent, it is, especially when it comes to comparisons between the geographies of different countries and to international scientific collaboration, or to legal issues about land rights in multilingual countries—as geographers increasingly come to recognize themselves (see, e.g., Mark and Turk 2003; Mark, Turk and Stea 2007; for discussion, see Bromhead 2013). But if terms like *river* and *mountain* are supplemented with more language-independent terms like "elevation" and "watercourse," and if these technical terms are defined through universal concepts like "above," "ground," "water," and "move," arguably, no great harm is done. Furthermore, additional precision needed for scientific purposes can, of course, be ensured by measurements and numbers.

When it comes to social cognition, however, there are no measurements and the need for technical terminology that can support measurements is more limited. For example, in the area of kinship, the use of terms like "harmonic and disharmonic generations," "alternating generations," and "odd-numbered generations" can be helpful in some contexts, but unhelpful or even misleading in others—far more so than the use of English-based technical terminology can be, for example, in geography. The reason is that a term like "odd-numbered generations" misrepresents the reality that it purports to portray, whereas a term like *elevation,* or even one like *mountain,* does not.

There can be many different and equally legitimate ways of thinking about places, and a lexical category like "mountain" is neither better nor worse than, for example, one like "puli" (see Chapter 2). But there aren't many equally good ways of representing other people's thoughts—arguably, a way of representing them that these people themselves can understand or articulate is better than any others.

Describing a conceptual category in a language like Dalabon as "disharmonic" saves space, and in that sense it is convenient and practical—for scholars who are familiar with this term. Describing it as referring to people "who are in odd-numbered generations" takes more space than saying simply "disharmonic," but at least it gives some inkling of understanding to English readers who are not students of the subject. But neither of these two ways can claim to be representing the conceptual reality in question, because neither of them could be translated into Dalabon itself and discussed with native-speaker consultants. By contrast, an explication formulated in simple words like *people*, *mother*, *father*, *the same*, and *other* can be, in principle, translated into Dalabon and discussed with Dalabon speakers. This fact of cross-translatability does not mean that this explication is perfect, but that it is a testable hypothesis about the conceptual reality it purports to represent. (For another extended discussion of the same fallacy that the meaning of grammatical categories can be captured in technical English terminology, see Chapter 11).

Anglophone scholars in social sciences often defend their use of technical terms by pointing out that it is natural for science—any science—to rely on technical terminology. This is a fair comment—up to a point. It is good to bear in mind, however, that, first, all technical terms need to be defined; second, that to be useful and viable, these definitions need to be couched in nontechnical and intelligible words; and third, that the use of technical terms is more necessary in sciences dealing with the external reality than in social and cognitive sciences dealing with people's thoughts.

The differences between studying the external (nonhuman) aspects of reality and the internal, human ones are profound and can hardly be overstated, and seemingly each generation of scholars needs to be reminded of it afresh. The visionary eighteenth-century Italian philosopher Giambattista Vico laid the blame for the misguided emphasis "on knowledge of the external world as the paradigm of all knowledge" (Berlin 1976: 25) at the feet of Descartes, but in the present-day globalized world, such a conception of knowledge is being spread, above all, by the English language. It is English, not French or any other European language, that has incorporated the paradigm of "natural sciences" and "exact sciences" ("hard sciences") into its very concept of "science," in the modern-English sense of the word. The French word *science* and the German word *Wissenschaft* are quite different in this respect from the English word *science*, since they apply equally to the humanities and the "exact sciences" (cf. Wierzbicka 2011b)[1].

Vico's insistence on the sui generis character of the humanities has important implications for present-day studies of "human sociality" and "social cognition," carried out through academic English in the name of a single paradigm of Science with a capital S. To quote from Isaiah Berlin's lucid rendition of Vico's thought:

> In the case of the external world the naturalists are right: all that we know is based on what the senses report. (....) Yet to say that this is all we can know about human beings, and that the techniques of our ways of apprehending the external world are, therefore, all that we can use in learning about each other, would be a grave understatement, a denial of what we know to be true. (...) If, following Descartes' rigorous rule, we allowed only that to be true knowledge which could be established by physics or other natural sciences, we should be confined to behaviourist tests, namely the uncritical assimilation of the human world to the non-human—the restriction of our knowledge to those characteristics of men which they

share with the non-human world; and consequently the attempt to explain human behaviour in non-human terms, as some behaviourists and extreme materialists, both ancient and modern, inspired by the vision (or mirage) of a single, integrated, natural science of all there is, have urged us to do. (...) [W]e should find ourselves debarred by such self-imposed austerity from saying or thinking some of the most natural and indispensable things that men constantly say or think about other human beings. (Berlin 1980: 23)

Following Vico's insights, we can resist the pressure to assimilate the study of "social cognition" to the paradigm based on natural and exact sciences. In particular, we can challenge the view that conceptual categories of speakers of any language (in Australia, Papua New Guinea, or anywhere else) can be adequately portrayed in English-based technical terminology. Such cross-linguistic understanding requires explanations based on shared concepts expressed in cross-translatable words—such as, for example, "above" and "below," "the same" and "other," "mother" and "father." This is different from scientific understanding of external reality, which relies on numbers and on technical concepts and terminology.

Unlike the "exact sciences," the "science of human thoughts" has to rely on the understanding of human words. Most human words differ in meaning substantially from language to language, but some do match. Potentially, these semantically matching words can give us better access to other people's thoughts than any technical terms synthesized from Greek and Latin morphemes or simply derived from English.

Science often needs, and has every right to use, technical terminology. This doesn't mean, however, that English expressions like, for example, "odd-numbered generations" can faithfully portray the "social cognition" of speakers of Australian languages. Phrases of this kind show how Anglophone scholars think, not how native speakers of these languages think. By themselves, therefore, they cannot evoke the social universe that those speakers mentally inhabit.

11

Thinking about "Things" in Yucatec and in English

In this chapter, I will look at the structure of the physical world as it is interpreted in two languages, English and the Mayan language Yucatec. The data on Yucatec will come from the work of John Lucy, who was quoted in Chapter 2 as a strong opponent of the Munsell color chart and of the putative color universals derived from it. At the same time, the chapter will examine the general approach to cross-linguistic comparison of meaning advocated by Lucy.

Like NSM researchers, Lucy strongly emphasizes the need for a neutral framework of description and comparison and opposes stimulus-based approaches that try to circumvent language and avoid in-depth semantic analysis. In some important respects, therefore, his ideas converge with those of NSM researchers. In other respects, however, Lucy's research program is quite different, and as I will try to show, also suffers from conceptual Anglocentrism and does not really try to enter other peoples' minds. (Unless otherwise indicated, the quotes from Lucy in this chapter will be from his contribution to the 2010 *Language and Bilingual Cognition* volume edited by Vivian Cook and Benedetta Bassetti (2011).)

Comparing the Nijmegen School's approach to language and cognition (which he calls "domain-centred") and his own (which he labels as "structure-centred"), Lucy (2011: 55) writes:

> The domain- and structure-centred approaches differ fundamentally, the former focussing on referential use and the latter on semantic structure. (....) However, (...) the two approaches have converged in some other ways that are significant and distinctive. They share the recognition that there must be a neutral framework of comparison.

A related feature (as Lucy sees it) that unites the two approaches is their cross-linguistic focus and their rejection of formalisms and speculative studies on human cognition divorced from cross-linguistic investigations. In this respect, both approaches contrast, in Lucy's view, with most other research on linguistic relativity, which Lucy characterizes as follows:

> research that adopts a metalanguage that is little more than a formalization of the categories of the investigator's own language, research that pays no

attention to the language as a structured system or to observable patterns of typological variation in such systems, research that speculates about effects on cognition but which never actually investigates them (e.g., most research in the color tradition exhibits all of these properties). From this vantage point, this anthropological approach to the effects of language diversity on thought represents the most theoretically coherent and empirically powerful approach currently available. (Lucy 2011: 55–56)

I fully agree with what Lucy says about metalanguages formalizing the categories of the investigator's own language, and about the need for wide-ranging cross-linguistic investigations. Needless to add, I am also in sympathy with what he says about "most research in the colour tradition." But what kind of metalanguage (other than technical English, with all its cultural biases) is Lucy himself envisaging? As we saw in Chapter 2, Goodenough believed that to overcome the ethnocentrism inherent in using one's own categories in cross-cultural description and comparison, we need some set of universally "applicable concepts." Lucy also writes that we need "to frame the comparison in neutral terms" (2010: 64). What are the neutral terms that he proposes for cross-cultural and cross-linguistic research?

There is no explicit answer to this question in Lucy's chapter in *Language and Bilingual Cognition* (2010), or in his other publications. To find out what answer he has in mind, therefore, we need to turn to his descriptive and analytical practice. There is no better place for that than the area that he himself uses to illustrate his approach: the semantic structure of nouns in English and in Yucatec (the central theme of his 1992 book, *Grammatical Categories and Cognition*).

Lucy notes that English and Yucatec treat most nouns differently, in that in English one has to choose for most nouns between a singular (e.g., *candle*) and a plural (*candles*), whereas in Yucatec one can say *kib'* regardless of the number of candles referred to:

> The two languages also contrast in the way they enumerate nouns. English speakers directly modify some nouns with a numeral (e.g. *one candle, two candles*), but for others they must provide an extra form indicating the unit to be counted (e.g., *one clump of dirt, two clumps of dirt*). By contrast, Yucatec requires that *all* constructions with numerals be supplemented by such an extra form called a 'unitizer' (or 'numeral classifier') that indicates a unit (e.g., *'un ts'iit kib,'* 'one long-thin candle,' *ká'a ts'iit kib'*, 'two long-thin candles'). (Lucy 2011: 53)

Lucy is making a big claim here: most of the concrete lexicon in the two languages, English and Yucatec, is structured differently, not just in grammar, but in meaning. The habitual way of thinking about candles, bananas, knives, books, and so on entrenched in the two languages is different. This claim is persuasive. But what exactly is the difference? Unfortunately, Lucy's answer to this more specific question is unclear and English-bound. It goes like this:

> English treats some of its nouns as indicating a quantificational unit (or form) in their lexical meaning, others as not indicating a quantificational unit. Yucatec essentially treats all nouns as if they were semantically unspecified as to the quantificational unit, almost as if they all referred to unformed substances. (p. 53)

This is difficult to understand, although a comparison with the English words *chair* and *mud* helps somewhat. Apparently, the idea is that in Yucatec, all or nearly all concrete nouns are like *mud.* This is why the same word *kib'* can refer both to candles and to wax: from a Yucatec point of view (Lucy suggests), candles are thought of not as candles (discrete objects, with a certain size, shape, and function) but as wax. In Lucy's own words, "the semantic sense of the Yucatec word *kib'* glossed as candle (...) actually refers to the substance and is better translated into English as 'wax.'" (p. 53)

But the division of all (concrete) nouns into just two classes: those like *chair* (*chairs*) and those like *mud* (no *muds*) is too simplistic. Even in English there are several other types of nouns: there are nouns like *wheat* (no *wheats*) and there are nouns like *oats* (no *oat*), there are nouns like *straw* (*one straw, a lot of straw*) and nouns like *hay* (*a lot of hay* but not *one hay), and so on (Wierzbicka 1985c; 1988; Goddard 2010). All these different classes of nouns, with different grammatical properties, reflect different habitual ways of thinking about things and substances of different kinds.

My own interpretation of the semantic structure of Yucatec nouns, based on Lucy's data but also on the more fine-grained analysis of English nouns developed by Goddard and myself just mentioned, is different from his. I do not believe that a phrase glossed by Lucy as "one long-thin wax" does justice to the Yucatec meaning. Surely, it must mean something like "one long-thin thing made of wax": a gloss like "one long-thin wax" simply doesn't make sense. This means that *kib'* has two meanings, not one: roughly speaking, kib'_1—wax, and kib'_2—something made of wax. This second meaning of *kib'* is not identical to the meaning of *candle,* but is comparable to it. It does not refer to a particular substance (wax), but to things of one kind made of that particular substance.

This appears to be a regular pattern of polysemy in Yucatec, comparable to what the Russian linguist Apresjan (2000) called "regular polysemy" with reference to languages like Russian and English. For example, English words like *pine, oak,* and *maple* can refer either to a tree of one kind or to one kind of wood (obtained from trees of this kind). Similarly, words like *chicken, duck,* or *turkey* in English can refer either to a bird of one kind or to one kind of meat (from birds of this kind). In some cases, regular polysemy can involve not just two but three different meanings, as in the case of *rabbit* (animal of one kind, meat of one kind, and fur of one kind). In languages like English and Russian, regular polysemy of this kind is fairly limited, but in languages with classi-fiers (like Yucatec) it appears to be often quite central to a language's semantic system.

The pattern of polysemy involving a particular "substance" and things of one kind made of that substance also has some parallels in English. For exam-ple, the word *glass* can refer to the substance called *glass,* but also to drinking glasses, to the amount of liquid contained in a glass, to *glasses* "spectacles," and with modifiers, to a *looking glass* or an *hourglass.* But in English, such cases are sporadic, whereas in Yucatec, it is a regular pattern. Furthermore, there are still differences between the overall semantic structures of *glass* (as in drinking glass) or *candle* and *kib',* as the explications below will show.

Building on the idea of regular polysemy, we can portray the difference in meaning between the English word *candle* and the Yucatec word *kib'* (in the second, "discrete" rather than "substance-like" meaning) as follows:

candle

a. one thing of one kind
b. people want there to be things of this kind in some places
     because people want to do something with these things in these places
c. if there is a thing of this kind in a place at a time when people can't see things in
     this place, someone can do something with this thing
d. after this, there can be something like a very small fire above this thing
e. when it is like this, people can see things in this place because of this
f. there can't be things of this kind in some places
     if some people don't do something with wax
g. things of this kind are like this:
h.   many parts of these things are wax
i.   often things of this kind are long
j.   often someone can hold something of this kind in one hand

kib'$_2$

a. something of one kind
b. there can be one thing of this kind in a place, there can be two things of this kind in
     a place, there can be many things of this kind in a place
c. many parts of a thing of this kind are wax (*kib'$_1$*)
d. people want there to be things of this kind in some places
     because people want to do something with these things in these places
e. if there is a thing of this kind in a place at a time when people can't see things in
     this place, someone can do something with this thing
f. after this, there can be something like a very small fire above this thing
g. when it is like this, people can see things in this place because of this

h.   there can't be things of this kind in some places

   if some people don't do something with wax

The first point to emphasize about these explications is that they are formulated in simple words (not all of them semantic primes), cross-translatable into Yucatec, and that they are intelligible to ordinary speakers and can be discussed with them. ("Fire," "hands," and "hold" are universal semantic molecules.)

There are three main differences between the meanings of the words *candle* and *kib'* (*kib'$_2$*) as portrayed here, one to do with shape (components (i) and (j) of *candle*), another with number (component (b) of *kib'$_2$*), and yet another, with the relative conceptual salience of function and material.

To begin with shape, the meaning of *candle* includes the component "things of this kind are often long," whereas the meaning of *kib'* doesn't. This is in keeping with Lucy's statement that Yucatec nouns, in contrast to English nouns, "do not draw attention to shape," and with a concomitant difference in "cognitive sensitivity" established by Lucy: English speakers attend more to the shape of the objects spoken about than Yucatec speakers do.

The second difference lies in the fact that the English word *candle*, in the singular, implies that the speaker is talking about one thing of the kind in question, whereas its Yucatec counterpart does not include any such information. This doesn't mean, however, that *kib'* is strictly analogous in this respect to *mud* or *wax*. Rather, the word indicates that what is being referred to is in principle "countable" (which is why it can combine with a classifier like "one long thing") but that the number of the objects in question is usually of no particular interest.

The third difference has to do with what is more salient, function or material. In the case of *candles*, the function comes very near the top (component (b)), whereas the material from which *candles* are made is first mentioned only in component (f). In the case of *kib'$_2$*, on the other hand, the material is mentioned first (in component (c)), and the function, later (component (d)). This is broadly consistent with Lucy's statement that "the Yucatec word *kib'$_1$* glossed as *candle* (...) actually refers to the substance" (p. 53). As I see it, the English word *candle* also refers to the "substance" from which *candles* are made (i.e., the material), but the emphasis on the material is indeed greater in the case of the Yucatec word.

My account of the difference between Yucatec and English nouns (in relation to number) is in fact very close in spirit to what Lucy himself said in his book *Grammatical Categories and Cognition* (1992: 73):

This account, that Yucatec lexical nouns are unspecified as to unit and somewhat like English mass nouns, is consistent with the fact that lexical noun phrases in Yucatec do not require pluralisation in the context of reference to a multiplicity of entities. (…) the multiplicity of these units is not *semantically* relevant.

Here, Lucy does not say that Yucatec words for candles, bananas, or bees are like English mass nouns (e.g., *mud* or *wax*) but that they are "*somewhat* like English mass nouns." This is better, I think, but it is not clear what exactly is meant. Since no definition of the Yucatec word is actually proposed, it is impossible to guess what (in Lucy's view) the Yucatec word actually means. All we hear are linguistic comments **about** Yucatec meanings and how they differ from English nouns.

But if we don't try to spell out what at least some Yucatec nouns actually mean, how can we really discover what the overall semantic structure of Yucatec nouns is and how it differs from the semantic structure of English nouns? Some of Lucy's general claims, not tested against any actual definitions, exoticize Yucatec people and their habitual ways of thinking (Keesing 1994). The main reason for this is that Lucy assumes unitary meanings for words that are actually polysemous and exhibit a regular pattern of polysemy.

Consider, for example, the word *hā'as*, which in some contexts can be translated as *banana* or *bananas*, but which can also be used to refer to banana trees, banana leaves, and bunches of bananas. According to Lucy, it is as if different phrases with this word, including different classifiers, "have reference to a common material or substance that can take a variety of meaningful shapes or forms" (1992: 77). But what could such a common material or substance be (in a Yucatec speaker's mind)? In the case of candles, it may be wax, but in the case of bananas it would have to be some generalized banana mash, including (crushed?) fruit, leaves, and even trees. This clearly doesn't make sense.

The ultimate test of a unitary meaning lies in the possibility of formulating a plausible unitary definition. It is not surprising that Lucy was not able to formulate such a unitary definition for either *kib'* or *hā'as*, and that in his gloss of the former he equivocated between "wax" and "anything made of wax" (hardly the same thing). By alternating his glosses in this way, he seemed to tacitly acknowledge that a plausible unitary definition of this word's meaning was not to be found.

If we recognize the regular polysemy of Yucatec nouns, however, we can posit two clearly differentiated meanings for *hā'as*, too (as we did for *kib'*). Schematically:

1. tree of one kind (called "banana-tree")
2. some parts of a banana-tree, people often do something with these parts

Depending on the classifier ("long," "flat," "a load"), this second meaning can be interpreted as referring to something of one kind that people often eat ("banana fruit"), something that they often wrap things in (banana leaves), or something that they often carry (banana bunches).

The need to recognize polysemy for most Yucatec concrete nouns is particularly evident in the case of the noun *hú'un*, which "can be used to refer to a type of tree, to the bark of the tree which traditionally was used to make a type of paper, to paper as a material, to any given piece of paper and to items made of paper such as books" (Lucy 1992: 201). I would defy anyone to produce a plausible unitary definition that would cover all these different uses and be adequate for each of them at the same time. To try to formulate such a unitary definition would be like trying to devise one definition covering all the uses of the English word *paper*: paper as the material from which *paper cups* and the like are made, *paper* in the sense of newspaper, *paper* as in *unpublished paper* (scholarly article), and *papers* as documents. Clearly, in the use of the Yucatec *hù'un*, too, a few different senses need to be distinguished. Schematically:

1. tree of one kind, called *hù'un* tree
2. parts of a *hù'un* tree, people often do something with these parts (bark)
3. something of one kind made of those parts of a *hù'un I* tree (paper)
4. something of one kind made of paper (books)

It seems clear that the reason why, in Lucy's presentation, such distinct senses can blur into one "unformed substance" is that he doesn't try to state what the meaning of the word under discussion actually is. In this respect, Lucy's approach is like that of the Nijmegen school: in both programs, a great deal is being said *about* indigenous meanings, but no indigenous meanings are ever actually presented.

Lucy's critique of the dominant paradigm in color studies is a milestone in the history of the "color wars," and his work on the cognitive effects of the grammatical differences between Yucatec and English will be seen to be of lasting value. However, despite postulating the need for such a thing, he has not provided a culture-neutral framework for the description and comparison of meanings across languages and cultures.

In the conclusion to his paper in the *Language and Bilingual Cognition* volume, Lucy writes:

> The anthropological approach makes clear that research on the impact of language diversity is inherently difficult because the bias of our own language pervades the research process. First, our understanding of the meaning structure of another language can be impeded by the categories of our own language (...) Second, our understanding of the nature of reality can be shaped by the categories of our own language (...). Our categories not only bias how we habitually see the world, they also seem to us uniquely suited to capturing that reality. Third, both of these effects (...) converge to create interpretive problems when we try to understand how another people are seeing reality. (Lucy 2011: 64)

All of these points are well taken. The key question, though, is: how can the biases Lucy identifies be overcome? Lucy seems convinced that they can be overcome if we try harder to study each language "on its own terms" and to focus on grammatical structure:

> They can be overcome only through embracing a theoretically informed methodology that forces us to follow the logic of another language on its own terms, to frame the comparison in neutral terms, and then to assess directly the contrasting views of reality held by ourselves and by others. (Lucy 2011: 65)

I agree that it is imperative to frame the comparison in neutral terms. This is what NSM theory and practice is in fact all about. But the only terms which are really neutral and which can really free researchers from conceptual Anglocentrism, are *shared* terms, that is, words which are cross-translatable, words with matching counterparts in the target language, words with which an Anglophone researcher can speak to his or her native-speaker consultants. Phrases like "quantificational unit," "unformed substance," "quantificational neutrality," and "malleable objects," in which Lucy frames his comparison of Yucatec and English, are not neutral and cross-translatable terms. They are terms of technical or semi-technical English.

12

Endangered languages, Endangered meanings

Endangered languages: repositories of thought, experience, and values

Most of the world's languages are dying out. Twenty years ago, Michael Krauss (1992) estimated that as things are going, within a hundred years, more than half of the world's six thousand languages could be extinct; by the end of the twenty-first century, most of the remaining languages will be endangered, and likely to be lost in the following century (for an update see Simon and Lewis 2013). Globalization, displacement, and the needs of communication between native speakers of different languages are resulting, all over the world, in languages falling silent.

In some parts of the world, vigorous efforts are being made to revitalize and "save" some endangered languages. Considerable successes are reported, in particular, in relation to the Māori language in New Zealand and to Hawaiian in Hawaii. These places are somewhat exceptional, however, because they both have only one main indigenous language, on which the revitalization program can focus. In many other parts of the world, the processes of language loss are regarded as irreversible, and the only rescue mission seen as feasible is that of "language documentation" rather than that of keeping the language alive.

Why should dying languages be documented? Two reasons that are often emphasized concern the knowledge and the interpretation of the world that are embedded in a language (any language). In relation to knowledge, Leanne Hinton, one of the editors of *The Green Book of Language Revitalization in Practice* (2001: 5) writes:

> the loss of language is part of the loss of whole cultures and knowledge systems, including philosophical systems (...) oral literacy, and musical tradition, environmental knowledge systems, medical knowledge, and important cultural practices and artistic skills. The world stands to lose an important part of the sum of human knowledge whenever a language stops being used. Just as the human species is putting itself in danger through the destruction of species diversity, so might we be in danger from the destruction of the diversity of knowledge systems.

137

In relation to indigenous ways of thinking, we have already seen Evans's comments (made with reference to Australian language Dalabon, with very few speakers left) that when a language like Dalabon dies, "no one's mind will again have the thought paths that its ancestral speakers once blazed" (p. xviii). The foremost student of indigenous languages of America and Australia, Ken Hale, put it like this: "When you lose a language, you lose a culture, intellectual wealth, a work of art. It's like dropping a bomb on (...) the Louvre." (*The Economist*, November 1, 2001, quoted in an unsigned obituary for Ken Hale.).

The ways of thinking and knowing of which a language is the repository are embedded, to a large extent, in the meanings of this language's words. Yet the meaning of words is seldom treated as a priority in the literature on language documentation and linguistic fieldwork. For example, in Claire Bowern's book *Linguistic Fieldwork: A Practical Guide* (2008), the chapter titled "Lexical and semantic data" focuses almost entirely on "getting vocabulary" (a section heading), "collecting words," and "getting one's consultants to name things": "One way to collect words is just to ask for them. (...) Get your consultants to take you on a tour of their house, street or village and name every item." (p. 107)

Bowern does mention discussions among consultants about the meaning of words, but she presents them as useful for vocabulary elicitation and for obtaining interesting conversational data rather than as a path to discovering indigenous meanings: "I've always found it easier to do vocabulary elicitation in small groups (three or four consultants). Consultants prompt each other and the arguments about definitions are usually interesting sources of conversational data." (p. 107)

In her article "Meaning and translation in linguistic fieldwork," Birgit Hellwig (2010: 804) observes that "there are very few methodological discussions on semantic fieldwork in general, with only a few articles dedicated to specific issues. (...) It is especially striking that many textbooks on linguistic fieldwork devote but little attention to questions of semantic fieldwork."

Hellwig quotes William Samarin's (1967: 208) observation made in his "Guide to linguistic fieldwork": "the chief failing of a field dictionary is that it indicates not so much the meanings of words but the fact that they exist." In the half century that has passed since, many fine and semantically revealing field dictionaries have been published. For example, in relation to Australia, Pitjantjatjara/Yankunytjatjara, Arrernte, Warlpiri, and Dalabon dictionaries (Evans et al. 2008; Goddard 1996; Henderson and Dobson 1994; Laughren et al. 2006) spring to mind. Nonetheless, the current needs for urgent semantic documentation of quickly disappearing languages are not being met, with prodigious numbers of concepts dying, unrecorded, all over the world. This includes cultural key concepts, which, properly analyzed, could have unlocked disappearing worlds of thought, experience, and feelings.

And yet the native speakers of endangered languages are often deeply concerned about the loss of their concepts. For example, in the *Green Book of Language Revitalization*, Leanne Hinton notes that "development of new words can be controversial because the language being developed might express certain values or traditions that could be lost if language is changed" (Hinton 2001: 16). She observes that an endangered language is often seen by its native speakers "as the carrier of traditional culture and values" and comments further:

> (...) Some members of the community will argue that the endangered language should be used to express traditional ideas and the mainstream language to express mainstream ideas. Some older Hawaiians argue this when they see the *Dictionary of New Words*, with thousands of vocabulary items not present in the language as they know it. It is reported that some Māori native speakers say the same thing of Māori children being educated in immersion programs: "They speak Māori, but they just spout English concepts." (ibid.)

In the same *Green Book of Language Revitalization*, another author, Sam L. No'eau Warner (2001: 138), quotes a parent of two students in a Hawaiian immersion school as saying (in Hawaiian) that "there is a critical need to preserve and restore the Hawaiian language—a natural treasure and resource—with its heart and spirit intact." An example of a Hawaiian cultural key concept that is evidently highly relevant to that Hawaiian "heart and spirit" is the word "mauli," discussed in another chapter of the *Green Book* (Wilson and Kamanā 2001). To quote: "Some features of mauli are covered by the English word "culture," but mauli also includes worldview, spirituality, physical movement, morality, personal relationships, and other central features of a person's life and the life of a people." (p. 161)

The discussion of "mauli" as a key to Hawaiian culture presented by Wilson and Kamanā is intriguing but the concept is not easy for an outsider to grasp. The evident importance of this concept for the insiders highlights the need for transparent semantic analysis of such cultural key concepts in endangered languages. Clearly, to be faithful to the vision of the insiders and at the same time intelligible to outsiders, such an analysis must be based on shared concepts expressible in simple English words (such as *do*, *live*, *want*, *people*, *good*, and so on), not in complex words such as *worldview*, *morality*, and *relationship*, which are not only English, but grounded in Anglo culture.

Semantic Documentation of Endangered Languages

"Language documentation has emerged as a response to the pressing need for collecting, describing and archiving material on the increasing number of endangered languages," writes Lenore Grenoble (2010: 289), one of the editors of a volume titled *Language Documentation: Practice and Values* (2010), in her "State of the field" chapter. While emphasizing the urgent need for such documentation, Grenoble notes (like many others have done) that in indigenous communities linguists are often seen as "unwelcome intruders" (p. 298), just as scholars from other disciplines collecting data in such communities can be: "medical researchers who have taken blood samples; geologists who have drilled and carried away samples; biologists who have sampled flora and fauna; and archaeologists who have taken 'artifacts' from the culture—all the while ignoring the people of the community, their knowledge, and their desires" (p. 291).

The introduction to the *Handbook on Linguistic Fieldwork* (Thieberger 2012: 1) states that the "recognition of the loss of linguistic diversity" has led to the emergence of a "new paradigm of research" associated with language documentation, and that "this paradigm focusses on collaboration with speakers." Further, the introduction states that "the project of language documentation includes recording aspects of a range of human knowledge systems" and documents "cultural information that provides new insights into local knowledge systems" (pp. 2-3).

But cultural knowledge cannot be somehow mechanically recorded and documented (with the help of new technologies) without talking to native speakers, that is, without collaboration with speakers. To be fruitful, such collaboration requires some attention to these speakers' words and to their meanings—and some readiness to divest oneself of some of one's own. Semantic documentation cannot be reduced to collecting words and pairing them with putative English equivalents.

I will try to illustrate the advantages of relying on simple and cross-translatable words in the documentation of endangered meanings by rethinking some glosses in Leanne Hinton's chapter in the *Green Book of Language Revitalization* devoted to the endangered American indigenous language Karuk. Hinton notes that the Karuk orient themselves in space in relation to the river and "instead of terms like 'north, south, east and west' use terms translatable as 'upriver, toward the river, away from the river'" (p. 191). Relatedly, Karuk "has a very large class of directional suffixes with highly specific meanings." Hinton's list includes the following suffixes and glosses:

> *-uraa* "up to a considerable height"
> *-unih* "down from a considerable height"
> *-vara* "in through a tubular space"
> *-kiv* "out through a tubular space"

Assuming that Karuk doesn't have words with meanings like "tubular," "space," "considerable," and "height," these glosses impose English meanings on the portrayal of Karuk ethno-topography. The same does not apply to the following explications, which seek to understand these meanings through simple and cross-translatable words:

-uraa "up to a considerable height"

someone is moving somewhere at this time because it is like this:

this someone wants to be after some time in a place far above the ground

this someone is far below this place at this time

-unih "down from a considerable height"

someone is moving somewhere at this time because it is like this:

some time before this someone was in a place far above the ground

this someone wants to be after some time far below this place

-vara "in through a tubular space"

something is moving at this time inside something long

some time before this something was on one side of the place where this long thing is

after some time, it can be on the other side of this place, inside something else

-kiv "out through a tubular space"

something is moving at this time inside something long

some time before this something was on one side of the place where this long thing is,

inside something else

after some time, it can be on the other side of the place

For the linguist, such explications may be harder to understand than phrases like "considerable height" and "tubular spaces," which for a speaker of English present familiar conceptual shortcuts. Such shortcuts, however, do not lead through the conceptual territory of the speakers of Karuk.

Language Documentation and Collaboration with Native Speakers

The literature on language documentation increasingly emphasizes the need for linguists to collaborate with native speakers, and on the training of native speakers as potential collaborators. For example, Peter Austin, one of the leaders in the field (see Austin ed. 2003-2010), writes: "Documentary linguistics should be embedded within a context of respect (...) that treats the speech community members with whom linguists work as partners in collaboration.". Arienne Dwyer (2010: 212) in the *Language Documentation: Practice and values* volume concurs: "In contrast to 50 or even 10 years ago, linguistic work foregrounds collaboration." Collaboration with native speakers as partners is often contrasted with their role as "consultants" in the traditional "lone-wolf" model.

Furthermore, given the current rate of "language death" and the urgent need for documenting as many languages as possible before they disappear from the face of the Earth, many linguists are pointing to the need not only for collaboration between linguists and native speakers but indeed for native speakers as documentors in their own right (Sapir's, and Boas', ideal).

For example, Frances Ajo and colleagues of the University of Hawai'i at Manoa write (2010: 275): "Emergent paradigms in documentary linguistics place emphasis on the role of native speakers as documentors (...)." Drawing on their own and their colleagues' experience in training native speakers in descriptive and documentary skills, they express the view that "native speakers are the best suited and most motivated participants to undertake and sustain language documentation programs" (p. 276).

The literature on language documentation often emphasizes that in the light of the need for collaboration with native speakers, many practices of linguistics as a discipline need to be rethought and reshaped. Increasingly, it is argued that "documentation material ought to be accessible to a wider audience, including the language community itself" (Ajo et al. 2010: 780). Many writers acknowledge that as things are, when a project carried out by a linguist within a community produces a reference work, this work "is often 'over the head' of the intended audience" (Gerdts 2010: 180). As Gerdts comments, people in the community often "find it impenetrable" (ibid.).

Clearly, if native speakers are to be enlisted as partners in documenting their own language, and also, if at least some people in the community are to be able to understand the products, this needs to change. Dwyer (2010: 212) goes as far as to say that "collaboratory research is [now] the baseline from which linguistic projects can be expected to be evaluated." This has implications, among other things, for basic practices such as the glossing and annotating of words and meaningful parts of words, and the annotating of sentences and texts.

In particular, standard linguistic practices include providing linguistic material with so-called "interlinear glosses," meant to identify or label the meanings of words and meaningful parts of words. Ajo et al. (2010) envisage training native speakers who are prospective "language documentors" in formulating such glosses. Yet traditionally, it was never expected that such glosses should be intelligible to the uninitiated, or indeed, that they should necessarily reflect the thinking of native speakers. To illustrate, I will adduce here two pairs of examples from Daniel Everett's 2005 article about the Amazonian language Pirahã, published as a target article for discussion in the journal *Current Anthropology* (2005). The first two examples here have to do with "wanting" (Everett's numbers).

31. *kohoai* *-kabáob* *-áo* *ti*
    eat -finish -temporal I
    gí 'aho*ai* *-soog* *-abagai*
    you speak -desiderative -frustrated initiation
    "When [I] finish eating, I want to speak to you." (lit. "When eating finishes, I speak-almost want.")

34. 'ipóihií   'i   gí   kobai   -soog   -abagaí
    Woman   she   you   see   -want   -frustrated initiation
    "The woman wants to see you."

The plain translations ("When I finish eating, I want to speak to you" and "the woman wants to see you") make perfect sense, but the same cannot be said of the interlinear glosses, or of the so-called "literal" translations. In particular, it is far from clear what the phrase "frustrated initiation" is doing in the interlinear gloss. Is this the Pirahã speaker's "literal" meaning or is it rather some intrusion from the conceptual repertoire of English?

It could be objected at this point that an academic article is intended for a specialist audience and that it is only to be expected that it may be impenetrable to the nonspecialist. It is not clear, however, what is gained by using such an impenetrable gloss for *any* audience. First, there is no evidence that such an element is indeed part of the meaning of the Pirahã sentence. Second, one could not defend this gloss on practical grounds (glosses need to be very short because of the limited space), because a gloss like "frustrated initiation" is long and doesn't save space.

The second pair of examples from the same source illustrates the use of so-called "evidentials," that is, elements that show the "evidential status" of what is being said (e.g., is it based on first-hand observation or on hearsay, is it certain or uncertain):

16. a. 'aoói   hi   paóhoa'ai   'isoí
       foreigner   he   anaconda   skin
       báaiso   *'oaboi*   *-haí*
       "whole"   buy   -relative certainty
       "The foreigner will likely buy the entire anaconda skin."

    b. *'aió*   *hi*   *báaiso*   *'oaob*
       affirmative   he   "whole"   buy
       -áhá   *hi*   *'ogió*
       -complete certainty   he   bigness
       'oaob   *-áhá*
       buy   -complete certainty
       "Yes, he bought the whole thing."

Presumably, there are no Pirahã words meaning either "relative" or "certainty." The closest English approximation of the Pirahã "evidentials" can no doubt be found in phrases like "I think" and "I know," constructed out of simple words cross-translatable into Pirahã itself: "I," "think," and "know." Yet such simple and cross-translatable words and phrases are not used in Everett's glosses, and abstract words taken from the English lexicon such as "relative" and "certainty" are used instead.

While phrases like "frustrated initiation" present a somewhat extreme example of Anglocentrism and academese in linguistic description, the practice of relying in glosses on terms like "desiderative" instead of "want," "relative certainty" instead of "I think," "factual" instead of "I know," or "dubitative" instead of "I don't know" is very widespread. There is little or no standardization in the use of such glosses, so that what one linguist glosses as "complete certainty" another may gloss as "factual" and what one may gloss as "direct" another may gloss as "immediate."

In the past, linguists often paid little attention to the question of glossing and invented their own labels ad hoc, drawing freely on the Latinate resources of English. But in the era of worldwide "language death" and the urgent need to enlist nonspecialists as collaborators and co-documentors of dying languages, such in-house practices cannot be relied on any more. In this context, the lack of standardization and the reliance on complex (often Latinate) English vocabulary to represent the meanings of "dying words" is a problem that needs to be addressed. To ensure that these meanings are preserved for a wider audience (as part of "human heritage") they have to be formulated in a widely accessible language such as English, in English words, but they don't have to be formulated in words with "English" meanings or in artificial and technical or semitechnical English phrases.

In fact, a move away from linguistic jargon and academese and toward simple cross-translatable words such as *know*, *think*, *true*, *say*, and *want* can help to address both problems at once: having a list of such simple and cross-translatable words at their disposal, language documentors seeking to document dying or endangered meanings can draw on it, thus increasing both the accuracy of their semantic analysis (from the point of view of a particular language) and their cross-linguistic comparability.

In the 2010 volume on *Language Documentation: Practice and Values* one scholar who particularly emphasizes the need for genuine cross-linguistic understanding between linguists and native speakers as co-documentors is Louanna Furbee. One way to build language documentation collaboratively is, Furbee suggests, to create "intermediate models" jointly with native speakers. She emphasizes that the practice of building such "intermediate models" attempts "to create a means for power and responsibility to pass increasingly into the hands of heritage speakers without requiring the enculturation of those speakers to a linguist's perspective, or the linguist to the native speaker's perspective, although it does ask all the parties to accommodate themselves to conceptions other than their own." (Furbee 2010: 8). As an example of such a joint enterprise, in which native speakers (. . .) can help describe their own language "while shaping an indigenous framework to guide their efforts," Furbee uses the ongoing analysis of the "evidentials" in the Mayan language Tojolabal.

The term "evidential" (mentioned earlier in relation to Pirahã) refers to a set of semantic categories particularly important in many American Indian languages and having to do (as linguists usually put it) with the "evidential basis" of what one is saying. Traditionally, the meaning of such categories is described by linguists in technical English terms such as "direct," "indirect," "circumstantial," and "inferential" (and, in Latin America, with similar terms in Spanish and Portuguese). But since the interviews with Tojolabal consultants were conducted not only in Spanish but also in Tojolabal, when the Tojolabal consultants were asked to explain the meanings of the different "evidentials" in their own words, not surprisingly, they did not come up with any such technical terms, but rather, with explanations that made sense to them in their own language. Furbee comments (p. 12):

> In analysing a series of interviews conducted in both Spanish and Tojolabal the five members of a bilingual team of Tojolabal Mayans working with me as a collaborating linguist stumbled onto a useful way of thinking about evidentials that was new to all of us.

In her discussion of the collaborative work with native speakers on the meanings of Tojolabal "evidentials," Furbee emphasizes the fact that "in that collaborative activity, the team more than tripled the inventory of evidentials previously identified" (p. 13) and that it used "a consensual discourse to arrive at the ranking" (p. 13) (in terms of "different strengths of certainty on the part of the speaker," p. 12).

From my perspective, however, what is even more striking about the results of this work is the simplicity of the language that is used in describing the meanings of the different "evidentials." For example, the "Table of 'Evidentials' in Tojolabal and Their Rankings" (p. 14) includes glosses such as "thus it is," "I say it's so," "it's true, always," "I think ... (it might be true, it might not)," "they said it," "perhaps he said it," "they say," "it is said," and "perhaps he said it."

This is not the usual English academese with words and phrases like "assurance," "veracity," "information," "responsibility for the truth," "likelihood of the truth," "reliable source," "the speaker certifies the truth of the information," "responsibility for its veracity," and so on (all of which are in fact present in Furbee's own accompanying commentary, but not in the glosses provided in the table). As the examples adduced above illustrate, the language of these glosses is very close to the language of universal semantic primes. It is also close to the language that I used in my own attempts at identifying the indigenous meanings embedded in the "evidentials" in a number of American Indian languages in Wierzbicka 1994 and 1996 (chapter 15). (One element which played a large role in my analysis and which is missing from Furbee's table is "know," and the phrase "I know," but this may well be due to the selective character of the examples included in her table.)

Collaboration with native speakers as co-documentors of their own language requires some common concepts and common words. In the case of "evidentials," such common concepts can be found in universal primes such as "true," "say," "know," "people," "I," "maybe," "like," and "this," and in combinations such as "I know," "I think," "people say," and "it can be like this." This is the kind of language used in NSM-based semantic fieldwork by, for example, Marie-Odile Junker (2003,, 2008), Junker and Blacksmith (2006) in East Cree (Canada); Carol Priestley (2002, 2008, 2009) in Koromu (Papua New Guinea); or Sophie Nicholls (2010) in Roper River Kriol (Australia). (For discussion, see Goddard and Wierzbicka, in press b.)

Clearly, the narrowing of the gap between language description and language documentation can lead to empowerment of native speakers as genuine collaborators and co-documentors. At the same time, it can free the linguist from the straightjacket of technical Latinate English, which often stands in the way of genuine understanding of how speakers of other languages, including dying languages, think.

Needless to say, a move away from technical language and reliance on simple words and collaboration with native speakers do not by themselves ensure that indigenous meanings will be identified precisely and reliably. More often than not, semantic analysis requires a great deal of time, experience, skill, and persistence. Yet **relative** progress can be easily achieved if these three basic guidelines are adhered to:

1. Try to avoid complex and technical English in the description of meanings;
2. try to use as much as you can simple words which are known to be cross-translatable (such as those in the NSM table of primes);
3. test provisional ideas about indigenous meanings in many different contexts, and in trying to state them go through several different versions and approximations—always trying to formulate them in simple and cross-translatable words.

I will shortly illustrate this approach by rethinking two key examples from Evans and Sasse's paper, "Search for meaning in the Library of Babel: field semantics and problems of digital archiving." First, however, I will show that in fact, even seemingly simple English words cannot always be trusted: only those that are both simple and cross-translatable can.

Leaving English Concepts Behind

In the attempts to document the meanings embedded in endangered languages, one of the greatest challenges lies in the need to leave familiar English concepts behind. The danger of unwittingly translating indigenous categories into English ones faces not only Anglophone scholars but also their bilingual consultants. Often, these consultants themselves speak English on a daily basis, and often they, too, are influenced by English concepts. In addition, there is also the pressure of traditional lexicographic models of definition. As a result, bilingual consultants are often caught in a paradox: they want to capture authentic indigenous meanings, but they find themselves glossing them with the nearest English words of the same general type, looking at these meanings through the prism of English concepts, and formulating them in a traditional lexicographic format unsuitable for the purpose.

I will illustrate the difficulties that bilingual consultants often encounter with two examples from a very valuable book on *Narungga Family Terms* published by the Narungga Aboriginal Program Association (2010) as a resource for documenting and revitalizing the South Australian language Narungga. In the foreword to this book, the authors write, movingly (p. 1):

> This Family book represents our history and our heritage. It is our past, present and future. It has been a remarkable journey, along the way we have found a living culture and a sense of pride. The strong, emotional ties that bind us to our family, bind us together as a people with a strong cultural history, rich in knowledge and worth. This book involved people on a journey that has been emotional and spiritually enlightening. It found a place within us that was special and held strong links to our past.
>
> This project has therefore been a significant step in the ongoing survival of the Narungga people, and provides for our future generations the opportunity to have a greater understanding of identity and culture.

Yet the meanings attributed to the Narungga family terms in this publication are influenced by English kinship categories and do not come as close to reflecting Narungga culture as the authors hoped. As discussed in Chapter 3, we can recover the meanings of family terms in a language like Narungga if we forget about the English family terms that have no counterparts in the language described and use only those English words in our explanations that do have such counterparts—that is, *mother, father, wife,* and *husband.*

Consider, for example, the word *banya,* glossed in the book as "younger brother or sister." Since Narungga doesn't have words meaning "brother" and "sister," such glosses could not be rendered in Narungga words. On the other hand, like any other language, Narungga does have words meaning "mother" and "father." Accordingly, the Narungga meaning of a word like *banya* can be captured through cross-translatable English words *mother* and *father,* as in the following explication:

banya ("younger brother or sister")
someone can say about someone else: "this is my *banya*"
   if this someone can think about this other someone like this:
      "this someone's mother is my mother,
      this someone's father is my father,
      this someone was born after me"

As a second example, let us consider the word *gawana,* described first as "uncle" and then assigned a "basic meaning" in simpler words: "mother's brother"

(p. 11). Again, the use of the English word *brother* (which has no counterpart in Narungga) introduces an English point of view. If we leave such culture-specific English concepts behind, we can try to capture the Narungga meaning as follows:

gawana ("mother's brother")someone can say about a man: "this is my gawana"

  if this someone can think about him like this:
    "his mother is my mother's mother,
    his father is my mother's father"

For an English reader accustomed to the English words *brother* and *sister*, glosses that rely on no family terms other than *mother* and *father* may seem somewhat strange. Why not use the short expression "mother's brother" instead of the two lines about mothers and fathers? And why use an unfamiliar format based on the frame "if this some can think like this" instead of the customary formula based on a noun and a modifier ("mother's brother")?

The reason is that the short expression "mother's brother" reflects an English (and more generally, European) conceptual shortcut and does not correspond to conceptual categories of the Narungga language. If we want to document indigenous concepts faithfully, then even simple and seemingly basic English concepts like "brother" and "sister" may need to be left behind. The effort of rethinking family terms in a language like Narungga without such English concepts pays off by allowing us to bring to light authentic indigenous meanings statable in the indigenous language itself, and thus to promote a greater understanding of a community's traditional ways of thinking and communicating.

Rethinking Two Key Examples from Evans and Sasse's 2003 Paper on Field Semantics

In this section, I will explore two indigenous categories from two endangered Australian languages, which serve as key illustrative examples in Evans and Sasse's 2003 paper on field semantics. The first one is the geographical concept from Kayardild expressed by the suffix *–ngunrrnga*. Evans and Sasse (2003: 11) use this example to illustrate the "difficulties in representing *construal* through external portrayal of examples" (i.e., through pictorial representations such as maps and photographs):

> For example, in Kayardild, there is a suffix *–ngurrnga,* added to directional terms based on compass points, meaning roughly 'beyond a significant geographical discontinuity.' Thus *ringurrnga* 'east-*ngurrnga*' can be used for an island, emerging from the sea to the east, but also to a stand of mangroves, or sandhills, as one leaves a saltpan travelling east. Though it is possible to photograph or map particular instances of *ringurrnga,* the

underlying meaning—what is construed as a significant geographical discontinuity—cannot simply be taken for granted, or immediately inferred from a couple of instances, and to really get to the bottom of it we need to probe an open-ended set of examples.

But to be able to grasp the indigenous construal—which, as the authors rightly note, cannot be captured by photographs or other pictorial representations—an open-ended set of examples is not enough: we also need to be clear about what semantic tools we can use to formulate hypotheses about this construal. The question cannot be just "what is construed as a significant geographical discontinuity?," because the very concept of "geographical discontinuity" is an English concept, not a Kayardild one.

In his Kayardild dictionary, Evans (1995: 759) glosses the same suffix somewhat differently, as "geographical boundary to X," but again, "geographical boundary" is an English concept, not a Kayardild one. The dictionary illustrates the meaning of the suffix in question with some examples based on the directional form *ra-* "south": "**rangurrnga** South across a geographical boundary. E.g. cliffs on south side of saltpan, or island south across the sea."

Since Kayardild doesn't have words for either "boundary" or "discontinuity" (or, for that matter, "geographical"), it seems clear that the glosses phrased in these terms do not express indigenous meanings but English-based approximations of these meanings. To have a plausible hypothesis about the Kayardild meaning, we need to scrutinize all the examples, thinking about them through meanings for which we know they do have words, such as "place," "far," and "near." We can also draw on the accumulated semantic knowledge about how such geographical notions tend to be construed in other languages. Taken together, the examples from the dictionary and from the joint paper by Evans and Sasse are in fact quite sufficient to allow us to formulate a hypothesis about the meaning of this suffix in words cross-translatable into Kayardild.

Drawing on Helen Bromhead's (2011a, 2011b, 2013) research into ethnogeographical concepts, I would venture to hypothesize that the meaning of the Kayardild suffix in question shows an anthropocentric perspective, and more specifically, the perspective of someone who wants to get to a certain place. The "discontinuity" in Evans's and Sasse's gloss seems to suggest that between the place where I am now and the place where I want to be, there is some place of another kind—a place where I can't move as I can in the place where I am now. This leads us to the following explication:

-ngurrnga (eg. rangurrnga)

a place on one side (e.g. South) of the place where I am now
I think about this place like this:
   "I want to be in this place
   I can't be in this place if I am not before in another place

I know that I can't move in this other place like I can move in the place where I am now

I am now on one side of this other place, the place where I want to be is on the other side"

The second key example from Evans and Sasse's 2003 paper concerns the Dalabon word *walu-no*, which appears to be a cultural keyword in Dalabon. In their paper on "field semantics," Evans and Sasse (2003) include a mythical Dalabon story about how humans came to have fire (and the way of living made possible by it): "in the original or dream-time when the story is set, only the freshwater crocodile (Korlomomo) had fire to cook with, until Berrerdberrerd (Rainbow Bee-eater), one of the various birds who were human forebears, managed to steal it away" (p. 13).

As the English translation makes clear, the story contrasts two ways of living: one linked with eating meat raw, dripping with blood, and a new way, linked with cooking meat with fire. These two "ways" of living are described in the English translation with the words *way* (twice) and *customs* (four times). In the interlinear glosses, the word *way* is used once, the word *custom* five times, and the word *rule* twice. The Dalabon concept apparently underlying these different glosses is given in the Dalabon text itself as *ru:l* (five times), presumably a version of the English word *rule,* and once as *walu-no*—presumably the indigenous term for the concept in question.

In the Dalabon dictionary (Evans et al. 2004), the word *walu-no* is assigned two meanings: 1. strength, power; 2. custom, law. In the folk explanations of the second meaning, the English words *law*, *custom*, and *rule* alternate, and again, the English word *rule* recurs as a loan word in the Dalabon sentences illustrating the use of the word *walu-no.* Below, I will quote the English glosses, omitting the Dalabon sentences themselves.

2. Custom, law.

> *The law of ours that we are telling you about, we are talking about our custom, our rules that we follow, we don't change our law. That law of ours, we follow it always.*
> *That law about that, we will always follow it.*
> **walu-no... –yung** verbal idiom.
> Ordain, lay down a custom or rule for how life is to be lived.
> *There by the light of the moon, when the moon is shining, the devil walks around, he says he has a sore foot, that a stick might have stuck into it, that's the custom that has been laid down for us humans, for all of us.*
> *syn:* walu-yung.
> **walu-yung** *v.t.* Ordain, lay down a custom or rule for how life is to be lived.
> *Old people, they blew paint around their hand, inside the humpy, in the cave (or enclosure), they blew around their hands with white paint... That was the rule that was laid down for him, that mimih,*

> *that Nardurrmi laid down the rule, the old people gave it to us, that*
> *Nardurrmi. Syn* walu-no ... -yung.

Maia Ponsonnet (2010) in her glossary of selected Dalabon words offers the following explanation of *walu-no*:

> *Walu-no* refers to the rules that define matters of cultural significance such as language and its meaning, country and landscapes, ceremonies, kinship, and life in general. *Walu-no* was laid down long ago by Nayunghyungki people. *Walu-no* is to be followed: it is not flexible (...) *walu-no* is associated with stories in what is called 'drimtaim' in Kriol (see *karru-no*), and also supernatural power.

Of particular interest are comments on *walu-no* made (in Kriol) by Ponsonnet's indigenous consultants, such as the ones I cite below (in Ponsonnet's English translations):

> *Walu-no, that's the one, that's the walu-no that the Nayunghyungki have*
> *laid down. Walu-no, that what we follow.*
> *Walu-no, like you know, it laid like every single thing now there.*
> *[Walu-no] you can't change it anymore. That all I can say about it.*
> *It laid rules, the law. It laid walu-no well, we follow walu-no. The old*
> *people laid names [for the country]. Well, we follow their judgment. In*
> *the same way. We can't make mistakes.*
> *Walu-no, yeah, walu-no that, Aboriginal law, it's good.*
> *A long time ago, walu-no was laid down.*
> *Yes, the old people. We didn't know, they laid that law.*
> *And it laid language there, it laid Dalabon language; before, us children*
> *were born. Now we know. We come to know.*

What the material provided in the dictionary, the glossary, and in the mythical story about the "new way" of living suggests is that *walu-no* is (was) a Dalabon cultural keyword, crystalizing a complex idea of human life: how people live now, how they have lived before, how they want to live, and how they have to live. Trying to understand this concept, evidently important to the traditional "Dalabon worldview," I would venture to propose the following explication:

walu-no (rule, law, way, custom)

a.   it is like this:

b.   people here live in one way, not another way

c.   they lived like this for a long time before, they live in the same way now

d.   this is good

e.   they want to live like this, they can't not live like this

f. people here think about it like this:

    "it is like this because a very long time ago, something happened in this place"

The English gloss *custom* corresponds, in principle, to components (b) and (c) (a distinct way of life, transmitted over a long time). The component "they can't not live like this" (c) is suggested by the repeated use of the English loanword *rule* and of the English gloss *law*. The evaluation "this is good" (component d) is suggested by the crocodile story and by the folk comments provided in the dictionary. Component (f) refers to a mythical event (in the Dreamtime).

The explication proposed here may of course not be quite right, but it is cross-translatable into Dalabon and can be discussed with native-speaker consultants. It seems clear that the concept in question is important to Dalabon culture and for this reason deserves careful semantic analysis that goes beyond conventional English glosses and does not involve what Evans and Sasse themselves describe as the "subtitling illusion" (p. 15).

The Importance of Cultural Keywords in Language Documentation

At the Indigenous Languages Conference held in Australia in 2007, a participant presented a paper on the first monolingual Maori dictionary for adults. The paper was written "with the revitalization of the [Maori] language and the preservation of a Maori worldview in mind" (Haumihiata Mason 2008: 35). Again and again, the author emphasizes that "our dictionary should reflect a Maori worldview" and that this can be done through "pinning down [Maori] meanings." But the motto introducing the paper and its English translation illustrate the difficulty of reflecting a Maori worldview without a workable semantic methodology. The Maori version of the motto reads:

> Tōku reo, tōku ohooho
> Tōku reo, tōku mana
> Ki te ngaro tōku reo, ka ngaro ko au.

This is rendered in English as:

> My language is of great value
> My language is my identity, my integrity
> Without my language I am lost.

Language translates here the word *tōku*, *my* translates the word *reo*, and *identity* and *integrity* translate the word *mana*. But can English phrases like *my identity* and *my integrity* really convey the Maori worldview?

Mana has long been recognized by Western scholars as a Maori key word, and indeed has been described as the foundation of the Polynesian worldview.

Anthropologists have long been fascinated by the concept of "mana," and as Keesing (1984: 137) puts it, "Early in this century *mana* became part of the metalanguage of anthropology." Keesing further comments that "Following Codrington and ethnologists of Polynesia, anthropologists assumed that *mana* in Oceanic religion was a kind of invisible medium of power, a spiritual energy manifest in sacred objects, a potency radiated by humans." Other glosses used at different times by different anthropologists to explain *mana* include "authority," "power," "prestige," "efficacy," "success," "potency."

The recent *Maori English, English Maori Dictionary* (Moorfield 2005) defines *mana* as "prestige, authority, control, power, influence, status, spiritual power, charisma," and adds (inter alia) the following comments (p. 76):

> *mana* is a supernatural force in a person, place or object.... *Mana* ...is inherited at birth, the more senior the descent the greater the *mana* (...) *Mana* gives a person the authority to lead, organise and regulate communal expeditions and activities, to make decisions regarding social and political matters. A person or tribe's *mana* can increase from successful ventures or decrease through the lack of success. (...) Animate and inanimate objects could also have *mana* as they also derive from the *atua* and because of their association with people imbued with much *mana* or because they were used in significant events.

As we have seen, a Maori linguist has recently added "identity" and "integrity" to the list of English glosses for *mana*. The wide range of these glosses highlights the fact that they all fail to capture the uniqueness of the Maori concept and that the whole approach that attempts to explain cultural key concepts of non-Western cultures and societies by means of English concepts based on Anglo ways of thinking is doomed to failure.

Clearly, glossing indigenous cultural concepts from Polynesia, Australia, or Africa by means of Anglo cultural concepts does not give us, in effect, "a view from many places" (Shweder 2003). Rather, it sets in concrete the "view from one place" brought to the ethnographic material by the Anglophone scholar and embedded in English words (e.g., *authority, power, identity, integrity, efficacy,* and so on).

In his conclusion to his article on "mana," Keesing emphasized that the exploration of this concept was a continuing task. "The task demands," he wrote, "not only painstaking hermeneutic skill, but comparative sociological vision. The coparticipation in this research of scholars who have the needed command of Oceanic languages and ethnographic evidence is urgent" (p. 153).

No doubt Keesing was right in stressing the importance of a comparative sociological vision and a command of indigenous languages and the ethnographic evidence. One crucial ingredient, however, was missing from his recipe: a workable semantic methodology, without which the would-be "explainer" and interpreter of other cultures cannot bridge the conceptual gap between the language that is being explained and the language of explanation. In the case of *mana*, it is only by breaking the concept into the parts that Maori shares with English that this key Maori cultural concept can be truly explained to speakers of English.

As the Maori scholar Haumihiata Mason pleads, "my language is of great value, without my language I am lost." But Maori cultural and conceptual treasures cannot be "saved" through English terms like *identity* and *integrity*. They can, however, be "saved" from obliteration if we draw on humankind's shared conceptual resources and try to articulate the meanings of Maori key concepts in universal human concepts. I would suggest that for *mana*, this could proceed along the following lines;

mana

something
people can't see it, people can't know well what it is
it can be part of some things, it can be part of some people
if someone has this part, this someone can do many things not like other people
when people think about this something, they can't not feel something good

This explication is framed exclusively in semantic primes; thus, all its terms are independent of English, transposable into Maori, and can plausibly represent part of the traditional Maori worldview. Unlike English glosses such as "authority" or "integrity," this explication does give us some insight into the traditional Maori worldview, reflected in the unique Oceanic concept of "mana." In more conventional English, the substance of this explication can be paraphrased as follows: "there can be in some things and in some people a mysterious, invisible power; this power is like a part of these things and these people; we call this power 'mana.'" This idea is foreign to cultural outsiders such as native speakers of mainstream English, but it is not unintelligible. It does give us a glimpse into a way of thinking about the world different from that embedded in, and encouraged by, English.

There are, of course, different genres and different contexts, and an accurate explanation of meaning may not be what is called for in a particular context. I am certainly not suggesting that an explication of "mana" in NSM English would be an appropriate gloss for the Maori motto quoted earlier. However, once we have such an explanation it may be possible to propose a gloss that would be close to the indigenous meaning without offending English readers' stylistic sensibilities and expectations, perhaps the following:

My language is an invisible power,
My language is part of me.

Invisible is close enough to "people can't see (it)," *power* is close enough to "can do many things," and *part of me* does not need to be replaced with "identity" and "integrity" to be understood through English.

As this example illustrates, in trying to document endangered meanings, some compromises may often be necessary, or desirable. This doesn't mean, however, that we can get insight into such meanings without making an effort to break away from culture-bound English concepts and trying to understand speakers of other languages on their own terms.

Speaking of human memory systems, with both their imperfections and their creativity, which allow us to assimilate much that comes from other people as our own, Oliver Sacks (2013: 21) writes that "indifference to sources allows us (…) to see and hear with other eyes and ears, to enter other minds, to assimilate the art and science and religion of the whole culture, to enter into (…) the general commonwealth of knowledge." *Mutatis mutandis*, the same can be said about languages. Accessing human meaning systems embedded in languages other than our own allows us to see and hear with other eyes and ears, and to enter into the general human commonwealth of knowledge and ideas. The condition is to become aware of the blinkers imposed on its speakers by any one language—including the one that J. M. Coetzee calls "the most imperial of them all": English.

13

Chimpanzees and the Evolution of Human Cognition

> Primates can obviously think.
> (Merlin Donald, *A Mind So Rare*)

> Though lacking language,
> they do not lack thought.
> (Rom Harré and Vernon Reynolds,
> *The Meaning of Primate Signals*)

Human Capacity for "Mindreading"

In their review of recent studies on human evolutionary origins, primatologists Andrew Whiten and David Erdal (2012: 2119) write:

> Hominin evolution took a remarkable pathway, as the foraging strategy extended to large mammalian prey already hunted by a guild of specialist carnivores. How was this possible for a moderately sized ape lacking the formidable anatomical adaptations of these competing 'professional hunters'?

Like many other writers on the subject, the authors attribute the human evolutionary success in large part to early humans' superior capacity for "mindreading." Comparing human hunter-gatherers with other primates, the authors describe the former as "mentalists, attributing to each other such states as seeing, desiring, and believing," and they explain:

> This means that the minds in a hunter-gatherer band interpenetrate each other in all these respects (...) the mutually interpenetrating mindreading provides a central information processing system unattained by other species (p.2122)

What exactly does it mean to say that "minds interpenetrate each other"? The notion of "mindreading" is mysterious enough, but at least it has some intuitive support in ordinary English usage. But the idea of "mutually interpenetrating mindreading" and the minds "interpenetrating each other" is truly mystifying: when one thinks about it carefully, it is far from clear what it actually means.

Referring to the other human features that they also regard as crucial and distinctive, namely "cooperation" and "egalitarianism," Whiten and Erdal conclude that "there is a profound connection between the evolution of mindreading and the features described earlier [i.e., "cooperation" and "egalitarianism"], in the ways they interact to facilitate the unique form that the human hunter-gathering adaptation has taken" (p.2122).

"Mindreading" is a nice metaphor, but not a self-explanatory one, and like many other such metaphors popular among scientists, it is bound to English, because "mind" is an English word with no exact counterparts in most other languages of the world. In its present-day meaning, *mind* focuses on thinking and knowing, to the exclusion of emotions and values, and it is quite different in this respect from the main counterparts of BODY encoded in other languages, for example, *psykhe* in ancient Greek, *duša* in Russian, *loto* in Samoan, *maum* in Korean, or *sind* in Danish (cf. Wierzbicka 1989, 1992; Mandler 1975; Yoon 2003; Levisen 2013).

As we have seen, Whiten and Erdal link the "mentalism" of human hunter-gatherers with the fact that they attribute to each other "such states as seeing, desiring and believing" (ibid). This formulation is clearer than the "mutually interpenetrating mindreading," but is not free of dependence on English, either: of the three verbs mentioned (*see*, *desire*, *believe*) only one (*see*) is universal, and the other two are also English-bound, or at least bound to a small number of European languages. In trying to clarify the underlying intended meaning of the culture-bound triad of *see*, *desire*, and *believe*, I would suggest that we need to replace it with the universal human concepts *see*, *want*, and *think* (I note that in one place the authors themselves describe "mindreading" with the verb *think* rather than *believe*).

Holding on to these three firm conceptual handles, we can try to clarify the authors' statement about the "mutually interpenetrating mindreading" of early humans as follows:

sometimes when someone in a place sees something
   someone else in this place can know it

sometimes when someone in a place wants to do something
   someone else in this place can know it

sometimes when someone in a place thinks something
   someone else in this place can know it

We cannot be sure, however, whether these restatements correspond precisely to what Whiten and Erdal had in mind: in this area as in many others, scientific statements phrased in complex English tend to be imprecise and compatible with many different interpretations.

If one attempts to clarify these statements by paraphrasing them through simple words cross-translatable into other languages, one may increase the clarity and precision of one's hypotheses, as well as decreasing their conceptual dependence on English.[1] And what applies to "mindreading" among humans, applies even more so to "mindreading" among chimpanzees.

What can Chimpanzees Know and Understand about Other Chimpanzees?

As Whiten and Erdal remind their readers, it is three decades since Premack and Woodruff (1978) first asked: "Does the chimpanzee have a theory of mind?," and the question has been the subject of heated debates in primatology ever since. Two decades after Premack and Woodruff, two high-profile participants in the debate, Michael Tomasello and Joseph Call, argued (1997: 340) that "there is no solid evidence that non-human primates understand the intentionality or state of mind of others." But as Whiten and Erdal note in a later article entitled "Does the chimpanzee have a theory of mind: 30 years later," Call and Tomasello (2008:187) "shifted far from their 1997 conclusion and instead argued that the spate of new studies shows that "there is solid evidence from several different experimental paradigms that chimpanzees understand the goals and intentions of others, as well as the perceptions and knowledge of others. At the same time however, there is currently no evidence that chimpanzees understand false beliefs."

Call and Tomasello (2008: 187) conclude their review of recent literature on the subject as follows: "Our conclusion for the moment is, then, that chimpanzees understand others in terms of a perception-goal psychology, as opposed to a full-fledged, human-like belief-desire psychology" (see also Tomasello and Call 2010).

This conclusion seems to me insightful and persuasive—but again, its phrasing seems unnecessarily dependent on English. Cross-linguistic lexical evidence suggests that humans share a "want-think psychology," rather than a "belief-desire" one. Concomitantly, a NSM-based rereading of the literature on the behavior of chimpanzees suggests that, strictly speaking, chimps have a "see-want" psychology rather than a "perception-goal" one.

What I mean by this reformulation is that, judging by their behavior, while chimpanzees don't have the concepts "perception" and "goal" in their "language of thought" (Fabrega, 2012; in press; forthcoming; Goddard et al., forthcoming), they do have analogues of the human concepts SEE and WANT. There is no evidence, however, that their "language of thought" includes an analogue of the human concept THINK (or, all the more so, of the English-specific concept "believe").

Elaborating on Call and Tomasello's conclusions, Whiten and Erdal (2012: 2125) write:

> The new thinking derived from this recent corpus of experiments is that the social cognition we should attribute to our common ancestors on the basis of shared human–ape capacities includes elements (perception-goal psychology) that are simpler than, yet logically were capable of providing a foundation for, the more advanced human forms (belief-desire reasoning, in this case) of mindreading that have evolved.

To extract the language-independent kernel of this hypothesis from its English lexical shell, I would propose formulations along the following lines:

Both chimpanzees and people can sometimes know what someone else can see.
Both chimpanzees and people can sometimes know what someone else can know.
Only people can sometimes know what someone else thinks.

This contention (to which I will return in section 5) is of course open to debate, but the use of universal semantic primes like *see, know, want*, and *think* (instead of English-bound terms like "perception," "intuition," "desire" and "belief" (not to mention "mindreading" and "the theory of mind")) allows us to clarify the issues, and at the same time free the debate from the conceptual shackles of English.

In the summary of their review article "Chimpanzee Social Cognition," Call and Tomasello (2008: 218) write: "chimpanzees, like humans, understand that others see, hear and know things." The clarity and precision of this statement is striking and is related to the fact that its content is not explained in more complicated (and thus more "scientific") English, but is phrased in more basic and cross-translatable words: SEE, HEAR, and KNOW.[2] But the elaboration, phrased in more conventional scientific language, is less clear and less transferable into languages other than English:

> all of the evidence reviewed here suggests that chimpanzees understand others as goal-directed agents who mentally represent desired states of affairs (i.e. goals) and who also perceive the world in order to devise behavioural strategies for meeting these goals; they understand something of the interrelations among perception, goal and action. (ibid)

Trying to clarify this elaboration and to detach its meaning from culture-specific English words and phrases, we could, first, avoid the phrase "goal-directed agents" by saying that chimpanzees "want something" and "do something because of this"; second, replace "devise behavioral strategies" with "see something, want something, think something, and do something because of this"; and third, replace "understanding something of the interrelations among perception, goal and action" with a statement that one chimp can know that another chimp "sees something, wants to do something because of this, and does something because of this." To illustrate more concretely what such "translation" of complex English-dependent generalizations into a more plausible "chimp language of thought" might look like, I will now present several concrete chimp scenarios drawn on the basis of observations reported in recent primatological literature.

Some Hypothesized Cognitive Scenarios for Chimpanzees: An Illustration

The last ten or fifteen years have brought an extraordinary expansion of knowledge about chimpanzees' behavior, especially their behavior "in the wild." As many primatologists see it, this new knowledge affords astounding new insights into chimpanzees' psychology, or as it is now frequently phrased, into "the mind of the chimpanzee."

As Anne Russon (2004: 93) puts it, "Virtually all experts agree that there is no longer any justification for reducing great ape cognition to associative processes or lumping together great apes with other non-human primates." Russon herself characterizes these new cognitive skills with the phrase "rudimentary symbolic cognition."

What, exactly, is the content of this new "symbolic cognition"? Russon credits great apes with a (limited) "fluidity of thought" (ibid). But if great apes "think" (in a limited, if "fluid" way), **what** do they think? What kinds of thoughts can be plausibly attributed to them—thoughts that would be consistent with their astonishingly human-like behavior in many situations?

On this point, primatological literature so far remains silent. Possible "chimp-thoughts" are characterized in various ways, but they are not modeled as possible mental representations of the chimpanzees themselves (that is, they are not modeled in a plausible "chimp language of thought"). By contrast, the use of NSM allows us to formulate quite specific hypotheses on this score— hypotheses that are consistent with observations made in the field and with the interpretations implied by field primatologists themselves, as the following example from Christophe Boesch and Hedwige Boesch-Achermann's book *The Chimpanzees of the Taï Forest* (2000:191) illustrates:

> *Forest scene* [A female chimpanzee, Héra, and her son Eros are on their own foraging]
> we follow Héra when she finds a nest of sweat bees in a large freshly fallen branch. The nest is hidden inside the branch, its small entrance betrayed by

some bees, but most must have already abandoned the nest. Héra quickly removes a stick from a sapling with her hand, approaches it to her face, and reduces its length to 25 cm by cutting it with her teeth. Then she dips one end of the twig into the hole, rapidly pulls it out with pieces of the drying honey sticking to it at the extremity. She licks the honey and dips again. Meanwhile Eros, 3 years old, sits nearby. When she removes the twig, he places his fingers tightly around it and she pulls it through his fist and he licks the delicacy that remains on his palm. She continues to dip, and soon she seems to collect more of the honey and Eros begs now directly for the loaded tool. Héra hands it over to Eros and rapidly makes a new one and now they exchange tools—empty for loaded. She dips while he licks. Héra shares every second dip and this goes on for about four minutes.

Using NSM, we can hypothesize that the core of what is going on in this situation can be interpreted in the following two behavioral-cognitive scenarios:

mother chimp dipping for honey with a stick (Hirata 2006a)

when the big chimp sees this tree in this place it does something because it thinks like this:
"there is something good inside this tree in one place
if I do something to this tree in this place with something long,
  this good thing can be on this long thing
after this, it can be inside my mouth
I want this"

mother chimp sharing some honey with her son

when the big chimp sees the small chimp in this place it does something
  because it thinks like this:
"this someone can see me now
my hand is on something long now, there is something good on this long thing
if I do something to this long thing now, after this,
this someone's hand can be on this long thing
after this, this good thing can be inside this someone's mouth
I want this"

Other common behaviors documented by primatologists can be interpreted along the same lines. For example:

dipping for ants (Sanz & Morgan 2010; Humble 2006; Boesch 2009)

sometimes when a chimp sees the ground in a place it does something
because it thinks like this:
"there are many very small living things inside the ground in this place
if I do something to the ground in this place with my hand,
  these very small living things can be on my hand

after this, they can be inside my mouth
I want this"

termite fishing (Sanz & Morgan 2010)

sometimes when a chimp sees the ground in one place it does something
because it thinks like this:
"there are many very small living things inside the ground in this place
if I do something to the ground in this place with something long,
   after this, these very small living things can be on this long thing
after this, they can be inside my mouth
I want this"

nut cracking (Boesch & Boesch-Achermann 2000; Biro et al. 2010)

sometimes when a chimp sees a place it does something
because it thinks like this:
"there are many small hard things in this place
inside these things there is something good
if I do something to these small hard things with something hard,
   after this, this good thing can be inside my mouth
I want this"

hiding from a dominant chimp (Boesch and Boesch-Achermann 2000; Hirata 2006b)

sometimes when a chimp sees another chimp in a place, it does something.
because it thinks like this:
"if this someone sees me now, this someone can do something very bad to me
I can't do something like this to this someone
because of this, I don't want this someone to see me now"

I will note that the attribution of "thinking" to chimpanzees, evident in the introductory frame, is consistent with Tomasello's (2012) unhesitating use of the word "think" in relation to the great apes. Furthermore, the use of the words "if," "because," and "not" in these scenarios is consistent with Tomasello's (2012) use of "proto-conditionals" (p.15), "causal inferences" (p.15), and "proto-negation" (p.19) in relation to chimpanzees' thinking. (See also de Waal 2003.)

Like these "logical operators," all the other words used in the "chimp scenarios" posited here come from a postulated vocabulary of seventy or so chimpanzee conceptual primes, which appear to be needed to account for the behavioral strategies described in recent primatological literature. (cf. Goddard et al., Forthcoming; Fabrega, 2012, Forthcoming.)

These seventy or so "chimp primes" overlap with the human repertoire of conceptual primes but are not simply a subset of human primes, because they include a dozen or so concepts that are not present as primes in human languages. As the cognitive scenarios presented here illustrate, they include "concrete" concepts such as "ground," "tree," "mouth," "hard," "long," and "hand." In human languages these concepts occur, too, of course, but they are analyzable in terms of the human language of thought because they are compounds of human primes, whereas in "chimp language of thought" they are not analyzable (cannot be broken down further).

The full set of "chimp primes" emerging from these and other scenarios suggested by recent primatological literature can be represented as in Table 13.1, below (for discussion and justification, see Goddard et al., Forthcoming).

The set of conceptual primes posited here for chimpanzees allows us to offer a coherent story consistent with a wide range of behavioral scenarios reported in recent primatological literature and to make sense of them, without at the same time attributing to chimpanzees implausibly large and complex representational resources. It also allows us to represent the import of chimpanzees' communicative gestures in the same framework as that of cognitive scenarios. The general schema for such gestures could look like this:

sometimes when a chimp sees another chimp, it does something with some parts of its body because it wants to say something to this other chimp

The topic of gestures is outside the scope of this chapter, but it will be useful to compare the schema above with that proposed for communicative bodily behavior of early humans later in this chapter in the section entitled "Four breakthroughs in human evolution".

The same seventy or so "chimp primes" enable us to try to articulate chimpanzees' apparent "knowledge of the world" from a chimpanzee's point of view. This can be illustrated by an instructive vignette in which Tomasello

TABLE 13.1:

Conceptual Primes Posited for Chimpanzees

∗CHIMP PRIMES MATCHING HUMAN PRIMES
I, SOMEONE, YOU, SOMETHING
KIND
THIS, OTHER, THE SAME; ONE, SOME, MUCH~MANY; LITTLE~FEW
BIG, SMALL; GOOD, BAD; VERY; MORE
KNOW, WANT, DON'T WANT, FEEL, SEE, HEAR
SAY
DO, HAPPEN, MOVE, TOUCH
LIVE, BE SOMEWHERE, THERE IS, BE (SOMEONE~SOMETHING)
WHEN, NOW, BEFORE, AFTER, A SHORT TIME, FOR SOME TIME
WHERE, HERE, ABOVE, BELOW, SIDE, INSIDE, NEAR, FAR
NOT, MAYBE, CAN, BECAUSE, IF, LIKE
CHIMP primes not present as primes in modern human languages
(Several of them are present in human languages as semantic molecules).
"CHIMPS," CREATURES
TREE, GROUND, WATER, LEAVES
MOUTH, "PENIS", TEETH, HAND, BLOOD, POO
SMELL
HARD, LONG; ON

(2012) peers into the mind of a foraging chimpanzee that is looking at a tree laden with bananas. Tomasello considers various factors that may influence this chimpanzee's decision to climb or not to climb.

"As described in English" (Tomasello's noteworthy qualification, p.11), these factors include, inter alia, the following: "there are many bananas in the tree," "the bananas are ripe," "there are no competitor chimpanzees already in the tree," "the bananas are reachable by climbing," "there are no predators nearby," and "escaping quickly from this tree will be difficult." Tomasello explains in this context that a tree without low hanging branches is preferable from a chimpanzee's point of view, "given its knowledge that leopards cannot climb such trees and its familiarity with its own tree-climbing prowess" (p.11).

Tomasello is prepared to say that "great apes know, for example, that a leopard does lots of things like climb trees" (p.231), but not that great apes have the concept of climbing, suggesting instead that "apes schematize acts of climbing not based on movements but on an understanding that the actor has the goal of getting up the tree" (p.24). All these observations are consistent with the hypothesis that the chimpanzee's knowledge can be articulated with the same seventy or so hypothesized "chimp concepts" that are both necessary and sufficient for formulating cognitive scenarios such as those outlined before. For example:

[Chimps know many things about the places where they live; because of this it is like this:]

a chimpanzee can think like this about a tree at some time:

"if a big creature of one kind is on the ground in this place now,

after a s hort time it can be somewhere on this tree, far above the ground

because of this I don't want to be somewhere on this tree"

In his "Comment" on Rom Harré's (1984) paper "Vocabularies and Terminologies," Frans de Waal (1984: 108) wrote: "Development of an adequate terminology and a set of methodological rules may allow us, to a very limited extent and only in theory, to enter the animal's inner world of intentions, expectations, thoughts and feelings." Arguably, the NSM terminology of postulated "chimp primes" (with words like KNOW, WANT, and FEEL, but without words like *intend* or *expect*) allows us to do just that: enter imaginatively into chimps' inner world, manifested in their astonishing behavior.

The blurb on the back cover of Christophe Boesch's fascinating new book *Wild Cultures* (2012) opens with the question: "How do chimpanzees say, 'I want to have sex with you?'" (The answers provided are: "by clipping a leaf" and "by knocking on a tree trunk.") From an NSM perspective, however, chimpanzees never say "I want to have sex with you" to anyone, because, arguably, neither the word "sex" nor the phrase "to have sex" are part of their mental lexicon. Indeed, as discussed in my paper "Sex in cross-linguistic and cross-cultural perspective" (Wierzbicka 2012d), the idea of "having sex with someone" is a modern Anglo invention (the first citation for "have sex" in the Oxford English Dictionary is dated 1929; see chapter 3).

So what is a male chimp saying to a female chimp by clipping a leaf or knocking on a tree trunk? In the light of the hypothesis about the chimp set of conceptual primes developed here, he is probably saying something far cruder and simpler, to wit: "I want my penis to be inside you now" (or perhaps: "I want to do something with my penis to you now"). Presumably, the meaning of a female display is similarly simple and basic, but given the asymmetry of roles and behaviors between male and female chimps, it is not identical with the male's message: "I want your penis to be inside me now."

As this example illustrates, whether or not we can avoid anthropocentrism in reading chimps' minds, the independently justified vocabulary of seventy or so chimp primes helps us at least to avoid projecting onto their minds culture-specific attitudes embedded in modern English. The more general point is that the modeling of chimp thoughts and meanings needs to go hand in hand with the modeling of the chimp language of thought.

Chimpanzees' Mental Scenarios and the Origins of Syntax

It is easy to see that the cognitive scenarios attributed here to chimpanzees (in order to make sense of their behavior in the wild) include not only a large number of "mental words," but also a relatively complex grammar. They feature several "parts of speech," including analogues of verbs like "do," "happen," "see," "want," and "feel," nouns like "mouth," "hand," "ground," and "tree," "adjectives" like "big," "small," "good," "bad," "hard," and "long," "adverbials" such as "a short time before" and "for some time," "pronouns" such as "I," "you," and "this," "conjunctions" such as "if" and "because," and "prepositions" such as "inside" and "on."

What is more, these different "parts of speech" combine in these scenarios according to relatively complex and sophisticated "rules of grammar"— quite unlike the kind of "primitive syntax" ("allowing different combinations of words representing objects and actions") that evolutionary psychologist Michael Corballis (2002: 36) was prepared to grant to the famous bonobo Kanzi studied in a laboratory by primatologist Sue Savage-Rumbaugh.

Of course, the syntax attributed to chimpanzees in the scenarios posited here pertains to hypothetical "thoughts" rather than to spoken utterances. All that this suggests, however, is that chimpanzees have a rich "language of thought," with a sizable mental lexicon and fairly developed mental grammar; and that in human evolution, too, a complex language of thought may have been in operation long before the emergence of speech.

If the cognitive scenarios in the minds of the chimpanzees are as developed as suggested here, this could have some implications for the controversial question of the origins of syntax in human languages. Perhaps the fundamentals of syntax were already there, in the minds of the "Ancestral Apes" (the last common ancestors of humans and chimpanzees), long before the first words were ever spoken. Perhaps the astonishing behaviors of "chimpanzees in the forest" such as those described in detail by Christophe Boesch and Hedwige Boesch-Achermann (2000) could be interpreted as "thinking in action" (by analogy with Condillac's (1746) "speaking by action," which he linked with the origins of language). Such "thinking in action" would require some "mental sentences in action," and therefore some mental syntax, as well as some conceptual lexical primes. (Corballis's 2002:39 notion of "combinatorial thought" is highly apposite here.)

In his book *Adam's Tongue*, linguist Derek Bickerton (2009:46) writes:

> The dream of strong continuists is to find precursors of words and precursors of syntax among other species. This would be the easiest and most obvious way to establish true continuity between ACSs [Animal Communication Systems] and language. But it isn't the right way. (...) It's a waste of time looking among other species for precursors of words or precursors of syntax. (...) So if we want to demonstrate real continuity in evolution, we should be looking not for linguistic precursors, but for some point of flexibility in ACSs (...) that might ultimately lead to the creation of words, and, later on, the creation of syntax. Because these things—words and syntax—are total evolutionary novelties, things useless and meaningless outside language.

I agree with Bickerton that there is little point in looking for precursors of human words and syntax in vocal communication systems that we find among nonhuman primates. Arguably, however, a strong case can be made for them having their analogues in "chimp primes" and "chimp syntax" hypothesized in the cognitive scenarios posited here for chimpanzees; and also, for having their precursors in primes and syntax needed for analogous scenarios that could be posited for our "Ancestral Apes."

My conclusion that the last common ancestors are likely to have had a rudimentary "mental syntax" as well as a set of mental primes is consistent with Michael Tomasello's willingness to attribute to chimpanzees (and, by implication, to the last common ancestors) logico-syntactic skills such as "proto-conditionals" (e.g., "if a tool with property A is used, then X will happen," Tomasello 2012:15).

Such rudimentary mental syntax could have set the stage for the emergence of "verbal syntax," just as the mental lexicon of a few dozen of conceptual primes that the last common ancestor is likely to have had could have set the stage for the lexical breakthrough in human evolution. The unique productivity and flexibility of human language was no doubt facilitated by the changes in the vocal tract that allowed early humans to become articulate. Arguably, however, the insight that "I can say things to people with words (spoken words)" was preceded by the realization that I may have something to say because at many times I have some thoughts in my head, and these incipient thoughts required some foundational words and syntax.

Four Breakthroughs in Human Evolution

In his book *Masters of the Planet: the Search for Our Human Origins*, one of the leaders in human evolutionary studies, Ian Tattersall (2012), writes:

> As far as we know, *Homo sapiens* is totally unique in significantly express-
> ing an ability to manipulate information symbolically. An understanding
> how we acquired this capacity is fundamental to any complete understand-
> ing of ourselves. (p.208)
> The changeover of *Homo sapiens* from a nonsymbolic, nonlinguistic spe-
> cies to a symbolic linguistic one is the most mind-boggling cognitive trans-
> formation that has ever happened to any organism. (p.220)

For his part, Tattersall links this "mind-boggling cognitive transformation," which allowed the members of the species Homo sapiens to become "masters of the planet," with the emergence of words and of the ability to combine words. This then led to "a change in the internal organization and wiring of our brains" (p.208)—a view epitomized by the title of his concluding chapter "In the beginning was the word." The ground was long prepared in prehuman anatomy and cogni-tion, but a stimulus was needed to release the potential that was already there:

> it seems justifiable to look upon what happened as analogous to the con-
> struction of an arch, which cannot function until the keystone has been
> dropped into place. What's more, whatever the "keystone" was in our case,
> the new potential it created then lay fallow for a substantial length of time,
> until its symbolic potential was "discovered" by its owner. (p.210)

Arguably, the conceptual primes and conceptual syntax that we need to attri-bute to our prehuman ancestors on the basis of what we seem to find in the thinking of chimpanzees served as the basic framework for the arch; but it was the emergence of words that provided the "keystone" for the unique cognitive capabilities of Homo sapiens.

As Tattersall puts it, "words are a crucial enabling factor of complex cognition" (p.219). He invokes in this connection the verbal awakening of a deaf and wordless man described by Susan Schaller in her book *A Man Without Words*:

> Schaller initially tried to teach Ildefonso the rudiments of American Sign
> Language (ASL), but soon perceived that he did not grasp even the concept
> of signs. Modifying her approach, she eventually achieved a breakthrough.

> Ildefonso, in a flash of insight, understood that everything had a name. "Suddenly he sat up, straight and rigid....The whites of his eyes expanded, as if in terror....He broke through....He had entered the universe of humanity, discovered the communion of minds." (Tattersall 2012: 217)

After this breakthrough, Ildefonso's perception of the world radically changed, and "he became hungry for signs, demanding new words" (Tattersall ibid). The emergence of words and of the ability to combine them (inaudibly inside one's head and audibly with the help of one's larynx) jointly constituted what can be called a "linguistic breakthrough," whose *fons et origo* must have lain in the "proto-lexicon of the mind" and the "proto-syntax of the mind" that we have every reason to attribute to the prelinguistic Homo-not-yet-sapiens.

Evidently, the linguistic (lexico-syntactic) breakthrough was accompanied at the dawn of human prehistory by a broader "symbolic awakening" (Tattersall 2012; Noble and Davidson 1996; Noble 2006; Davidson 2010), which found its expression in phenomena such as cave art in Europe and rock art in Australia; and presumably it was preceded by two intermediate evolutionary stages, describable in technical language as the "mimetic" stage and the stage of "metacognition" (Donald 2001). Using NSM we can portray the hypothetical critical breakthroughs in human evolution in a language free from conceptual dependence on English, relying on simple concepts like SAY and SEE, BODY and WORDS, as follows (see Goddard et al. Forthcoming):

1. The "mimetic" breakthrough (early Homo, not yet *Homo sapiens*)

[someone can think like this:]

"I can say something with my body if I do something with my body
if someone sees me, this someone can know something because of this"

2. The "meta-cognitive" breakthrough (early Homo, not yet *Homo sapiens*)

[someone can think like this:]

"I can say something inside my head
if I say something inside my head,
someone else can't know it"

3. The "symbolic" breakthrough (Early *Homo sapiens*)

[people can think like this:]

"I can say something with some things if I do something with these things
if other people see these things,
they can know something because of this"

4. The "linguistic" breakthrough (Early *Homo sapiens*)

[people can think like this:]

"I can say something with some words if I do something with my mouth
if other people hear these words,
    they can know something because of this"

The first of these breakthroughs corresponds to Merlin Donald's (2002) "mimetic" stage of human evolution, linked with phenomena such as "mimetic" (that is, bodily) representation of events and actions or "imaginative reenactment of an event" (Donald, p. 263), potentially for the purpose of sharing knowledge.

The second breakthrough can be seen as a logical consequence of the first: if I realize that I can "say something," visibly, with my body (and thus make this something publically available), I can also realize that I can "say something" **not** with my body, that is, invisibly, and that so can others. Furthermore, once our early ancestors (such as perhaps "Homo Ergaster") started showing "many of the hallmarks of *Homo*," including "its high degree of sociality and cooperativeness stem[ming] from the closeness among group members" (Tattersall p.113), it is likely that they increasingly wanted to know what the other members of their group may be thinking—or, if they didn't yet have the concept of "thinking," what they may be saying "inside their heads."

The two breakthroughs distinguished here as "symbolic" and "linguistic" correspond to what evolutionary scientists such as Tattersall (2012:202) call "symbolic cognition" (see also Noble and Davidson 1996; Donald 2002), applying this term to both language and art. The interpretive framework adopted here and relying on universal concepts such as "I," "say," "do," "see," "something," "body," and "word" allows us to construct a transparent and English-independent schema based on "saying something with one's body" (the "mimetic" mode), "saying something with some things" (the "symbolic" mode), and "saying something with words" (the "linguistic" mode), as well as self-conscious "saying something inside one's head"—a precursor of "thinking about thinking" (see next section). In addition, the same set of primes allows us also to portray the baseline for these four developments: judging by the chimpanzees, our ancestral apes (LCAs) may have had communicative gestures with the basic meaning "I want to say something to you," but no insight into their own cognitive capacities (no "I can say something with my body" concept).

Using gestures like chimpanzees do (Tomasello and Call 2010; Call and Tomasello (eds) 2007) is not the same thing as having a "mimetic awareness," that is, the conscious knowledge that one can say something to others by doing something with one's body. Such knowledge is likely to have emerged at a later stage of evolution, giving rise, in time, to the realization that one can also say something in one's head. The "symbolic awakening," that is, the realization that one can say something with "things" (material objects such as personal adornments or paintings) and with words, appears to have been a revolutionary innovation of Homo sapiens.

Finally, we should point out that the four breakthroughs postulated here are, so to speak, both cognitive and communicative: they represent different ways of thinking, three of which open up new ways of communicating with others, and one (labeled here as "meta-cognitive") that paves the way for the realization that "I can think" ("inside my head") and that others can, invisibly and inaudibly, think ("inside their heads"), too.

Thinking about Thinking

Returning to chimpanzees, I must stress that while all the simple "chimp scenarios" posited for them earlier in this chapter are introduced by a frame with the word "think," this word does not appear inside the hypothetical "chimp thoughts" themselves. This is consistent with the distinction that Call and Tomasello (2010) draw between, on the one hand, "mental representations" (which chimpanzees do have) and, on the other, "understanding false beliefs" (which they don't have). When this distinction is translated into simple language, it boils down, in essence, to a difference between "thinking" and "thinking about thinking": I read Call and Tomasello as saying that a chimp can "think" something (for example, "this someone wants to do something now") but not "think that someone else thinks" something (e.g., "this someone thinks like this now...."). Clearly, this is why for these authors, like for many other evolutionary scientists, a key question is whether or not chimpanzees can "understand false beliefs": if a chimp could differentiate conceptually between "know" and "think," it could think like this about another chimp:

"I want to do something now
I don't want this someone to know it
I want this someone to think that I want to do something else"

According to Call and Tomasello (as I understand them), a chimpanzee cannot think like this, because while it can "think something" (for example, that someone wants to do something), it cannot "think that someone thinks something." This is, in fact, they suggest, a key difference between human cognition and chimpanzee cognition:

> Human cognition is clearly different from that of other species; nothing we are saying here threatens this unassailable claim. At the moment, in the domain of social cognition we believe that one key difference is that humans understand that peoples' actions are driven by their beliefs, even false beliefs, whereas chimpanzees and other apes do not understand this. (p. 248)

Both the words "understand" and "belief" imply "thinking." Roughly, if one "understands" why some people are doing something, one *knows* why they are doing it because one has *thought* about it, and if one "believes" that some people are doing something because of X, one *thinks* that they are doing it because of X without necessarily *knowing* it (one's "belief" that these people are doing it for reason X may be false).

The words *believe* and *belief* are problematic in such discussions for a number of reasons. *Believe* is a complex English concept, which arose in the context of post-Enlightenment thinking in Britain (Wierzbicka 2006a, chapter 7; Gladkova 2007). The distinction between chimpanzees and humans that both Call and Tomasello and Whiten and Erdal are seeking to draw does not depend on this complex English concept and can be more clearly formulated in terms of "think."

A distinction between an ability to "think something" (which both people and chimpanzees have) and an ability to "think that someone thinks something" (which only humans have) is articulated quite explicitly by Whiten and Erdal. A study of Baka hunter-gatherer children by Avis and Harris (1991) showed, they write, "that 5-year-olds would take into account others' false beliefs just as do children in urban and other communities." They go on to comment:

> The attribution of false beliefs is recognized as a watershed stage in which the child grasps that others may hold mental representations of the world fundamentally different from their own, and it develops through a series of steps that incorporate the attribution of states that include emotions, seeing and knowing. Moreover, some later achievements such as higher order attributions (thinking about what another person may be thinking about one's own ideas, for example) rest on the recursion of the first-order achievements in place by age five. (p. 2122)

Thus, the ability to "think about what another person may be thinking" appears to be a *human* achievement.

From an NSM perspective, evidence reviewed in studies such as those mentioned above suggests that the "representational resources" of chimpanzees include conceptual primes KNOW, SEE, WANT, and DO, but do not include THINK, which we find in the human language of thought (Goddard and Wierzbicka, eds., 2002). Whether or not one accepts this conclusion, the methodological point still holds: here as elsewhere, issues can be clarified if the debate is freed from the conceptual dependence on English and articulated in simple, stable, and cross-translatable words such as *see, want, know*, and *think* (and, as noted before, *say*).

Discussing the NSM list of human conceptual primes in his "state of the art" survey of evolutionary psychology, anthropologist Doug Jones (1999, 562) comments that "a subset of these concepts is probably phylogenetically ancient." Among the elements that are likely to be shared by humans and other primates, Jones includes, inter alia, SEE, KNOW, and WANT. At the same time, he suggests that "representations of beliefs (*think* versus *know*) may be limited to our species" (p. 564). This suggestion is consistent with the reconstruction of the chimp set of primes attempted here. Schematically, we can represent this shift in conceptual resources and abilities as follows:

People can think like this about some other people:

a. "this someone sees something now"

b. "this someone wants (to do) something now"

c. "this someone is thinking something now"

Chimpanzees can think like this about some other chimpanzees:

a. "this someone sees something now"

b. "this someone wants (to do) something now"

Chimpanzees can't think like this about some other chimpanzees:

"this someone is thinking something now"

The contrast in ways of thinking shown in the schematic formulations above appears to reflect a significant psychological breakthrough in the evolution of human cognition.

[people can think like this:]

I can say something with my body if I do some things with my body	ACTING
if someone sees me when I do it	
this someone can know something because of it	

I can say something inside my head if I do something inside my head	INNER SPEECH
if I say something inside my head	
someone else can't know it	

I can say something with some things if I do something with these things	ART & CRAFT
if someone sees these things	
this someone can know something because of it	

I can say something with words if I do some things with my mouth	ORAL SPEECH
if I do some things with my mouth	
other people can hear these words because of it	
they can know some things because of it	

Can a Chimp Understand Another Chimp's Feelings?

While the articles quoted here do not explicitly consider the question of chimpanzees' feelings, the evidence strongly suggests that the concept FEEL, too, belongs to the chimpanzees' "language of thought" (Fabrega, In press; Forthcoming). This can be illustrated with the following two hypothetical cognitive scenarios:

thirst

sometimes a chimp does something because it thinks like this:

"I feel something bad inside now

I want some water to be inside my mouth now"

Apparently, feelings can also be attributed by one chimp to another, for example, when one chimp licks the wounds of a fellow chimp injured in a leopard attack and bleeding.

licking the wounds of another chimp

sometimes when a chimp sees another chimp in a place

it does something because it thinks like this:

"something very bad happened to this someone a short time before

this someone feels something very bad because of this

I want to do something good to this someone with my mouth because of this"

Thus, a fuller description of "chimpanzee psychology" would be a "SEE-WANT-FEEL" psychology rather than just a "SEE-WANT" one. Concomitantly, its human counterpart would then need to be described as a "SEE-WANT-FEEL-THINK" psychology.

Are Chimpanzees Capable of "Empathy"?

In their article devoted to "contagious yawning" in chimpanzees, James Anderson and Tetsuro Matsuzawa (2006: 233) write:

> Although many people who work closely with these primates [great apes] are convinced that they are capable of reflecting about what other individuals might be thinking, others express doubts about the extent and level at which they do this.

The statement should perhaps not be taken literally: it seems unlikely that any primatologists really believe that chimpanzees can "reflect" about what other individuals might be thinking.

One suspects that in attributing such a belief to many primatologists, the authors may be influenced by their own definition of empathy: "By empathy, we mean the ability to identify with another individual's emotions and cognitive states" (ibid.). The phrase "the ability to identify with" could be interpreted in many different ways, but "contagious yawning" is a long way from "reflecting" on what somebody else may be thinking or feeling.

As evidence for chimpanzees' "empathetic abilities," Anderson and Matsuzawa cite the fact that "chimpanzee bystanders often approach to offer reassuring friendly contact to victims of an aggressive act" (p.234). Such "reassuring" approaches are consistent with the following scenario (similar, but not identical, to the "wound-licking" one):

"reassuring contact"

sometimes when a chimp sees another chimp,

    it does something because it thinks like this about this other chimp:

        "something very bad happened to this someone a short time before

        this someone feels something very bad because of this

        I want to be with this someone for some time because of this"

It is, however, a far cry from thinking that another chimpanzee "feels something very bad" to *reflecting* on what another chimpanzee might be thinking.

Anderson and Matsuzawa emphasize the continuity between chimpanzees (or the last common ancestors) and humans by highlighting chimpanzees' capacity for "empathy." Whiten and Erdal, on the other hand, emphasize the discontinuity, highlighting, inter alia, early humans' interest in "fairness." Since "fairness" is a highly culture-specific English concept, which emerged in the context of changes in modern Anglo culture (Wierzbicka 2006, chapter 5; cf Fischer 2012), such an attribution is unhelpful; and I would argue that to some degree at least, the same applies to "empathy" (Gladkova 2010).

Can One Get into the Mind of a Chimpanzee with Academic English?

Some of the long-standing controversies in primatology may be due, in part, to the complex and culture-specific English vocabulary in which the competing hypotheses and counter-hypotheses tend to be framed. Can chimpanzees take one another's perspective? Are they capable of empathy? Do they have a theory of mind? Do they practice deception? And so on.

Many such questions hinge on the distinction between KNOW and THINK. One relevant question is: "Can a chimpanzee know (in a concrete situation) what another chimpanzee (in this particular situation) *knows*?" Another question is: "Can a chimpanzee (in a concrete situation) *know* what another chimpanzee (in this particular situation) *thinks*?." Arguably, these are very different questions. Yet the difference between them is often blurred by the use of complex English terms such as "perspective," "empathy," and "identification," whose precise intended meaning is never clear.

In their article in the edited book *The Mind of the Chimpanzee,* Tomasello and Call (2010) take a step in this direction themselves when they raise questions about "knowing what others see" (p.243) and "knowing what others know" (p. 248), or when they state that a "chimpanzee, like humans, understands that others see, hear, and know things" (p. 248). When it comes to "thinking," however, they appear to be reluctant to use the simple word "think," and speak instead of "beliefs," "mental representations," and a "coherent understanding of the psychological functioning of others" (p. 248). For example, they write:

> Chimpanzees may not have a more human-like belief-desire psychology in which they understand that others actually have mental representations of the world which drives their actions, even when those do not correspond to reality—but why should beliefs be the only mental state thought worthy to be called theory of mind?

Seemingly exasperated by the pseudo-controversies due to the metaphorical phrase "theory of mind," Tomasello and Call continue:

> We ourselves think that most of human cognitive uniqueness derives less from their "theory of mind," narrowly defined, than from some species-unique social-cognitive skills and motivations for sharing intentional states with others in special types of cooperative and communicative activities. (p.249)

While fully agreeing with these authors that the phrase "theory of mind" has outlived its usefulness in the studies of human evolution, I would nonetheless suggest that human cognitive uniqueness lies not only in the development of *socio*-cognitive skills but also in the emergence of the concept THINK in the primate repertoire of primes, that is, in the expansion of the "theory of mind" from KNOW, SEE, WANT, and FEEL, TO KNOW, SEE, WANT, FEEL, and THINK.

A Theoretical Vocabulary for the "Natural History of Human Thinking"

In his new monograph "The natural history of human thinking," Tomasello (2012) raises what I see as a key question: what is an appropriate "theoretical vocabulary" for talking about the origins of human thinking? Tomasello quotes in this context philosopher Donald Davidson's comment:

> In both the evolution of thought in the history of mankind, and the evolution of thought in an individual, there is a stage at which there is no thought followed by a subsequent stage at which there is thought...What we lack is a satisfactory vocabulary for describing the intermediate steps. (Davidson (2001), quoted in Tomasello 2012: 117)

Recognizing the critical importance of this question of an appropriate theoretical vocabulary, Tomasello (2012: 120) acknowledges that "modern humans reify and objectify what are essentially socially created entities." This applies, of course, to English concepts reified in the language of evolutionary social science: "nowhere is this tendency stronger than in language, where we all, many linguists and philosophers included, have a tendency—correctable but only with much effort—to reify the concepts codified in our own natural language" (ibid.). Coming from someone of Tomasello's standing in the field, this implicit recognition of the dangers of conceptual Anglocentrism to our understanding of the evolution of human thinking is particularly significant and promising.

In the conclusion to their (2010) paper "Chimpanzee Social Cognition," Tomasello and Call (2010: 248) write:

> the fundamentals are the same for both chimpanzees and humans: perceptual-goal psychology enabling the understanding of important aspects of intentional, rational action and perception. Humans may go beyond this in also understanding false beliefs, but that additional social-cognitive skill is built upon the general *Pan* foundation (...).

"Primates can obviously think," says the evolutionary psychologist Merlin Donald (2002: 277). It seems equally obvious that they don't think in academic English. Naturally, when we write about them in English, we have to model their thinking through English words, but we don't have to try to model it through words specific to modern English and Anglo culture. The closer we keep to universal words like THINK, WANT, and KNOW, the closer we can get to that "general *Pan* foundation"—without compounding our inevitable anthropocentrism (cf. Asquith 1984) by avoidable Anglocentrism.

In any case, it seems clear that the simple concepts THINK and KNOW allow us to develop a wider range of hypotheses about human and prehuman cognition than the complex English phrase "false belief" does. In particular, the prime THINK can help us to articulate a possible link between humans' expanded "theory of mind" and their new socio-cognitive skills and interests.

It is easy to see how the psychological breakthrough epitomized by the ability to think about someone else, "this someone is thinking something now" can be related to the social breakthrough epitomized by the ability to think about someone else, "I want to do something with this someone." Obviously, when one wants to do things with other people, it is desirable to be able to know what these people are thinking.

In an article titled "On Defining Emotions" within a recent special issue of *Emotion Review*, anthropologist Richard Shweder (2012b: 383) expresses some doubt about the usefulness of the concept of "emotions" and its various definitions "as a means of making sense of mental life and cultural psychology of peoples wherever you go." Referring to my 1999 book *Emotions Across Languages and Cultures: Diversity and Universals,* Shweder is willing to accept the NSM primes KNOW, WANT, FEEL, THINK, GOOD, and BAD as a plausible basis for human cultural psychology:

I am quite willing to conduct interpretive research on cultural differences in human mentalities relying on a theory of mind that presumes that all normal human beings wherever you go in the world want things, know things, feel things, and value things (as good or bad), and think about the things they want, know, feel, and value. (p.383)

I would suggest that—as the chimp scenarios and the evolutionary break-throughs presented earlier in this chapter illustrate—the same primes can furnish a toolkit for interpretive research into the psychology of chimpanzees and into the origins of human cognition, and thus go a long way toward solving D. Davidson's problem of finding a satisfactory theoretical vocabulary. They can help to free evolutionary social science from conceptual dependence on English-specific words and phrases such as "inferential reasoning" (Call 2010: 75), "mindreading" (Whiten & Erdal 2012: 2119), "cooperative and communicative activities" (Tomasello & Call 2010: 248), "metacognition" (Donald 2002: 292), and "publicly shared mentalistic framework" (Whiten & Erdal 2012: 2122).

Last but not least, what applies to "emotion," "cognition," "empathy," and "communication" (Goddard 2009), applies also to terms like "shared intentionality" (cf. e.g., Tomasello 2012) and to "intersubjectivity" and "the shared mind" (cf. Zlatev 2008)—key concepts in today's cutting-edge evolutionary social science. Unlike words such as *know*, *think*, *want*, and *say*, such terms cannot be translated into other languages and their meaning is neither precise nor intuitively clear. For all their purported emphasis on what is shared and what is "inter-" (rather than "intra-"), such terms unwittingly lock the debate, conceptually, within one language: English. I contend that these concepts, too, will sooner or later need to be reconceptualized and clarified through universal human concepts, independent of the conceptual vocabulary of English.

Six Million Years of Cognitive Evolution in Six Stages

As we have seen, it is possible to develop a hypothesis about the conceptual repertoire of chimpanzees in terms of simple and universal human concepts such as SEE, KNOW, WANT, DO, HERE and NOW. This hypothesis may be more or less anthropocentric, but is not Anglocentric. The same applies to the hypotheses that can be developed in relation to the Last Common Ancestor and to all the intermediate stages between LCAs and modern humans. The conceptual repertoire posited here (on the basis of observed behavioural scenarios) for chimpanzees gives us a good basis for reconstructing the conceptual repertoire of LCAs and allows us to develop a coherent story about our ancestors' conceptual journey over the last six million years. Having a reasonable idea of the starting point of this journey and of its end point (that we find in modern human languages), we can engage in semantic reconstruction in stages, relying to some extent on the internal logic of the system(s) of primes.

Some conceptual primes presuppose some others, so while we may not know for sure when particular primes emerged, we can formulate reasonable hypotheses about the relative order. By positing four intermediary stages between the LCA and fully modern humans we can establish a timeline consistent with such an order. At the same time, we can try to correlate the stages arising from such a semantic reconstruction with the results of archaeology, paleoanthropology, evolutionary biology and other evolutionary sciences.

It is not possible to present a detailed account of such semantic reconstruction in the chapter. All I can do here is to give a brief summary of the discussion presented more fully elsewhere (see in particular Goddard, Wierzbicka, and Fabrega, Forthcoming). The six stages that we have singled out in that fuller account are as follows (this is not an attempt at dividing those six million years into well-defined periods but a glimpse into six "moments" during that large span):

Stage   I: Last Common Ancestors/Ancestral Apes (6 million years ago)
Stage II: Archaic Hominids/Bipedal Apes (4-3 million years ago)
Stage III: Proto-Humans (1 million years ago)
Stage IV: Early Humans (200,000 years ago)
Stage V: First Modern Humans (80,000 years ago)
Stage VI: Cognitively Fully Modern (60,000 years ago)

If I were to nominate three new primes most likely to have been critical to human cognitive development and to involve major shifts in neurocognitive development, then I would single out three: THINK at Stage III (Homo Erectus/ Homo Ergaster), PARTS at Stage IV (e.g. Homo Heidelbergensis), and WORDS at Stage V (First Modern Humans). A full list of the new primes acquired at Stages II-VI posited in Goddard, Wierzbicka, and Fabrega (Forthcoming) looks as follows:

Stage II: LEGS, HANDS, HEAD, FACE; SHARP
Stage III: THINK, TWO, BODY, "PEOPLE"
Stage IV: PARTS, ALL, SOME, LITTLE (small quantity), A LONG TIME, DIE
Stage V: WORDS
Stage VI: TRUE, WHOSE (personal possession)

It is not possible to provide here a lengthy discussion and justification of the proposed timeline for the emergence of primes over the evolutionary time. What I can do, however, is to illustrate the links between habitats, lifestyles, and cognitive developments with some examples (drawing on Goddard,

Wierzbicka, and Fabrega, Forthcoming). I will focus on the concepts PARTS, THINK, and WORDS.

From LEGS, HANDS, and HEAD, to BODY and PARTS

The "new" (post-LCA) primes LEGS, HANDS and HEAD are all related to the new upright position of Bipedal Apes/Archaic Hominids. The idea of 'legs' – because of which they could move quickly in the open terrain running away from predators or following prey – must have forced itself on their attention compellingly. The hands, too, must have become more noticeable than ever before – no longer occupied most of the time with tree-climbing, they were free to do things with, and when on the move, to carry things (or babies) with; and they were frequently visible in front of one's body, together, doing things.

Once the concepts of LEGS and HANDS were firmly in place, the paired character of certain body parts would have forced itself onto the humans' attention, and the concept of TWO could have clearly emerged. Furthermore, when the ideas of LEGS, HANDS, and HEAD were well established (at stage II), the idea of BODY may well have suggested itself to Proto Humans (Stage III). And the presence of the prime PARTS at the next stage (Stage IV), which must have developed, first of all, in relation to "parts of the body", suggests that between Stage II and Stage IV (that is, at Stage III) the idea of BODY was already in place.

The concept of 'parts of the body' may well have emerged at Stage III, more or less together with the concept BODY, as a way of rethinking the earlier primes LEGS, HANDS and HEAD. At Stage IV, however, we find a well established prime PARTS independent of the prime BODY and applicable in other areas, in particular, in relation to making tools and shelters. The invention of "composite tools", such as stone axes attached to a piece of wood, is particularly telling in this respect. Tattersall (2012: 141) calls the invention of such tools "a major innovation in the technological history of hominids" and speaks in this connection of "a new layer of cognitive complexity". Boesch (2012) also speaks of composite tools as a key invention that is "totally missing from chimpanzee technology" (p. 235), and he too invokes in the connection differences in cognition:

> Why have chimpanzees not been able to use composite tools? Axes and lances, which appear to be the first human composite tools, were used to hunt prey from a distance. This requires an open habitat and was proposed to be essential to the evolution of our ancestors. So chimpanzees have either rarely encountered the conditions that necessitate the use of such tools (...) or they cannot cognitively conceive of such tools. (p. 225)

Using NSM, we can pinpoint the cognitive difference in question in terms of the prime PARTS. An expanded technology depended on the expanded conceptual repertoire: having acquired a firm grip on the concept of PARTS and having learned to think in terms of 'parts' about 'things' as well as bodies, early humans were able to combine different materials into complex objects such as 'hafted' axes, hammers and lances. Or, from another point of view, the emergence of such technology suggests, and provides evidence for, an earlier emergence of the prime PARTS.

From SEE, KNOW, WANT and FEEL to THINK (Stage III)

The most important acquisition of Stage III (Proto-Humans, Homo Erectus) is the prime THINK. Being able to attribute thinking to others ("this someone thinks like this now...") enabled Proto-Humans to coordinate activities with others and to achieve better interpersonal understanding. As we have seen, there are good reasons to posit the primes SEE, KNOW, WANT and FEEL for chimpanzees, and, by extension, for the Last Common Ancestor. THINK, however, was evidently an invention of the hominids, and its development may well have depended on the earlier emergence of the concepts HEAD and FACE (see Goddard, Wierzbicka, and Fabrega, Forthcoming). Furthermore, as noted in relation to "shared mind" and "shared intentionality", the ability to coordinate activities with many other group members suggests thinking in terms of "think the same" and so it points to the emergence of the prime THE SAME, possibly around the same time as THINK.

From SAY and THINK, via PARTS, to WORDS

Perhaps the most momentous breakthrough in human cognitive evolution was due to the emergence of the concept of WORDS. As Tattersall (2012: 219) says, "... words are a critical enabling factor in complex cognition". There are good reasons to think that it was precisely this concept which enabled "the spurt of symbolic innovation" around 80 thousand years ago – a time at which Tattersall locates the emergence of "cognitively modern humans who eventually took over the world" (p. 222). Tattersall links the importance of 'words' with the notion (attributed by him to the neurobiologist Norman Geshwind) that words enable the discrete identification of objects by naming them, and that, concomitantly, the emergence of the idea of WORDS provided "the foundation of symbolic cognition" (ibid.).

   As Tattersall points out, important support for this idea comes from what we know about the WORD-based cognitive breakthrough in the life of Helen Keller and others like her. He quotes in this connection Susan Schaller's description of such a breakthrough in the life of a 'wordless' deaf man named Ildefonso, who "in a flash of insight understood that everything had a name", and Schaller's account of how this "changed everything about his perception of the world" and how, as a result, he "discovered the communion of minds". (Tattersall 2012: 217).

The hypothesis that the idea of 'words' enabled the birth of symbolic cognition at some time between a hundred thousand and sixty thousand years ago fits in with the internal logic of semantic reconstruction. The prime SAY appears to be truly ancient (present already in the language of thought of chimps and the ancestral apes). While the chimpanzees cannot "say things with words", they can of course communicate – and they can even communicate about communicating, as in the case of so-called "attention getters", that is gestures conveying the message "I want to say something to you now".

For modern humans, the concept of SAYING something is so closely linked with the concept of WORDS, that it may take some effort to disentangle the two. Nonetheless modern humans, too, can sometimes "say something not with words", but with global gestures, winks, arrows in the ground, and so on. In the case of chimpanzees, saying things *not with words* is the only way, and obviously so it was for the LCAs. It was a limited way, but it represented an important step on the way to articulated thought and speech dependent on the idea of WORDS.

The prime THINK is likely to have emerged at Stage III; but perhaps it was only the emergence of PARTS at stage IV that enabled early humans to learn to break their complex thoughts and 'messages' into word-like components and to conceive the idea of WORDS. Furthermore, the dependence of the concept 'true' (present, as evidence suggests, in all human languages) on the concept of 'words' supports the hypothesis that the prime TRUE, apparently acquired at the latest stage of human cognitive evolution (that is, Stage VI) was building on the earlier emergence of the prime WORDS (at stage V).

As I will discuss further in Chapter 17, the debates about the emergence of "language" in evolutionary time are hampered by the variable and opaque use of the word *language*, which is neither self-explanatory nor universal. By contrast, the universal concept of WORDS allows us to obtain a greater clarity and precision in our attempts to date the emergence of human symbolic cognition than that afforded by the fuzzy and historically shaped English concept of 'language' – just as the universal concept THINK helps us to gain a greater clarity and precision in our attempts to pinpoint human cognitive uniqueness among primates than the fuzzy and English-specific notion of "the theory of mind". At the same time, both WORDS and THINK help free our account of the cognitive evolution of primates from LCA to modern humans from its entirely unnecessary conceptual dependence on one language among thousands: English.

PART FIVE

Breaking Down the Walls of the Prison

14

From Ordinary (Anglo) English to Minimal English

The idea that language is shaped by culture is not new. It was one of the central themes of the German reflection on language from Herder and Humboldt to Weisgerber and Spitzer, and it is alive to this day in the German intellectual tradition. Through the German immigrants Franz Boas and Edward Sapir, this idea was transplanted onto American soil, resulting in a strong linguistic and anthropological tradition that has survived the decades of Chomskyan dominance in linguistics, blind to culture and indifferent to meaning.

What *is* new in this book (and in its two predecessors, *English: Meaning and Culture* (2006a) and *Experience, Evidence and Sense: The hidden cultural legacy of English* (2010a)), is the thesis that like all other languages, English, too, is culturally shaped, and that this has profound consequences for today's globalizing and English-dominated world. I have amply illustrated the cultural shaping of English—especially in its dominant variety, which I have called "Anglo English"—in these two earlier books. In the present book, aimed at a wider audience, I have focused above all on the implications of the cultural legacy of English for today's English-dominated global discourse—in social sciences, psychology, philosophy, education, and, in many countries, in people's everyday thinking influenced by the English language.

In this chapter, which concludes Parts I to V of the book, I take these ideas a step further, illustrating them with some additional examples from contemporary thinking on moral themes, and introducing two twin concepts of "Basic Human" and "Minimal English."

In a book on "conditions of psychiatric interest" in human history and prehistory, psychiatrist and anthropologist Horacio Fabrega writes: "'Insanity,' 'madness' and 'mental illness' are terms with a long pedigree and heavy baggage in the cultural history of the West." In an effort to look at the phenomena in question afresh, Fabrega refrains from using not only pejorative terms like "insanity" and "madness," but even the seemingly more neutral term "mental illness":

> Conceptual and emotive dissonance raised by labels such as "madness," "insanity," "lunacy," and "mental illness" beclouds and mars efforts to study the phenomena referred to by such terms in more neutral ways. In other words, we seek to understand the phenomena with their heavy Western cultural baggage left out. (Fabrega, In press)

Fabrega's conscious attempt to look at human beings afresh and to "let go of inherited constructs" is as remarkable as it is rare in contemporary human sciences. As illustrated throughout this book, "inherited constructs" are part and parcel of the language we speak; and in the era of worldwide domination of English, constructs embedded in the English lexicon are often taken for granted in scientific discourse, where, to use Fabrega's words, they becloud the phenomena referred to, and mar efforts to understand them.

When the limitations and distortions imposed on "human understanding" by English-bound thinking are illustrated with a wide range of examples, reactions of Anglophone scholars differ. Some speak of a new insight, even a sense of revelation. Others, however (and we have seen examples of this in this book), fight such observations tooth and nail. "Basic color terms like "blue" are culture-bound? Basic emotion terms such as "anger"? Basic kinship terms such as "brother" or "sibling"? Basic social terms such as "reciprocity," "cooperation," and "fairness"? And not just culture-bound in some broad abstract sense (because science itself is a culture-bound enterprise, in a broad sense), but tied, specifically, to Anglo culture and English language?" This is totally unacceptable, protest more than a few psychologists, philosophers, and even anthropologists and linguists.

When the culture-dependent and historically contingent character of such concepts is shown (as it seems to me) in black-and-white, one common defensive strategy is to affirm that such concepts (which can be crucial to their defendants' theories) are *scientific* concepts, not to be confused with their vernacular English counterparts. As a further defensive strategy, it is often proposed that the relevant English words should be printed in scientific writings in capital letters, or better still, in capitalized initials, for example, not *anger* or *sadness,* but ANGER and SADNESS (cf. e.g., Griffiths 1997), not *white* and *red* but W and R (cf. e.g., Kay et al. 1997), not *cooperation,* but C (as in CP, "cooperation principle"), not reciprocity but REC (cf. e.g., Dalrymple et al. 1998).

Disguised in this way as "scientific" notions, English folk concepts live on in many areas of contemporary global science, serving as props for theories that depend on English words but are divorced from ordinary intuitive understanding of what these words mean, and thus unverifiable and seemingly immune to criticism.

This book puts forward the idea that ultimately, the basic criterion for intelligibility and thus intellectual validity of claims made in human sciences is their translatability—*salvo sensu*—into languages other than English. In particular, this book argues that if claims are made about "human nature" and the human condition that can only be stated in English, then such claims can tell us something about speakers of English, and the impact of English on their ways of thinking, but not really about human beings in general.

This criterion of translatability may not apply in natural sciences, interested in the structure of the external world (including the bodies of animals and humans), but it is important, I believe, in human sciences, interested in human thoughts, feelings, and values. It is worth recalling at this point Giambattista Vico's observations on the misguided emphasis on "knowledge of the external world as the paradigm of all knowledge," "the uncritical assimilation of the human world to the non-human," and "the vision (or mirage) of a single, integrated natural science of all there is" (Berlin 1976: 25; see chapter 10).

As evolutionary psychologist Merlin Donald said, words define reality for us. Scholars in humanities and social sciences are not exempt from this generalization; if they habitually think, speak, and write in English, English words such as *color, anger, fairness, mind, interaction, brother,* or *male* and *female* may come to "define reality" for them. Scholars working in natural and exact sciences are not in the same position, because they can rely, ultimately, on numbers rather than words. As Galileo put it, mathematics is the language of the physical world. It is not, however, the language of the human mind.

Thus, if the words that define reality for us—especially *human* reality—are English words shaped by history and culture, and if moreover we are not aware of this and take the "reality" as defined by them for granted, then our view of the world is slanted: the English words on which we rely most create a conceptual barrier between us and the speakers of other languages, and preclude a neutral, culture-independent perspective.

For example, Marc Hauser's claim that human beings have a "universal sense of right and wrong" (reflected in the title of his book, *Moral Minds: How Nature Designed our Universal Sense of Right and Wrong*) is not translatable into languages other than English, as it relies on the English-bound concepts of "sense," "right," and "wrong" (Wierzbicka 2006a, 2010). This doesn't mean, of course, that Hauser's intended meaning could not be rephrased in a way that would make it transferrable into other languages. After all, a title is just a title, and in choosing a title, the author has the right to aim at a rhetorical effect rather than complete intellectual clarity or accuracy. But then one would expect the intended meaning to be clarified in the body of the book. Yet Hauser doesn't go beyond the English-bound concepts "right" and "wrong" in the body of the book, either—maybe because he doesn't realize that they are English-bound (as is also the concept of "sense," in the relevant meaning of the word, see Wierzbicka 2010a), maybe because he doesn't think this matters. This book argues, however, that it matters a great deal.

Trying to rethink Hauser's conception in terms of universal concepts "good" and "bad," we could suggest the following formula:

A hypothesis about the main point of Marc Hauser's theory

in all places, many people think like this at some times:

"I can do something good, I can do something bad, I know this."

when people think like this, they can feel something because of this

But is this what Hauser really means? We can't be sure.

Let us consider, in turn, the conception of a philosopher who, in contrast to Hauser, takes a relativist view of such matters. In his book *Beyond Human Nature*, philosopher Jesse Prinz (2012: 312) acknowledges that "morality is widespread in humans," but emphasizes the "dramatic variation and fluidity in morality" (p. 328), arguing that "morality is not innate" (p. 328) but rather that "morality is learned" (p. 322).

What exactly does Prinz mean by "morality"? Opposing current theories that attribute some sort of "morality" to animals, and especially to chimpanzees, Prinz writes:

> There is no reason to infer an understanding of morality from the fact that chimps do things we might applaud. Some chimp kindness may be motivated by fear.... Much human decency has little to do with morality, so we shouldn't assume chimp decency is morally motivated. (p. 318-319)

Thus, Prinz seems willing to attribute to chimps "decency" and "kindness" but not "morality." Since he doesn't define any of these terms, seemingly crucial to his argument, it is difficult to be sure what he means. A possible clue to what he might mean comes from the word "motivated," which he uses repeatedly, and also from statements like the following: "There is a difference between doing something because you hate to see others suffer and doing it because it is right." But if that is what "morality" means for Prinz—"doing something because [you think] it is right"—then his conception is not only locked within the European tradition, with its key concepts "moral" and "morality," but more specifically, within the Anglo tradition, with its key concepts of "right" and "wrong."

We might note that in this respect at least, Prinz's thinking is similar to Hauser's: both rely, crucially, on the English concepts "right" and "wrong." But other aspects of their conceptual framework differ in some significant ways. Hauser, following the Anglo empiricist tradition (and the tradition of British moralists like Hutcheson and Hume), links "morality" with a particular "sense," that is, with something *felt* by the experiencer (cf. Wierzbicka 2010a, Chapter 7). Prinz, on the other hand, thinks in terms of "motivation" and conscious thinking (about what is "right" and what is "wrong").

Since many languages of the world don't have a word matching in meaning Hauser's and Prinz's key term "morality" (let alone "right" and "wrong") and since neither Hauser nor Prinz explain what they mean in simple and cross-translatable words, their claims cannot be translated into other languages.

Furthermore, it is not quite clear where exactly Prinz disagrees with "nativists" and "universalists" such as Hauser. Hauser describes human minds as "moral minds" and, as we have seen, attributes to people an innate "sense of right and wrong." Prinz, on the other hand, affirms that "morality is not innate." These two positions appear to be incompatible, but since neither author defines his key terms in simple and intuitively clear words, it is impossible to be sure of the extent and exact nature of their disagreements.

Here as elsewhere, the debate could be sharpened and clarified if the two positions were formulated in the simple and intuitively clear terms "good" and "bad," instead of complex, unclear, and English-bound words and phrases like "moral minds," "the sense of right and wrong," "decency," "kindness," and, last but not least, "altruism." Given the role that *altruism* plays in contemporary scientific discourse, including evolutionary psychology, ethics, and social sciences, this word deserves a special mention in the present context. A quote from Prinz can serve here, too, as an illustration:

> There are remarkable tales of altruism in the animal word. Rats will press a lever to help another rat in distress, vampire bats will regurgitate blood for unrelated bats...There is remarkable behavioural continuity between chimps and humans when it comes to pro-social behaviour. (p. 318)

Despite such "tales," for his own part, Prinz chooses to emphasize discontinuities between animals and humans as far as "pro-social behavior" is concerned (distancing himself from evolutionary biologists such as, for example, Frans de Waal). But what, exactly, does he mean by *altruism*, a word that he is willing to use about rats and vampire bats, as well as human beings? If "morality" is uniquely human but "decency" and "kindness" are shown also by chimps, and "altruism" by rats and bats, and if these words are neither defined nor used in a stable and consistent fashion, then it is hard to see how clear mutual understanding can be achieved between different participants in these debates, even if they all are Anglophone scholars. When it comes to speakers of languages other than English, including students in different countries who are learning about current debates through translation, the chances for achieving much understanding are, of course, even slimmer.

Hauser's "sense of right and wrong" suggests thoughts couched in terms of "knowing what is a good thing or a bad thing to do" rather than "wanting to do good things for others," as implied by much of the writing on evolutionary "altruism." Prinz's use of "motivation" (wanting to do the "moral" thing) also suggests a focus on "doing what [one thinks] is good" rather than "wanting to do good things for others" (his statements seem to suggest that the latter is sometimes more applicable to rats, bats, and chimps than to humans.) But the distinction between "wanting to do what [one thinks] is good" and "wanting to do good things for others" is usually blurred in the recent literature of evolutionary psychology and anthropology, and in fact, Prinz moves between the words "moral" and "pro-social" without any clear explanation of what he means by either.

As these examples illustrate, framing one's conception in cross-translatable terms can achieve several goals at once: it can liberate the theory from English-bound thinking, it can make it potentially intelligible to speakers of other languages, and it can ensure some clarity and precision in what exactly is being claimed. This paves the way for genuine debates rather than pseudo-debates where different writers argue past one another, each relying on basic terms that are sometimes different and sometimes identical, but always undefined.

Neither Prinz nor Hauser posit any substantive universals concerning human thinking about "good" and "bad." Prinz's view that "morality" is learned, not innate, is not inherently incompatible with the idea that there may be some human consensus on certain specific "moral norms," but he is at pains to deny this and to emphasize only the variability and "flexibility" of all norms. Hauser, on the other hand, speaks of an innate "moral grammar" but doesn't posit any specific norms as universal. On the other hand, some writers on "altruism" and on human evolution do appear to suggest certain areas of consensus among different human groups across time and space, along the lines of what from my perspective could be articulated as "it is good if people want to do good things for (some) other people" (cf. e.g., Harman 2010). Presumably, it could be argued that from an evolutionary point of view, "pro-social" thinking of this kind would make good sense. Such a generalization would seem consistent with what, for example, Fabrega (In press, p. 106) says about early humans:

> Contexts of behavior among individuals at the threshold of Upper Paleolithic social life were experiencing emerging categories of awareness of self, other, personal and social identity, and the value and disvalue of social commitment compared to selfish pursuits. It was behavioral milieus such as these which became emotionally and cognitively associated with scrutiny of oneself, one's situation, and the actions and belief psychologies of group members.

Thinking in evolutionary terms, one might even consider the following scenario. At some time in human prehistory, when our ancestors started to live in relatively small groups (rather than in large "hordes"), there may have emerged (in some places) "pro-social" and "proto-moral" thinking along the following lines:

[A] I live with many people
    these people do many good things for me
    it is good if I do some good things for these people

Drawing on Fabrega's (2012) discussion of the cognitive evolution of early humans, I would in fact suggest that the key evolutionary breakthrough in human "moral" thinking may be more faithfully represented in a fuller formula, reflecting early humans' "group thinking," along the following lines:

[B] I live with many people
    all these people are like one something
    I am one of these people
    these people do many good things for me
    it is good if I do some good things for these people

Speaking of early social and cultural psychology among "late hominins," Fabrega stresses both the emergence of the idea of self (and others) and "behavior pointing to a social self based on high group interdependence" (Ch. 3, p. 36). Formula [B] above is consistent, I think, with both these emphases.

This is all, needless to say, contested territory. The purpose of the present discussion is not to express particular views on the subject-matter as such, but to show that the debates on these matters can be sharpened and clarified if a more precise conceptual language is used. The prevailing language of evolutionary social sciences, with its heavy reliance on the undefined and variably used word *altruism* (cf. Goddard and Wierzbicka in press; Th. Dixon 2008) makes it difficult to see what exactly is being claimed by different scholars about the conceptual evolution of our species.

The evolutionary perspective on human cognition can be helpful for anyone interested in breaking out of the English-bound thinking common in contemporary social sciences. Even those scholars to whom conceptual constructs of modern English such as "cooperation," "politeness," "kindness," "reasonableness," and "fairness" seem to be common human concerns equally applicable to all cultures, may nonetheless agree that early hominins were more likely to think in simpler terms, such as NSM primes DO and WANT, THINK and KNOW, and GOOD and BAD.

Current discussions about "moral universals," "moral sense," "the sense of right and wrong," and "altruism" suffer from the same conceptual problems as discussions about "mental illness" noted by Fabrega: they carry with them a heavy cultural baggage, in some cases, Western (or European), and in others, Anglo/English. To reach a fresh and culture-independent perspective on this domain, so central to human interests and concerns, this heavy cultural baggage needs to be identified, and at times, set aside, at least as a thought experiment. One can, of course, choose to be nourished by the ideas that one has inherited from one's own cultural tradition, through the patterns of one's native language. But it is one thing to use distinctions and values embedded in one's language freely and consciously, and another, as the literary scholar David Parker (2004: 31) put it, to "get used by" them. At some times at least, we need to (in Fabrega's words), "let go of the inherited constructs" and search for "more clearly descriptive formulations (...) shorn of heavily freighted preconceptions" (Fabrega, In press, p. 3). This applies both to preconceptions entrenched in various prestigious scientific paradigms and to those embedded in the privileged language of contemporary science—English.

The historically shaped vocabulary of English can be a conceptual prison for those who absolutize it and never look at it from a historical and cross-linguistic perspective. No one stands in danger of such unwitting self-imprisonment more than those who place a boundless trust in Science as a guide to reality, including the reality of what goes on in human minds. A good example of such an attitude can be found in cognitive scientist Steven Pinker's book *The Language Instinct* (1994: 58):

> there is no scientific evidence that languages dramatically shape their speakers' ways of thinking. The idea that language shapes thinking seemed plausible when scientists were in the dark about how thinking works or even how to study it. Now that cognitive scientists know how to think about thinking, there is less of a temptation to equate it with language just because words are more palpable than thoughts.

More than a decade later, in his book *The Stuff of Thought,* Pinker (2007a: 132) speaks in pretty much the same tone, by and large dismissing, for example, psycholinguist Dan Slobin's research into "thinking-for-speaking" (i.e., thinking geared toward the particular language in which one's thoughts are going to be expressed). Slobin (2000: 107) wrote:

> One cannot verbalize experience without taking a perspective, and (...) the language being used favours particular perspectives. The world does not present "events" to be encoded in languages. Rather, in the process of speaking or writing, experiences are filtered through language into verbalized events.

Pinker accepts that "every language forces speakers to pay attention to certain aspects of the world" (p. 131), but not that "a lifelong habit of attending to certain distinctions and ignoring others" can have an effect on how they think. In particular, he is convinced that English speakers "have no trouble grasping the distinctions that some other languages make and English doesn't" and that "clearly we command these distinctions as we negotiate the social and physical world" (p. 150). Armed with this confidence that English speakers have no trouble grasping any distinctions drawn by other languages, Pinker shrugs Slobin's insight off: "It shouldn't be surprising that the effects of thinking-for-speaking or thinking itself are small at best" (ibid.).

The irony is that Pinker himself is arguably an example of someone whose thinking appears to be strongly influenced by his native language (English)—for example, when he interprets human evolution through the prism of the modern English concepts "violence" and "cooperation" (see Chapter 6), or when he characterizes the concept of "story"—a highly culture-specific conceptual artifact of English (Wierzbicka 2010b)—as a human universal and a product of evolutionary adaptation (Pinker 2007b).

I have tried to show in this book that modern English—the language on which most contemporary science and popular science relies—carries with it many ideas and assumptions that are culture-specific (in the words of the Australian writer David Malouf (2003), "made in England"), and that if one fails to recognize this, one can become conceptually imprisoned in English. If one is a victim of such (self-)imprisonment, one is disadvantaged in three different ways.

First, there is a wall between ourselves and other people: we cannot put ourselves, conceptually, in the shoes of someone whose conceptual categories are different from ours and who doesn't think in terms of categories like "color," "river," "brother," "depression," "cooperation," "fairness," "story,", "mind" or "right" and "wrong." We tell ourselves that if such fundamental (as it seems to us) categories are absent from their lexicons, surely they must be present in their thinking: after all (we reassure ourselves), the absence of a word does not prove the absence of a concept. At the same time, we remain blind to conceptual categories which *are* constructed through the lexicons of other languages and assume that they must correspond to our own.

Second, one gets a slanted picture of what it is to be human: one may not see that the givens of human life, recognized, evidence suggests, in all languages, include being born, living for some time, and dying; having a body, and being able to think, feel, want, and know; and at the same time, we may imagine that they include certain things that in fact are conceptual artifacts of the English language and Anglo culture, such as, for example, "having a mind," being "male" or "female," and "having a sense of right and wrong."

Third, one cannot understand *oneself*: one takes one's own conceptual categories and cultural scripts for granted, one doesn't appreciate their distinct character, shaped by a unique history and culture, and consequently, one cannot get an insight into what it is to be an "Anglo"—a bearer of a particular culture and an inhabitant of a particular conceptual and cultural universe.

None of this means that evidence from cross-linguistic and cross-cultural semantics corroborates postmodernist claims such as those of which the doyen of modern anthropology, Clifford Geertz, wrote:

> Postmodernists have questioned whether ordered accounts of other ways of being in the world—accounts that offer monological, comprehensive, and all-too-coherent explanations—are credible at all, and whether we are not so imprisoned in our own modes of thought and perception as to be incapable of grasping, much less crediting, those of others. (Geertz 2000: 102)

Nor does cross-linguistic semantics lend any support to the intellectual trends of which historian and philosopher Felipe Fernandez Armesto (1998: 194) wrote:

No development of our times is more terrifying to those who hope to sustain the truth or revive it than the breakdown of confidence in the power of language to express it. Any certainties left unscathed by other disciplines have been declared inexpressible by philosophers of language. (...) We are left with dumbstruck tongues and hands too numb to write, despairing of ever saying anything true because language is trapped in self-reference, unable to reach reality, never expressing truth and, at best, only able to 'represent' it.

Like Geertz and Fernandez Armesto, I do not believe that we are imprisoned in our own modes of thought and perception and are incapable of grasping those of others, or of ever reaching reality and expressing truth. To the extent to which our thoughts can be translated, without distortion, into languages of other people, we can make them intelligible to speakers of other languages, and vice versa; and we can say many things that are true regardless of the language in which they are being said.

I do, nonetheless, believe that neither truth nor understanding can be reached, in all areas, through complex English. English is one language among many, and like other languages, it bears the imprints of its users. At the same time, evidence suggests that, like other languages, English includes a core that is free of such imprints and can therefore be used for talking about the world in culture-independent ways.

Despite my critique of Pinker, I am not against the idea of a "language instinct" in the sense of our innate capacity for language: both the culturally shaped language of one's local community (such as, in the case of Anglophone societies, the historically shaped "maxi English"), and the local version of the universal language of the mind (such as, in the case of English speakers, the "mini-English" embodied in NSM English). If these two varieties of English, "maxi" and "mini," are distinguished, then English does not need to be a conceptual prison for anyone. On the contrary, in its "mini" version, which in the title of this chapter I have called "Minimal English," it can serve, whenever needed and appropriate, as a common auxiliary inter-language for speakers of different languages, and a global means for clarifying, elucidating, storing, and comparing ideas.[1] Such a mini-version of English, trimmed to the bone and detached from the culture-specific conceptual heritage of "Anglo English," can, I believe, fulfill a vital role in the globalized and English-dominated world.

I have called the mini-language derived from English but matching the mini-languages hidden within all the languages of the world, "Minimal English," to emphasize the aspect of radical reduction, linguistic and cultural. Thus, Minimal English is not another simplified version of English analogous to Ogden's 1930 "Basic English" or Jean-Paul Nerrière's "Globish" (2004), both pruned for practical purposes but not reduced to the bare essentials. Building a semiartificial language that matches the lowest common denominator of all languages is an entirely different undertaking.

The mini-language described here as Minimal English is not a simplified English, "basic" and "decaffeinated" (as the English writer Robert McCrum (2010) describes Nerrière's "Globish").[2] Rather than being a form of "Basic English," it is, essentially, the English version of "Basic Human," with its minimal vocabulary matching the full repertoire of shared human concepts.

The vocabulary of Ogden's Basic English includes 850 words (and in its expanded versions, 2,000) and that of Nerrière's "Globish"—1,500. The great majority of the words on these two lists do not have matching equivalents in most languages of the world, and some carry meanings that are highly English-specific (for example, Ogden's "suggestion" and "science," or Nerrière's "fairness"). Neither Ogden nor Nerrière aimed at identifying a minimal set of words with counterparts in many (let alone all) languages, and in fact they were not looking at English from a cross-linguistic perspective at all.

By contrast, "Basic Human" includes not much more than a hundred words: on present estimates, less than seventy semantic primes, "hardwired" in the human mind (such as "someone" and "something," "do" and "happen," and "good" and "bad") and no more than thirty universal semantic molecules (such as "man," "woman," and "child," "mother" and "father," "hands," "water," and "fire"). All these words have been located through extensive cross-linguistic investigations.

Given such a skeletal lexicon, "Basic Human" cannot be an all-purpose practical global means of communication. It can be, however, a global lingua franca for the elucidation of ideas and explanation of meanings—and not only in scholarship but also in international relations, politics, business, ethics, education, and indeed in any context where it is important to explain precisely what one means.

In an article entitled "Moving political meaning across linguistic frontiers," political scientist Richard Collin (2011) writes: "Diplomacy, international commerce, and the academic study of international relations are all based on the assumption that we can cross linguistic borders with very complicated words and concepts in our cognitive luggage" (see Chapter 16). As I see it, in this one sentence Collin puts his finger on the central problem in many areas of today's global English-based communication: the assumption that one can cross linguistic and conceptual borders by relying on complex (but seemingly ordinary) English words and concepts.

This is the key difference between words of "ordinary" (Anglo) English, such as *fairness, mind, cooperation*, and *moral sense*, and words of Minimal English, such as *do* and *the same*, *think* and *know*, or *good* and *bad*. Obviously, the language of international negotiations, discussions, and debates cannot be limited to Minimal English, but if full mutual understanding is to be achieved, it cannot be limited to "ordinary (Anglo) English," either. As an auxiliary language of explanation and elucidation of key points across language barriers, Minimal English, which is culture-independent, can fulfill a role that a simplified form of Anglo English (such as Basic English, Globish, Plain English, or so-called Simplified English) cannot.

In his introduction to a volume entitled *Universals of Human Thought*, philosopher Ernest Gellner (1981) wrote: "Unconvertible currencies are not suitable for trade." A key characteristic of Minimal English is that (unlike Basic English or any other reduced form of English) it is fully convertible.

Theoretically, a mini-version of any language (Russian, Chinese, Arabic, etc.) could fulfill such an auxiliary function; but given the realities of today's globalizing world, at this point it is obviously a mini-English that is the most practical way out (or down) from the conceptual tower of Babel that the cultural evolution of humankind has erected, for better or for worse.

Thus, this book is not an attempt (futile as it obviously would be) to dethrone English in contemporary scholarship and other areas of global communication (as, for example, Robert Phillipson's 1992 book *Linguistic Imperialism* apparently was). It is, however, an attempt to dethrone English as the putative language of human cognition, hardwired in the human mind and, as van Brakel (1994: 188) ironically put it, "the pinnacle of the evolution of naming of the structure of the experiential world."

There are good reasons for a mini-English to be, in today's world, the paramount auxiliary language of interpretation, explanation, and intercultural communication. There are no good reasons, however, for historically shaped Anglo English to be treated as the voice of Truth and Human Understanding. This book argues that it is time for many areas of human sciences and other English-based fields of activity to set about breaking down the walls of the conceptual prison that they have unwittingly built themselves by their parochial and ahistorical Anglocentrism. And it seeks to shows how it can be done.

PART SIX

Kindred Thinking
Across Disciplines

PRELIMINARY REMARKS

The main message of this book—that much of contemporary research in the social sciences needs to liberate itself from an excessive conceptual dependence on English—will not necessarily be welcome in all quarters. For many linguists who have had occasion to hear this message but have preferred to ignore it, it may prove irritating; and for many scholars outside linguistics who have not previously heard it, it may come across as idiosyncratic.

It is important for the author, therefore, to point out that she is not actually as isolated as it may seem. The NSM program of research is unique in proposing a solution to the problem but not in the recognition that there *is* a problem. This final part of the book looks at the work of scholars who have either explicitly or implicitly acknowledged the danger of Anglocentrism in the contemporary social sciences and who recognize the cultural shaping of all languages (including English) as well as the existence of a universal shared core.This final part of the book seeks to be broadly based and to let voices from a range of disciplines be heard, including anthropology, psychology, philosophy, and evolutionary social science, as well as linguistics. Some of the scholars to be cited here refer explicitly to the NSM program and its practitioners, while others don't. Needless to say, they don't all agree on every point with either myself and my colleagues, or with each other. As the numerous quotes adduced in this part testify, however, there is a great deal of convergent thinking among those chosen here to represent a variety of disciplines.

15

Anthropology, Psychology, Psychiatry

Robin Horton: A View from Cultural Anthropology

Robin Horton, a British anthropologist working in Africa, devoted his life to the study of African thought patterns in the context of a broader inquiry into the history and sociology of thought, science, and religion. In his book *Patterns of Thought in Africa and the West: Essays on Magic, Religion and Science* (1993), Horton explores the contrasts between Africa and "the West," as well as the shared core of the two, which, he surmises, is likely to be universal. He characterizes this shared core as "primary theory," "coeval with Man himself" and "the product of the period of accelerated gene-culture coevolution" among early humans (p. 11). On the basis of that universal and presumably innate "primary theory," every language and culture develops its own "secondary theory." "Whereas there is a remarkable degree of cross-cultural uniformity about the way the world is portrayed by primary theory, there is an equally remarkable degree of cross-cultural variation in the way it is portrayed by secondary theory." (p. 121)

Horton characterizes "primary theory" as follows:

> Primary theory gives the world a foreground filled with middle-sized (say between a hundred times as large and a hundred times as small as human beings), enduring, solid objects. These objects are inter-related, indeed inter-defined, in terms of a 'push-pull' conception of causality, in which spatial and temporal contiguity are seen as crucial to the transmission of change. They are related spatially in terms of five dichotomies: 'left/right'; 'above/below'; 'in-front-of/behind'; 'inside/outside'; 'contiguous/separate.' And temporally in terms of one trichotomy: 'before/at the same time/ after.' Finally, primary theory makes two major distinctions amongst its objects: first, that between human beings and other objects; and second, among human beings, that between self and others. (p. 121)

This description of the pan-human interpretive framework, which "provides the cross-cultural voyager with the intellectual bridgehead" (ibid.), is, in the main, remarkably consistent with the corresponding parts of the NSM picture of the "naïve" human physics and metaphysics.

I have used the word "metaphysics" here advisedly, to signal my agreement with Horton's objection to Bernard Russell's denigration of ordinary human ways of thinking and speaking as "Stone Age Metaphysics."

> At this point, we can truly appreciate both the aptness and the irony of Russell's famous characterization of 'Ordinary Language' as 'Stone Age Metaphysics.' With this striking phrase, he was one of the first to draw attention to the fact that 'Ordinary Language,' far from being a 'Neutral Observation Language,' embodied a theory like any other, and an ancient and in many respects outmoded one at that, tailored as it was to age-old and rather limited human capabilities and interests. Russell, however, used the characterization as a means of denigrating 'Ordinary Language' and of pouring ridicule on those philosophers who devoted their lives to studying it. What he failed to consider was the possibility that, through the operation of evolutionary processes at the dawn of human history, 'Stone Age Metaphysics' had left an indelible imprint on the human brain. If indeed it has left such an imprint, then, like it or not, we are stuck with it. (Horton 1993: 326-7)

Speaking from the vantage point of empirical cross-linguistic semantics, we can say that "Stone Age Metaphysics" of the kind sketched by Horton has also left an indelible imprint on all human languages. Horton's speculative universals such as "above" and "below," "inside," and "before," "after" and "at the same time," have been confirmed in empirical cross-linguistic investigations as lexically present in all sampled languages (ABOVE, BELOW, INSIDE, BEFORE, AFTER, AT THE SAME TIME). Some of the dichotomies posited by Horton require, from an NSM point of view, some adjustments, but the universal semantic prime SIDE and universally available composite concepts such as "on one side" and "on the other side" come very close to Horton's suggested concepts "left/right," and the prime TOUCH, to Horton's dichotomy "contiguous/separate." The universal primes PEOPLE, I, SOMEONE, and OTHER are also highly consistent with Horton's ideas.

Horton's basic premise is that "the same foundational universals provide us with the crucial 'bridgehead' through which to gain understanding of the thought of other people and other cultures" (p. 381). Consequently, from his point of view, explanations of non-Western patterns of thought should be based on universal concepts, not on concepts drawn from the anthropologist's own language and culture.

This means, in effect, that a quest for understanding non-Western (or, more specifically, African) ways of thinking is inseparable from an effort to understand ways of thinking embedded in one's own language and culture (in

Horton's case, specifically, English language and Anglo-American culture). Thus (commenting on his own scholarly journey), Horton writes: "the scholar in quest of the appropriate translation instruments for African religious thought had to be prepared to enquire deeply into the intentions and structures embodied in various areas of Western discourse. This meant his spending a lot of time and effort in activities which were similar to or even indistinguishable from those of the analytic philosopher whose primary concern was with Western discourse." (p. 2)

This is reminiscent of Sapir's observation that "To a far greater extent than the philosopher has realized, he is likely to become the dupe of his speech forms, which is equivalent to saying that the mould of his thoughts, which is typically a linguistic mould, is apt to be projected into his conception of the world" (1949: 157). Sapir adds that "the philosopher needs to understand language, if only to protect himself against his own language habits" (1949: 165). Horton addresses a similar warning to his fellow anthropologists, who in his view may tend to impose the "secondary theory" of their own language and culture on "indigenous ways of seeing things" or "what American anthropologists like to call the 'emic' aspect."

Referring in particular to anthropological studies of religious life and religious thought in Africa, he writes:

> Especially where Western colleagues based in Western universities are concerned, it seems to me that although the emic aspect may be very vivid to them when they are in the field, it tends to lose its hold over them on their return to the groves of Western academe, to be replaced by pseudo-emic visions more congruent with the latter's world-view. The reality of the spirits is apt to fade, to be replaced by visions of people engaging in elaborately veiled power-plays, composing secular poetry, or participating in complicated semeiological parlour games. (Horton 1993: 386).

Horton is an anthropologist, not a linguist, and his scholarly objectives are, of course, different from those of NSM researchers. At the same time, however, his emphasis that "comparisons between (...) thought-systems required a standard, universally-current medium" (p. 2) and that "a culture-bound label is of no use in cross-cultural comparisons" (p. 32) matches the central themes of the NSM research program: that cross-cultural comparisons between thought systems require a standard universal conceptual currency, that such currency can be found in the "Stone Age Metaphysics" imprinted in human brains and languages, and that culture-bound labels of academic English cannot reveal indigenous ways of seeing things or lead to genuine cross-cultural understanding.

Richard Shweder: A View from Cultural Psychology

Like Horton, Richard Shweder is a cultural anthropologist. His special interest, however, is the relationship between cultures and psyches, and so he often
identifies his type of anthropology as "cultural psychology." For example, his
1991 book *Thinking Through Cultures* bears the subtitle "Expeditions in cultural psychology." Shweder's emphasis is on the diversity of cultures and culturally shaped psyches, but the question of diversity is closely linked for him with
questions about "human nature" and the "psychic unity of humankind" (which
is, as he says, "one of the central themes of *Thinking Through Cultures,*" p. 2):

> The problem presents itself to anthropologists and other students of
> cultural psychology in the following form: What inferences about human
> nature are we to draw from the apparent diversity of human conceptions
> of reality, and what justification is there for our own conceptions of reality
> in the light of that apparent diversity? (p. 3)

As the quote indicates, there are in fact three central questions in Shweder's
conception of "thinking through cultures": human diversity, human unity,
and the status of one's own conceptions of reality. In Shweder's case, "one's
own" means, primarily, those of a twentieth-/twenty-first-century Anglophone
American anthropologist.

Richard Shweder is a kindred spirit for NSM researchers because, like them,
he stands both for human diversity and (properly interpreted) human unity. He
emphatically rejects the claims that "all differences [between peoples] are merely
apparent, or superficial, or idiomatic" and that deep down, "that faraway place
that seemed so different, is not so different after all" (1991: 4). And yet, he says,
this insistence on genuine and profound differences between cultures cannot
mean that the other is fundamentally alien. "Others are not fundamentally alien
to us, just inconsistently and importantly different in their conception of things
(as expressed in their texts, in their discourse, in their institutions, in their per-
sonalities) from our conception of things, at the moment." (Shweder 1991: 5).

The qualifying phrase "at the moment" emphasizes the contingency of
"our own" conception of the world, as do the references to "our prejudices."
Yet it is precisely because we tend to take our own culture's prejudices for
granted that we are able to get astonished when we are confounded by other
cultures. Thus, the essays in the volume are variations on the themes:

> that our prejudices make it possible for us to see; that traditions not only
> obscure but also illuminate; that our differences make us real; the freeing
> of consciousness goes hand in hand with feeling "astonished" by the vari-
> ety of ways there are to see and to be. In other words, reason and objectiv-
> ity are not in opposition to tradition, and they do not lift us out of custom
> and folk belief. (Shweder 1991: 8)

The important thing, then, is to learn to get astonished at our own culture. The world of [the Indian mother-goddess] Kali is astonishing to a secular Anglophone social scientist, but "thinking through cultures" may lead one to see one's own cultural world as equally astonishing. "Or perhaps what is most truly astonishing of all is that when 'thinking through cultures' there is no place else, no mental place, for us to stand." (Shweder 1991: 23)

Like Horton, Shweder is an anthropologist, not a linguist, so naturally language is not at the center of his attention to the degree it must be for NSM researchers. Nonetheless, he is deeply aware of the dangers of Anglocentrism facing those who take the lexical categories of their own native language for granted and regard them as a neutral place from which to interpret and compare categories embedded in other languages.

Shweder has pursued this idea in particular in relation to emotions (see, e.g., Shweder 1994, 2004, 2012b). For example, in *The Handbook of Emotion* he and his coauthors stress that in writing about human emotions, there is a constant danger of "assimilating them in misleading ways to an a priori set of lexical items available in the language of the researcher" (Shweder et al. 2008: 424). In presenting these ideas, Shweder has often referred to my own work and that of Cliff Goddard. For example, in his 2004 paper "Deconstructing the Emotions for the Sake of Comparative Research," he wrote:

> Wierzbicka and Goddard have argued that the complex mental states referred to with the English words for "emotions" (words such as "sadness," "envy," "guilt" or "love") should be theoretically decomposed into more elementary mental processes such as wanting, knowing, feeling, and evaluating things as good or not good. They have suggested that the ideas of "thinking," "feeling," "wanting," "knowing," and evaluating things as "good" (or not "good") are semantically simple, intuitively obvious, readily available universal folk concepts, which is why those ideas have been found by linguists to be natural language "primes." (Shweder 2004: 82)

Shweder emphasizes the convergence of NSM with his own thinking: "A cognate argument can be found in some of my own writings in cultural psychology (e.g., Shweder 1994, Shweder and Haidt 2000)" (Shweder 2004: 82). From an NSM point of view, as well as Shweder's, what applies to emotions applies also to various other areas of human psychology: lexical items from different languages don't match in meaning, and using English labels for describing other people's psyches always carries with it the danger of Anglocentric distortion. Thus, referring to my cross-cultural work on emotions, Shweder made (as early as 1994) a more general comment:

> Undoubtedly most anthropologists will appreciate Wierzbicka's sensitivity to the all too often glossed over problem of translation. In my own experience the mapping of lexical items across languages has always seemed especially

hazardous when it comes to the characterization of psychological states, in part because of the way culture and psyche are interdependent and make each other up…to adequately understand the meaning of the terms in either language is to understand a good deal about different local systems of values and particular ways of life (1994: 33)

The point is made even more emphatically in Shweder's 2004 paper, where it is suggested that the NSM primes WANT, FEEL, KNOW, GOOD, and BAD can be seen as fundamental to mental life of peoples in all cultures. In his most recent work, Shweder is willing to accept the NSM mental primes WANT, FEEL, KNOW, and THINK and the evaluative primes GOOD and BAD, as a basis for comparative research in cultural psychology in general.

> Informed in part by Anna Wierzbicka's (1999) corpus of research in which she nominates certain concepts as universally available across all cultural traditions, I am quite willing to conduct interpretive research on cultural differences in human mentalities relying on a theory of mind that presumes that all normal human beings wherever you go in the world want things, know things, feel things, and value things (as good or bad) and think about the things they want, know, feel, and value. (Shweder 2012b: 383)

As the quotes adduced here illustrate, for Shweder—as for NSM researchers—a crucial question is (as he put it in his 2013 commentary on my paper "Translatability and the scripting of other peoples' souls"): How can we "do comparative research without ethnocentrism?" Emphasizing the affinity between his own approach and that of NSM researchers, he applies to the NSM program the words of the French anthropologist Louis Dumont:

> The oneness of the human species, however, does not demand the arbitrary reduction of diversity to unity—it only demands that it should be possible to pass from one particularity to another, and that no effort should be spared in order to elaborate a common language in which each particularity can be adequately described. The first step to that end consists in recognizing differences. (Dumont 1970: 249).

While combining notes of generous endorsement with a note of skepticism and "some concerns (…) about the limits of the Natural Semantic Metalanguage approach," Shweder refers to Dumont's words as follows:[1]

> Very few anthropologists have systematically taken up that challenge, which requires one to be a universalist without reducing diversity to uniformity. Anna Wierzbicka's Natural Semantic Metalanguage is a monumental and heroic attempt to take up the challenge. It deserves to be seriously engaged by all cultural anthropologists. (ibid.)

Richard Shweder is an important ally of the NSM program. His emphasis that "the knowable world is incomplete if seen from one point of view" and that "the view from only here (. . .) [is] ethnocentric" (2003: 6) deeply resonates with the main theme of *Imprisoned in English.*

Roy D'Andrade: A View from Cognitive Anthropology

Roy D'Andrade is an eminent cognitive anthropologist and one of the acknowledged leaders of the "cognitive revolution" of the 1950s and 1960s. As Richard Shweder (2012a: 2) recently noted, early on, D'Andrade (together with fellow cognitive anthropologist A. Kimball Romney) organized "an influential interdisciplinary conference (. . .) which was published as a special issue of the *American Anthropologist* as 'Transcultural Studies in Cognition'" (Romney & D'Andrade, 1964).

As Shweder further notes (ibid.), "By 1980 Roy D'Andrade was a major voice (arguably *the* major voice) for cognitive studies within anthropology (see D'Andrade 1995)." In this connection, Shweder quotes D'Andrade's talk of March 14, 1980 (given at a planning meeting for an international conference on "symbols and meanings"), in which he commented on the origins of the "cognitive revolution" as follows:

> Before 1957 the definition of culture was primarily a behavioral one—culture was patterns of behavior, actions and customs. The same behavioral emphasis was there in linguistics and psychology. The idea that cognition is where it's at struck all three fields at the same time. (. . .) I think it was a nice replacement. But the thing is now breaking—that force set in motion in the late fifties. And I feel it is breaking in psychology, it's breaking in linguistics, and it's breaking in anthropology.

The reason why "the thing" [the anti-behaviorist cognitive revolution] was breaking was that it was felt that this revolution was, as Shweder describes it, hijacked by "cognitive science" dominated by "brain scientists," "process oriented experimental psychologists," "artificial intelligence researchers," and other scholars uninterested in the study of cultural and linguistic diversity. By contrast, for D'Andrade—as for Shweder himself—cognitive researchers ought to be interested not only in the discovery of universal "laws of thought" and in people's language- and culture-independent "thought processes," but also in "the actual content of their goals, values, and pictures of their world" (Shweder 2012a: 1), that is, "in the study of mental things (what people know, think, feel, and want, and value as good or bad) as one way of understanding what people and peoples habitually or customarily do within and across cultural groups" (Shweder 2012a: 8).

This was the perspective from which D'Andrade viewed the past and present of his discipline in his 1995 book *The Development of Cognitive Anthropology,* in which there were many references to NSM research. For the most part, these references are sympathetic, but support is mixed with reservations. D'Andrade presents a much stronger endorsement of the NSM program in his more recent work published in *Cross-Cultural Research* (2001), where he writes:

> Over the past 25 years, a strong case has been made by Anna Wierzbicka that a small number of universal concepts are found as lexical items in all languages (Wierzbicka, 1972, 1992). Wierzbicka argued that these words are conceptual *primes* or *primitives* that form the basic units from which all other concepts are constructed. Wierzbicka's goal is to construct a simple, clear, universal semantic metalanguage, a language made up of the ordinary little words that everyone knows. Wierzbicka's universal metalanguage offers a potential means to ground all complex concepts in ordinary language and translate concepts from one language to another without loss or distortion in meaning. The idea of developing a universal metalanguage has often been proposed by philosophers and linguists. Wierzbicka's work is the most thorough and complete working out of this agenda to date. (D'Andrade 2001: 246)

It is interesting to note D'Andrade's references to Cliff Goddard's critique of the use of complex technical English terms in social sciences. Thus, reproducing the inventory of NSM primes, he writes:

> As an aside, an interesting use of Wierzbicka's natural semantic metalanguage is to construct clear definitions for technical terms in the social sciences. For example, using Wierzbicka's metalanguage, Goddard (1998) critiqued writers who present definitions that are more complex semantically than the original term to be defined.

In D'Andrade's opinion, NSM offers a helpful tool for defining, explaining, and comparing shared ideas, meanings, and folk knowledge in cross-cultural cognitive research:

> If one defined culture as shared ideas/meanings/knowledge/understandings, then these shared ideas must either be composed of indefinable prime terms or they must be composed of chunks made up of prime terms. To the extent that Wierzbicka has succeeded in finding a universal metalanguage, all cultural ideas/meanings/knowledge/understandings are definable within this metalanguage. (D'Andrade 2001: 248)

D'Andrade takes up the metaphor of "semantic atoms" and "semantic molecules," which has, over the years, played a key role in NSM-thinking.

Wierzbicka's universal terms are analogous to the atoms of the physical world (unfortunately, use of this analogy seems to annoy many anthropologists). Of the enormous number of combinations of these terms that make up the sentences that correspond to the possible ideas/meanings/knowledge/understandings of a person, some are cultural—that is, are intersubjectively shared by collectives within a society. Just as more than a hundred kinds of atoms can combine into more than 20 million kinds of molecules, so the 50 or more universal concepts can combine into hundreds of thousands of ideas. This puts the anthropologist who knows and is able to use the Natural Semantic Metalanguage in the same position as the chemist who knows about atoms (...).

D'Andrade goes on to emphasize that "most of the actual things in the world are molecules, and it is their properties that one wants to investigate (...) knowledge about atoms is helpful to the chemist only because it helps in understanding the nature of molecules (...) A few simple elements can be chunked or combined into a huge variety of complex things" (D'Andrade 2001: 249). D'Andrade is using the word "molecules" here to refer to all the complex meanings that are of special interest to the anthropologist (e.g., in the domain of values, emotions, kinship, categorization, or religion). This is, in fact, what the bulk of ongoing NSM research consists in. As noted by the evolutionary anthropologist Doug Jones (1999: 560), "much of the work of this [NSM] school consists of showing how secondary, cultural-specific concepts can be defined by composing sentences using the conceptual primitives and a simplified version of natural language syntax."

Gananath Obeyesekere and Christopher Dowrick: a View from Anthropological and Clinical Psychiatry

In his essay "Depression, Buddhism, and the Work of Culture" anthropologist Gananath Obeyesekere quotes a description of "depression" by two American psychiatrists, Brown and Harris (1978), commenting: "This statement sounds strange to me, a Buddhist, for if it was placed in the context of Sri Lanka, I would say that we are not dealing with a depressive but a good Buddhist" (1985: 134). In a nutshell, the problem is that from a Buddhist point of view, hopelessness lies in the nature of the world and salvation lies in understanding and accepting one's personal miseries as part of the nature of existence in general.

Obeyesekere asks: "How is the Western diagnostic term 'depression' expressed in a society whose predominant ideology of Buddhism states that life is suffering and sorrow...?" (p. 135). He acknowledges that symptoms of "depression" as described by Western psychiatrists do occur in Sri Lanka, and he agrees that "on one level it is possible to prove that depression in its various forms is universal" (p. 136). Noting that the symptoms of depression as defined in the successive editions of the *Diagnostic and Statistical Manual* of the American Psychiatric Association "seem to exist everywhere even if culture bound," Obeyesekere questions nonetheless the orthodox conclusion that "depression in its Western sense is a disease universally present" (ibid.). Above all, he draws attention to the problematic nature of the language in which the phenomena in question are conceptualized and described:

> One of the problems of contemporary psychiatric methodology is the assumption that the language that expresses "depressive affects" can be (...) operationalized. Yet the attempt to give operational specificity to the vocabulary of emotion is to destroy what is integral to that form of speech. (...) Furthermore, and I specifically refer here to the vocabulary of suffering and despair, that speech is linked to specific traditions, such as those of Buddhism and Christianity. It is almost impossible for a Sinhala person to use words expressing sorrow without articulating them in the Buddhist tradition. (p. 144)

Obeyesekere makes three important observations in this connection: first, that even technical or semi-technical English medical terms such as "depression" derive from certain folk concepts of ordinary English; second, that in countries associated historically with Christianity, certain aspects of vocabulary may reflect Christian ways of thinking; and third, that in order to understand indigenous conceptualizations of "suffering" and "sorrow" in places with a long Buddhist tradition, such as Sri Lanka or India, one would need, above all, to grasp the meaning of indigenous words, including Buddhist terms such as *sōkaya* (roughly, "sadness or sorrow"), *kampanaya* (roughly, "the shock of loss"), *dukkha* (roughly, "suffering"), *kalakirírma* (roughly, "a sense of hopelessness or despair with life"), and so on—all directly or indirectly colored by Buddhism.

Referring in particular to a study of "mental disorders" in an Indian village by Carstairs and Kapur (1976), Obeyesekere comments:

> can these terms from ordinary English-language use be transferred to designate entities expressed in another language? A reverse procedure may be more justifiable, that is, formulating a list of psychiatric terminology employed in the native language and then seeking appropriate terms or phrases in English.
> Furthermore, though the authors claim to construct a value-free instrument, are not Western theoretical and commonsense notions implicit in psychiatric terminology such as "depression" (no. 15) (...), "phobia" (no. 14), "delusions" (no. 24) and especially "pathological worrying" (no. 20)?

Indeed: terms coming from ordinary English, even if somewhat "technicalized," carry with them a particular culturally shaped perspective, and the same applies to native terms from Sinhala or Kota. If we want to grasp what the Sinhalese or the Kota understandings of phenomena comparable to "depression," "suffering," and "hopelessness" are, the first thing to do is to find out the exact meaning of the relevant terms in these languages.

But how is this to be done? Obeyesekere suggests that we should seek appropriate terms or phrases in English—and this, too, is an excellent point, as long as by "appropriate terms or phrases" we don't mean lexical equivalents, because, as he notes himself, words like *dukkha* or *kalakirirma* don't have lexical equivalents in English, just as English words like *depression* or *delusion* don't have lexical equivalents in Sinhalese or Kota.

Obeyesekere doesn't discuss in detail where such appropriate words or phrases can be found in English. However, British clinical psychiatrist Christopher Dowrick, in his book *Beyond Depression* (2004), takes up Obeyeskere's theme and points to the Natural Semantic Metalanguage as one possible solution to the problem.[2] Drawing on an ethnographic study of sixteen women of Asian backgrounds living in London (Fenton and Sadiq 1993), Dowrick acknowledges the importance of the fact that words that speakers of English take for granted, like *depression*, "do not translate readily into other languages and cultures" (p. 122).

But Dowrick goes further than that and stresses that it is not just a matter of specific words that don't match across language and culture boundaries: "It is more that different cultures and languages are constructed in such different ways that there may be no room for a concept like depression, rendering it virtually meaningless." (p. 123) Concurring with Obeyesekere, Dowrick notes, with reference to Anglophone psychiatry, that "our decision to afford depression that status of a diagnosis may derive not so much from our scientific knowledge as from our system of values" (p. 12).

Instead of relying on conceptual categories embedded in English words like *depression*, "it may be safer to start from some simple premises which seem to have validity across cultures, some universal describable categories of human experience from which culturally-derived emotions may emerge" (Dowrick 2004: 130). In this context, Dowrick discusses the NSM-based approach to emotions developed in my 1999 book *Emotions Across Languages and Cultures: Diversity and Universals* and emphasizes the usefulness of NSM-based components such as "something bad is happening to me," "I don't want this," and "I feel something bad because of this" to psychiatric understanding of patients regardless of their cultural background.

Rom Harré: A View from Psychology and Philosophy of Science

In one of the introductory chapters of *Psychology for the Third Millennium*, edited by philosopher of science Rom Harré and psychologist Fathali Moghaddam, Rom Harré (2012: 22) writes:

Methods of research in the cultural/discursive psychology that partners neuroscience in hybrid psychology are focused on the way people use symbolic systems in thinking and acting. We now know that such systems are also involved at a very fundamental level in the way people feel and what they perceive in other people and in the world around them. The most deeply studied of these systems is language.

There is a great diversity of languages and each is the bearer of core features of the culture in which it is used as a major instrument for managing everyday life. Each language is the bearer of a distinctive psychology. The way the users of particular languages think, act, feel and perceive is shaped by their cultural inheritance, of which a major component is their mother tongue.

In contrast to many other philosophers and psychologists, Harré has no doubt that what applies to other people's mother tongue applies also to his own, English; and he sees "the implicit psychology" of English as an important part of the "psychology for the third millennium."

This is an unusual statement for a textbook on psychology. Harré has no doubt about the dominant role of English in today's world and today's science, but this doesn't prevent him from recognizing that, like any other language, English, too, has an "implicit psychology" which is a cultural and historical creation of the past generations of its speakers.

As we set out the implicit psychology of one form of English, roughly middle-class Anglo-American, we will draw attention to some of the ways other languages differ from it in their implicit psychologies. It is not our intention to privilege English as a source of cognitive standards and proper social relations in any way except as the most useful place to start our studies. There will be some very general concepts that find a representation in every language (Wierzbicka, 1992), but local variants will often be important psychologically. (Harré 2012: 22)

Refusing to absolutize concepts of scientific English and recognizing the need for human sciences to be anchored in ordinary human words, Harré writes further:

The concepts of neuroscience must conform to the semantics of vernacular psychological concepts—or we are not studying the same subject matter...all psychological research must begin with vernacular concepts which identify the field of interest and the psychological processes that comprise it. (Harré 2012: 23)

Harré sees the main objective of "qualitative cultural psychology" in "extracting the meanings and rules that shape the meanings of human activities." "Our task is to display and illustrate methods for the discovery of the cultural matrices of human thought, feeling, perception, and action" (ibid.). Crucially, these meanings cannot be identified through concepts imported from another cultural matrix: "Cross-cultural research, in so far as it transports Western methods and concepts to attempt to understand alien life forms, has little to offer a hybrid scientific research program (Cole 1996)."

The insistence on the inappropriateness of "Western concepts" as tools for understanding how human beings think and feel corresponds closely to the NSM program. Harré's and Moghaddam's attitude toward this program is reflected in the short bio of the present writer included in *The Psychology for the Third Millennium* among other bios of scholars whom these authors regard as influential. To quote:

> [Wierzbicka's] work has become very well known in recent years for her creation of the 'Natural Semantic Metalanguage' together with her Australian colleague Cliff Goddard (Goddard & Wierzbicka, 2002). This proposal, based on the empirically established intersection of all sampled natural languages, has important consequences for psychology. The central hypothesis is that this metalanguage corresponds to the innate and universal 'lingua mentalis'—the hardwired language of the human mind, and that the small lexicon of this metalanguage constitutes the 'alphabet of human thoughts' once envisaged by Leibniz. This intersection between neuroscience and language is of great significance for the project of this book.
>
> She is also very well known for her studies of emotions in their cultural and historical diversity. Most recently her book, *Experience, evidence and sense: The hidden cultural legacy of English* (2010), opens up the fundamental question of how far the current lingua franca shades the psychology of most of humanity. (Harré and Moghaddom 2012: 14)

Horacio Fabrega: A View from Evolutionary Psychiatry

Horacio Fabrega is a physician and psychiatrist with a special interest in the origins, history, and culture of mental illness. He is the author of books such as *Disease and Social Behavior: An Interdisciplinary Perspective* (1974); *Evolution of Sickness and Healing* (1997); and *Origins of Psychopathology: The Phylogenetic and cultural basis of mental illness* (2002). In his recent work, Fabrega has increasingly focused on the evolution of the human mind and the possibility of recapturing some thoughts of early humans without modernizing (and thus distorting) them through scientific English. Fabrega sees in NSM a tool with the help of which his goal could be realistically pursued.

Fabrega's special interest lies in the conceptualization of "psychiatric conditions" among early humans (which he doesn't want to label "mental illness" because he wishes to avoid the culturally shaped implications of this modern English phrase). In exploring those conditions, Fabrega is trying to look not just at behaviors, but at what may have been happening inside our ancestors' minds, and moreover, to look at it from their own rather than a modern perspective. His questions concern the early humans' subjectivity—their thoughts and feelings.

From the point of view of evolutionary social science, the project of getting inside the heads of early humans and trying to comprehend their own self-understanding is unusually bold. From a linguistic point of view, however, it is not altogether different from an attempt to get inside the heads of speakers of an endangered (or dead) language, and to endeavor to see the world from their point of view (see Chapter 11). As Fabrega recognizes, for an Anglophone scholar, the first step toward either of those goals must be to divest oneself of the layers of culturally shaped English in one's own mind, and to try to imagine possible conceptual perspectives of people whose thinking was not similarly shaped by English and by Anglo culture. For example, there is good evidence that the languages of hunter-gatherers (in Australia, Papua, or Africa) do not have words corresponding to *depression, self-esteem, phobia,* or *paranoia.*

Presumably, it is safe to assume that there were no such words and concepts in the thought of early humans and proto-humans in ancestral environments, either. Fabrega suggests that in trying to model that thought from within, we need a simple metalanguage such as NSM:

> One can presume that to the extent that NSM grips the logical and semantic core of human thought that underlies all languages, its resources serve as a model or exemplum of what language and communication may have been like in early human history. Something like NSM, then, probably undergirded early modes of thought and language use. (In press: 86)

Fabrega points out that NSM, which he calls an "exemplum of early human thought," presupposes a mental or psychological faculty and is consistent in this respect with "ideas about cognitive modules (e.g., theory of mind, social cognition more generally) and underpinnings of cognitive models of persons and minds" put forward in evolutionary social sciences. At the same time, he notes, "the 'folk psychology' that permeates NSM formulations of behavior is miles away from similar sounding ideas about minds, persons, and which are regnant in modern Western societies."

Referring to "conditions of psychiatric interest," which are at the center of his attention, Fabrega sketches conceptual components couched in terms of NSM primes such as "someone," "something," "bad," "happen," "do," "want," and "feel," saying that "NSM delineates a conceptual space around a social context wherein conditions of psychiatric interest would have been placed" (in press: 88). As he observes elsewhere, "NSM enables one to get inside the heads of hominins as they acquired resources for representing and sharing ideas" (Fabrega 2012: 319). Fabrega makes this observation with special reference to ideas about "bad, unwanted things happening to me" (such as "pain"), and in his commentary on my article "Is Pain a Human Universal?" published in the *Emotion Review,* he writes:

> Three decades of empirical research enabled Wierzbicka and coworkers to perfect an objective way of studying language and thought. Natural semantic metalanguage (NSM) is based on self-evident, self-explanatory concepts which all natural languages build on. Such conceptual primes, Wierzbicka and coworkers have concluded, represent foundations or building blocks of all languages. (Fabrega 2012: 318)

Applying these ideas to ethnomedicine, Fabrega notes that thoughts such as "something bad is happening to my body" are central to the awareness that one is sick and in need of treatment and healing, and that such simple NSM formulations can provide an effective framework for comparative "ethnomedical science":

> Anthropologists and historians of medicine have documented the diverse interpretations that peoples across space and time have had about sickness and healing (Fabrega, 1974, 1997). (...) A schema of concepts and propositions derived from them which explain the logic and function of ideas and beliefs about sickness and healing constitute a theory about ethnomedicines worldwide. Such a theory would derive from and be reducible to dicta of NSM.

In Fabrega's view, simple "NSM dicta" referring to the body and to "bad things" happening to the body can also offer a framework for exploring ethnomedicine in an evolutionary perspective:

> NSM exemplifies the semantic information (conceptual primes) which enabled language-ready brains of Homo sapiens to describe and communicate about matters relevant to fitness and well-being. It provides a way of formulating how sickness and healing were understood during later phases of human biological evolution.

According to Fabrega, these developments in the understanding of sickness and healing must have taken place in the context of wider evolutionary changes in human cognitive resources and communicative capabilities:

> This was the time during which the biological capacity for intentional and communicative sharing of human subjectivity (i.e., culture) was consolidating (Tomasello, 1999). NSM enables understanding of how the morbidity of disease was reasoned about through universal semantic and

grammatical primes based on self-perceptions and observation of behavior of group mates. Thus, it provides a handle with which to grip the beginnings of the culture of medicine (i.e., ethnomedicine) and its evolution thereafter.

The convergence between evolutionary psychiatry and NSM semantics is further explored in Fabrega, Forthcoming and Goddard et al., Forthcoming.

16

Philosophy, Theology, Politics

Thomas Dixon: A View from Philosophy and History of Science

British philosopher and historian of science Thomas Dixon places particular emphasis on "chronocentrism" rather than "Anglocentrism" in contemporary social science, but the two are very closely related. In his 2003 book *From Passions to Emotions*, this chronocentrism (Bromhead's 2009 term, not Dixon's) was illustrated with the ascent of the word *emotion* in modern English and the reification and absolutization of this word's modern meaning in scientific discourse:

> Emotions are everywhere today. Increasing numbers of books and articles about the emotions are being produced for both academic and broader audiences; by neuroscientists, psychologists and philosophers. The existence and the great value of the emotions are obvious to academics and non-academics alike. It is surprising, then, to discover that the emotions did not exist until just under two hundred years ago. (Dixon 2003:1)

Dixon does not deny, of course, that before the nineteenth century, English-speaking people felt, thought, and wanted many different things, and were aware that their various feelings, thoughts, "wants," and "diswants" were interconnected. What he has in mind is that the way of thinking about these various psychological states that in present-day English is linked with the word *emotion* was born in a particular place and time: eighteenth-/nineteenth-century England.

As the title of Dixon's book indicates, the earlier English words for feelings, which the word *emotion* succeeded and largely superseded, was *passions:*

> It is an immensely striking fact of the history of English-language psychological thought that during the period between *c.*1800 and *c.*1850 a wholesale change in established vocabulary occurred such that those engaged in theoretical discussions about phenomena including hope, fear, love, hate, joy, sorrow, anger and the like no longer primarily discussed the passions

or affections of the soul, nor the sentiments, but almost invariably referred to 'the emotions.' (Dixon 2003: 4)

The "historical puzzle" of why this "wholesale change" occurred is at the heart of Dixon's book. Dixon's answers, though extremely interesting, cannot be discussed here in detail, beyond noting that as he shows, the shift from *passions* to *emotions* represented a cultural and conceptual, and not only lexical, change. The direction of that change can be gleaned from the lexical and conceptual networks to which the two words belonged. The network to which *passions* belonged also included words such as *soul, conscience, sin,* and *grace,* whereas the one to which *emotions* belonged included words such as *psychology, evolution, organism, brain, nerves, expression, behavior,* and *viscera.*

Thus, Dixon sees the all-important item of Anglophone psychological discourse—the term *emotions*—as conceptually and culturally dependent on one language, English, and as stemming from a specific recent period in this language's history. The idea that such a doubly contingent conceptual category can accurately match language-independent psychological realities is one that Dixon emphatically rejects:[1]

The assumption that psychological theories, regardless of their language and categories, pick out theory-independent mental states that we can identify with our own current English-language psychological terms is one of the assumptions that this book challenges. (...) [T]his book reveals that our modern-day category of emotions is rather a blunt instrument when it comes to constructing histories of ideas about feelings, passions, affections and sentiments; its employment has led to several misconceptions and confusions.

"Emotion" is not the only such "blunt" instrument favored by contemporary scientific discourse: the same can be said about many other terms of Anglophone social science discussed in this book. All these key terms of present-day academic English are both language-bound and time-bound; and yet they are often taken for precise instruments suitable for scientific study of people in a cross-cultural, cross-linguistic, and cross-temporal perspective.

According to the NSM theory, precise instruments that are both "English-proof" and "time-proof" can be found in shared, stable, pan-human concepts such as FEEL, WANT, KNOW, and THINK (cf. Bromhead 2009). This is a theme that is not part of Dixon's story. Nonetheless, the themes of conceptual Anglocentrism and chronocentrism in contemporary social sciences run deep in both approaches.

Dixon's groundbreaking study, *The Invention of Altruism: Making Moral Meanings in Victorian England* (2008), I will note, goes even deeper into the question of dependence of social science and global scientific discourse on the vicissitudes of the English language and the historical semantics of some key

English words. The story of "altruism" told by Dixon is highly illuminating. In his "conclusion," Dixon (2008: 361) writes, "The semantic progression that has been revealed by tracing the dissemination of the language of altruism through Victorian culture like a marker or a dye, culminated in the naturalization of an ethical term fraught with paradox and confusion."

Pointing out that "while 'altruism' is a single word, it is one that has historically been used to signify a multiplicity of different concepts," he emphasizes that he cannot, in his conclusion, make any statements about "the" meaning of *altruism*; and he states

> What I can do, however, is to end by drawing attention to some of the recurring intellectual and political conundrums to which debates about 'altruism' gave rise during the nineteenth century, in the hope that doing so might give present-day users of the language of altruism pause for thought.

Expressing this hope, Dixon appears to be thinking in particular about practitioners and popularizers of evolutionary science, where the word *altruism* has come to play a crucial role. Addressing the same issue and some of the same examples in our *Words and Meanings*, Cliff Goddard and I reached similar conclusions, and sought to show how the problem can be solved (or at least alleviated) with the help of NSM techniques.

Wacław Hryniewicz: A View from Theology

Wacław Hryniewicz is the author of more than thirty books, devoted largely to the hermeneutics of the interpretation of the Bible. Questions of language and cross-cultural communication (over languages, civilizations, and millennia) are at the heart of his work.

In his most recent book, *God's Spirit in the World: Ecumenical and Cultural Essays,* (Washington 2012), Hryniewicz addresses, in particular, "miscommunication" between, on the one hand, the prophets of the Hebrew Bible and the authors of the four canonical gospels, and on the other, modern Western readers (and especially, Anglo readers), who have absorbed certain assumptions of post-Enlightenment "rationality" with their mother's milk, and to whom the cultural and linguistic world of the Bible is often completely alien.

In this context, Hryniewicz discusses the cross-linguistic and cross-cultural analysis presented in my 2001 book *What Did Jesus Mean? Explaining the Sermon on the Mount and the Parables in Simple and Universal Human Concepts.* Referring in particular to a chapter entitled "The hyperbolic and paradoxical language of Jesus," he writes:

> Anna Wierzbicka rightly draws attention to language as a key issue in understanding his message. Many Western readers of the Gospel continue

to find Jesus' way of speaking extraordinary, strange, striking, riddle-like, paradoxical, hyperbolic, humorous, or even absurd. Examples of such utterances can be quoted in large numbers: remove first the beam from your own eye before you take the mote from your brother's eye; do not strain out the gnat and swallow the camel; camels passing more easily through the eye of a needle than rich people entering into the kingdom of God; mountains hurled into the sea by strong faith; "hating" one's own family and own life as a condition to become Jesus' disciple; let the dead bury their dead; plucking out one's right eye and cutting off one's right hand when they would cause you to sin. (Hryniewicz 2012: 71).

Many such sayings, which are widely recognized by scholars as indisputably authentic and characteristic of Jesus, are, Hryniewicz notes, deeply rooted in ancient Judaism, and notwithstanding the new content of Jesus's teaching and his distinctive personal style, continue the rhetorical heritage of the Hebrew prophets.

In analyzing the clash between the rhetorical and stylistic traditions of the Hebrew Bible and modern "Western" [Anglo] values of "accuracy," "logical consistency," "epistemological caution," and "rationality," Hryniewicz draws on the NSM theory of cultural scripts (cf. Goddard and Wierzbicka eds. 2004; Goddard ed. 2006), and in particular, on my 2004 article, "Jewish Cultural Scripts and the Interpretation of the Bible."

> When we read texts belonging to other epochs, peoples, and traditions, we need to know something about the so-called "cultural scripts" or "cultural rules" which shaped the ways of thinking and speaking reflected in those texts. To understand the ways of speaking which belong to a culture alien to us we must learn to perceive them in their proper cultural context and acquire some knowledge of this culture's established speech-forms. The culture of Jesus' times was profoundly influenced by the tradition of the biblical prophets. He spoke a language of the prophets shaped by Jewish scripts and cultural rules which contained certain shared linguistic patterns. (Hryniewicz 2012: 72)

In his analysis of Jesus's ethical teaching, Hryniewicz draws on the NSM-based comparison of Jewish and Anglo cultural scripts and linguistic cultures.

> In his ethical teaching Jesus would often say something which could not be taken literally, because it was logically impossible. This way of speaking about God in a figurative language aimed to challenge people to think and to see for themselves, and so to discover the intended meaning. Wierzbicka rightly calls it "an attention-catching and thought-provoking device." One says things which on the surface look self-contradictory but in fact reveal

deeper insights. That is why Jesus often preferred paradoxical ways of speaking about God instead of using unambiguous and simple language. (Hryniewicz 2012: 72)

Such deliberately self-contradictory, exaggerated, and paradoxical ways of speaking are contrary to those that have become the norm in modern English-speaking countries.

As discussed by anthropologists Richard Bauman and Charles Briggs in their 2003 book *Voices of Modernity,* seventeenth-century England was the scene of a massive campaign to "re-make language" (that is, to remake English). The main goal of that campaign, aimed at "making language safe for science and society," was fighting "rhetoric" and thus, in Locke's words, "removing some of the rubbish that lies in the way to knowledge" (Locke 1959, vol. I: 14).

The "father of British empiricism," Francis Bacon, saw language as the greatest obstacle to progress and modernity and mounted a concerted attack on rhetoric, warning that "the juggleries and charms of words" (Bacon 1860: 61) can subvert reason and stand in the way of knowledge. This was taken up by the scholars associated with the Royal Society, who denounced words as intrinsically unreliable instruments in scientific thinking, rejected rhetoric, and promoted a new style of discourse characterized by understatement and moderation (rather than hyperbole and rhetorical amplification), epistemological caution (rather than a tone of certainty), dispassion (rather than passion), and rationality (rather than emotionality and flights of imagination).

As Bauman and Briggs further note, "much of Locke's legacy has simply become common sense" (2003: 32). It is important to bear in mind, however, that this legacy has become "common sense" not for everyone, but, above all, for speakers of English. (The "voices of modernity" to which Bauman and Briggs listen so attentively are, above all, English voices).

The "common sense" widely shared by speakers of contemporary English may lead them to look for coherence at the surface of biblical texts (that is, in their literal meanings) instead of trying to find it at a deeper level. This can lead, in turn, either to literalist interpretation or to rejection of these texts as inconsistent or incoherent. Such rejection, Hryniewicz stresses, is often based on deep cross-cultural misunderstandings.

A literalist reading distorts the essential message of the Good News as a whole and misses its internal coherent. Any doctrine of the infallibility of the letter of the Bible leads to insurmountable difficulties, because it ignores their proper cultural content. The authors of the Books of the Bible multiplied metaphors, paradoxes and antinomies; they used dramatic expressions, in order to impress the reader and the hearer ever so strongly, so that people could feel what those authors actually wanted to say. Such modern values as accuracy, logical formulation, consistency, absence of contradictions and exaggerations, calm and fair reasoning, concern for a precise scientific information were unknown to them. One should not take contradictions at their face value or stop at the outer surface of the formulations. (Hryniewicz 2012: 83)

Hryniewicz's choice of words (e.g., *fair, reasoning, precise, accuracy, consistency*) is instructive. The "modern values" that he refers to are, above all, Anglo values—a fact that is highlighted by Bauman and Briggs's historical account, and which has many visible effects in modern English lexicon, phraseology, and even grammar (cf. Wierzbicka 2006a, 2012b).

Hryniewicz emphasizes that "the failure to understand the Jewish prophets' discourse may obscure some of the central aspects of Jesus' teaching" (p. 72), and that "to many Western Christians (...) the paradoxical sayings of Jesus present insurmountable difficulties and become great stumbling blocks" (p. 72). It could also be said, however, that for many contemporary Anglophone readers, their own "cultural scripts" (which are invisible to them) can become great stumbling blocks on the way to cross-cultural and cross-temporal understanding. In the conclusion to my *English: Meaning and Culture* (2006a: 313), I wrote: "It is important to 'denaturalise' Anglo English, and to identify and acknowledge the historically shaped cultural meanings embedded in it, if only so that they are no longer taken for granted as the voice of 'reason' itself." Hryniewicz's biblical hermeneutics points to the same conclusion.

Richard Collin: A View from Political Science

Richard Collin opens his recent article in *Political Studies*, entitled "Moving political meaning across linguistic frontiers," with a reference to Ingmar Bergman's classic film *The Silence*, in which a professional translator named Ester, her sister Anna, and Anna's son Johan are traveling through an unnamed war-torn country whose language they don't understand. Collin sees the world of international relations as similar to "the nightmare of being caught without a phrase book in a country where we do not speak the local language and where no-one speaks ours" (2012: 1). Except, Collin implies, that travelers like Bergman's Ester, Anna, and Johan are likely to be aware of their predicament, whereas those involved in international politics may not be. This is the problem to which Collin seeks to draw general attention, starting with the linguistic aspect of the Middle East conflict.

None of the major American and British politicians actively involved in the Israeli-Palestinian conflict, for example, speak either Arabic or Hebrew. Negotiations are conducted in English which is not spoken competently by many Palestinians and is only a second language for most Israelis (Cohen, 2001, p. 25). Somewhere in the process, is there a supremely competent Ester able to move what a Palestinian leader says into Hebrew via English without loss of semantic cargo? (Collin 2012: 2)

As Collin explains, however, problems with "moving political meaning across linguistic frontiers" cannot be solved simply by relying on competent translators, not even "supremely" competent ones, especially when cultural key words on which political discourse depends don't match in meaning. Miscommunication is a constant danger—a problem in which "traditional political science has shown little interest" (Collin 2012: 2).

As Collin emphasizes, often the greatest difficulty lies in cross-linguistic mismatches between words that are both very important for the speakers' thinking and very complex in meaning—mismatches of which the speakers are usually not aware. "Diplomacy, international commerce and the academic study of international relations are all based on the assumption that we can cross linguistic borders with very complicated words and concepts in our cognitive luggage." (Collin 2012: 2)

One extended example that Collin uses to illustrate the problem is "the fundamental political word 'democracy'" (Collin 2012: 16). He refers in this context to Frederic Schaffer's (1998) book, *Democracy in Translation: Understanding Politics in an Unfamiliar Culture*, which warns that while "Xhosa speakers today talk of *idemokrasi* (...), Chinese students demonstrated for *mizhu*, and Václav Havel attempted to institute *democracie*, (...) translating *mizhu*, *demokracie*, or *idemokrasi*, by 'democracy,' as journalists and scholars regularly do, is potentially problematic" (Schaffer 1998, 14). Collin quotes, in particular, Schaffer's findings about the use of the word *demokaraasi* by Wolof speakers in Senegal and wonders what this word really means for them.

> Schaffer (1998, pp. 51–65) found that *demokaraasi* in Wolof referred less to electoral behaviour (voting leaders in and out of office) and more to the search for consensus (achieving community unity), solidarity (taking care of friends and neighbours in times of need) and a structured equality or even-handedness (in the sense that a polygamous husband would treat his wives equally or a mother her children fairly). (Collin 2012: 16)

Reflecting on examples such as this, Collin ponders the idea of "a comparative or multilingual political semantics" (p. 6). In this context, he refers (inter alia) to my own analysis of the meaning of the English word *freedom* and its closest counterparts in several other languages (in my 1997 book *Understanding Cultures Through Their Key Words*):

> One of the major advocates of seeing language in terms of a specific culture is Anna Wierzbicka. In her studies of the English language,

Wierzbicka (2006, pp. 5–14) maintains that there is an 'inner circle' of anglophone countries (the UK, the US, Ireland, Australia and New Zealand) where political and legal systems have led to the creation of a vocabulary that does not render successfully into other languages. In what she calls 'Anglo-English,' Wierzbicka (2006, p. 16) argues that words like *fair*, *bias*, *commitment* and *compromise* are rooted in English common law tradition and shed much of their original sense when translated into a different language culture. Strongly influenced by the Sapir-Whorf perspective, Wierzbicka (2006, pp. 103–40) dwells convincingly on the oft-used word *reasonable*. In English, we make *reasonable* effort to obey laws within a *reasonable* time. If we are arrested on *reasonable* suspicion, we count on a jury of *reasonable* people to determine that there is a *reasonable doubt* about our guilt. This usage works well within the common law judicial tradition, which depends heavily on precedents established by earlier cases; what is *reasonable* is what a judge and a jury have found *reasonable*. Outside the anglophone world, however, civil law systems are inspired by the Roman and Napoleonic legal traditions in which legislators attempt to define very carefully what is and what is not legal, leaving judges very little latitude to decide whether behaviour had been reasonable or not (Collin 2012: 14).

Such historical, cultural, and semantic complexities lead Collin to the conclusion that many political terms simply cannot be adequately translated, and that in this domain as in many others, translation may need to be supplemented at times with extended commentaries and background explanations. He illustrates this with two further examples from my 1997 book *Understanding Cultures Through Their Key Words*:

And explanation and/or decipherment is not translation. In comparing two German words for *country*, Wierzbicka (1997, pp. 157–77) dedicates 21 densely written pages to the difference between *Heimat* and *Vaterland*. Her discussion is brilliant, but no translator/interpreter will ever be allowed a 21-page parenthesis in the middle of a European Union speech by the German Chancellor (Collin 2012: 17)

Obviously, NSM explications of political keywords can't be inserted into the translator's or interpreter's rendering of a political text, but they can *inform* translation and thus assist in "moving political meaning across linguistic frontiers." Collin ends by appealing to students of politics to pay greater attention to the questions of cross-linguistic semantics ("As students of politics, we need to take political translation as seriously as language professionals do," p. 17.). He even goes as far as calling the absence of political scientists from cross-disciplinary conversation about the interaction between language and society "a tragedy." He concludes: "International politics is an exercise in language, and without a studied appreciation of that fact, we find ourselves like Ingmar Berman's Ester and Anna, cognitively marooned in a world of words that are forever foreign to our ears." (ibid.)

17

Linguistics: Cognitive and Cultural Approaches

Vivian Cook: A View from Cognitive Linguistics

British cognitive linguist Vivian Cook has no doubt that for speakers of English, English words play a very significant role in organizing and interpreting the world. This applies both to humble "concrete" words such as *car* and to weighty "abstract" terms such as *truth*, *globalization*, and *education*. In his book *All in a Word*, he writes:

> The word *car* links something that exists in the world with a concept in our minds. There's no way of linking the word and the world without the mind. Cars don't usually come labelled as *cars*; it's us who call them *cars*. The word *car* shows how a speaker of English organizes the world. (2009: 26)

Echoing Sapir's and Whorf's famous words "we do not live in the objective world alone" (Sapir 1949: 162) and "we dissect nature along lines laid down by our native languages" (Whorf 1956: 213), Cook emphasizes that both the physical and the mental world are "parcelled up by the words of our language" (2009: 27).

English is not an exception to the general rule: it is not a "neutral language" whose words parcel the world up more objectively than those of other languages and reflect the structure of the reality itself. On the contrary, English (including scientific English) is also shaped by history and culture. In his coedited book *Language and Bilingual Cognition*, Cook applies this point to the important English word *language*.

Referring to my own contribution to that volume, which "discusses the dangers of treating English as a universal metalanguage for discussing cognition" (Cook 2011a: 12), he notes that the word *language* is often taken for granted in academic discussions in various disciplines. And yet, "the meanings of the English word *language* are not necessarily found in other languages" and, for example, the French distinction between *langue*, *langage*, and *parole* "has always been a bugbear for English-speaking linguists" (ibid.). Cook's concludes: "Given that the language of academic discussion for most research in language and cognition is English, researchers may indeed be constrained by the English interpretation of *language*."

When one considers the huge role that the English word *language* plays, for example, in debates about human evolution and human uniqueness, one can appreciate the far-ranging implications of Cook's remarks (cf. also Harris 1982; Goddard 2011b). What distinguishes humans from apes? What makes us unique? What made humans the "masters of the planet"? Some scholars reply, "language," and some others argue, "not language." But if *language* is an English, or at best European, concept, then clearly, the use of this word in evolutionary social science can skew debates and impede, instead of facilitating, clarity, precision, and what John Locke called "human understanding." From an NSM point of view, I would add that since cross-linguistic research indicates that WORD is a universal human concept (as is also SAY) whereas "language" is not,[1] there is a strong case for using WORD and SAY as the most basic conceptual tools in evolutionary debates—noting at the same time that "cognition" itself is also an untranslatable English concept, less reliable in comparative research than the universal concept THINK.[2]

Recognizing the dangers of conceptual Anglocentrism in human sciences, Cook is sympathetic to the NSM project of trying to identify the common core of human thought and use it as a metalanguage for human sciences. (2011a: 9). In *All in a Word*, he (2009: 272–273) reproduces the full NSM list of "semantic primes expressed in all languages" and comments: "These words are the core of what human beings express through language, common to all cultures and races"; and in the introduction to *Language and Bilingual Cognition,* he writes:

> At its most general, language and cognition research concerns language as a property of human beings: The semantic primes of Wierzbicka (1996) such as 'part,' 'kind' (the relationship between things) or 'big,' 'small' (the size of things) make good candidates for a central inalienable core of human language and human cognition. (Cook 2011a: 9)

Cook stresses that from the perspective of cognitive linguistics (at least of the kind that he identifies with), languages influence their speakers' thinking but do not determine it: "From the perspective of cognitive linguistics, semantic structure encoded by language can influence our conceptualization, and other outputs of cognitive function, such as categorization, for instance. However, language does not determine them" (Cook 2011b: 85).

This is also the NSM position: every language, including English, influences the ways its speakers think, but it does not fully determine them, because in addition to all the cultural "accretions," there is also that "central inalienable core of human language and cognition." (Cook 2011a: 9).

James Underhill: A View from Ethnolinguistics

In his recent book *Ethnolinguistics*, James Underhill, a British linguist working
in France, characterizes the field of ethnolinguistics as "the study of the way
worldviews construct the complex and flexible framework within which we think
and feel." Underhill emphasizes that we are not "confined" by language: our
language shapes us but we also shape our language.

> Studying thinking-in-language involves investigating the geography of our
> understanding. Like land developers we can transform our linguistically
> painted landscape. Ultimately language is not a prison. But nor is it a mere
> tool, a means: it is an ongoing act of creation. Consequently, at one level we
> are as much the producers as the products of language. (Underhill 2012: x)

Underhill has no doubt that many different worldviews, visions, and ideologies
can be expressed in any language. At the same time, he recognizes that there
can also be a conceptual world inherent in the language itself, a world of which
the speaker may not be aware. Underhill illustrates this idea with in-depth cor-
pus-based analyses of four concepts: "truth," "love," "hate," and "war" in four
European languages, English, French, Czech and German, in a historical and
cultural perspective. He concludes:

> there is a worldview which is implicit in the deeper frameworks of the lan-
> guage system we speak. At this level French and German shape the imagi-
> nation, the understanding and the desires of the French and Germans.
> Their sensitivity to the world, all of the conceptual connections which
> French and German people take for granted, appear to us [Anglos] curi-
> ous, at times almost incomprehensible. Learning to navigate within
> their waters, we come to realize that we are entering another worldview.
> (Underhill 2012: x)

Crucially, what applies to "foreign" languages, applies also to English.

> And at this stage we realize that the world is always grasped and repre-
> sented 'in' language. We realise that our English language imposes its own
> constraints upon us, just as the richness and depth of expression in English,
> both past and present, has opened up for us a wonderful means of expres-
> sion: one which allows us to enter the worlds of philosophers such as John
> Locke and the worlds of writers such as Shakespeare. (Underhill 2012: xi)

Since English is neither neutral nor transparent, "believing that we can understand other cultures and languages (…) 'in' English" is often an illusion. In
this context, Underhill refers to my own emphasis on the cultural shaping of
English. Summarizing the main themes of my 2010a book *Experience, Evidence
and Sense: the Cultural Legacy of English*, he writes:

One essential aspect of Wierzbicka's work is that it exemplifies what I will call 'the ethnolinguistic challenge.' Wierzbicka forces us, the speakers of the world language, English, to face up to something which inevitably leaves us feeling uncomfortable, something which less prolific cultures feel goes without saying: that our language does not offer us direct unmediated access to the world and all that is in it, but rather provides us with a series of concepts which construct reality along culturally specific lines. Language organizes our concept of the world, and that process of organisation imposes limits, blindness and insensitivity just as it is through the medium of language that we open up to the world, see it, feel it, and manipulate our conceptions of it in our conscious and unconscious thought. (Underhill 2012: 37)

Underhill ends his summary of the main themes of *Experience, Evidence and Sense*, with a generous endorsement: "Essentially, one of the great services Wierzbicka is doing is alerting English speakers to the underlying patterns of understanding and expression with which our language culture has equipped us for interpreting the world."

Underhill also gives a good deal of attention to the Lublin School of Ethnolinguistics led by Jerzy Bartmiński, and to Bartmiński's 2005 book *Aspects of Cognitive Ethnolinguistics*. In fact, one of the sections, in the introductory chapter of Underhill's book, is titled, somewhat incongruously, perhaps, "Humboldt, Bartmiński, Wierzbicka, and the ethnolinguistics project."

Underhill expresses his admiration for Bartmiński's "vast and multi-faceted project" of investigating many key concepts and themes in several European languages, with a view to comparing "European worldviews" (a project with many participants from many countries):

What is refreshing about Bartmiński's approach, though, is its rigour, and the vast nature of its comprehensive research into literature, popular idioms, discourse and etymology. In contrast to the linguistic anthropology of the States, and in contrast to the incisive but fragmentary studies made by Whorf, Bartmiński's studies give an infinitely more profound insight into the linguistic imagination into which he is reaching. The paradigms his study provides are inevitably both more detailed and more reliable (though of course it should be remembered that he was dealing with his own mother tongue, while Whorf, to his credit, was reaching into entirely different frameworks of understanding when he studied foreign languages.) (Underhill 2012: 33)

Since the present chapter has to be selective, I have not devoted a separate section to Bartmiński and the Lublin Ethnolinguistic School, but obviously the work of this school is also an excellent example of what I call here "kindred thinking."

Jurij Apresjan: A View from Lexicography

Jurij Apresjan, the leader of the "Moscow Semantic School," is regarded by many linguists as the world's foremost lexicographer. As he writes in the introduction to his 2000 book *Systematic Lexicography,* the two areas that concern him most and that for him are intimately related, are linguistic theory and lexicography:

> Until quite recently in some quarters lexicography *was* looked down upon as a purely practical enterprise unworthy of scholarly interest. The present author is convinced, however, that sound lexicography can only be based on sound linguistic theory and that recent theoretical developments are of paramount importance for the practical skills of compiling a dictionary. (Apresjan 2000: xi)

This deep conviction that linguistic theory and practical dictionary-making can and should go hand in hand has borne fruit in Apresjan's and his coworkers' unique lexicographic output. As another prominent theoretician and practitioner of semantics and lexicography, Igor Mel'čuk, put it in his preface to Apresjan's (2011) Festschrift, "Apresjan is unique: I don't know of any other linguist of his class who would have comparable experience of lexicographic work. It is precisely this lexicographic base that allowed him to undertake his colossal—both in scope and in importance—investigations of the Russian lexicon" (Mel'čuk 2011: 15).

Two features of Apresjan's linguistic philosophy and lexicographic practice make his work especially close in spirit to the NSM program of research: first, his search "for the 'naïve' picture of the world" embedded in lexical and grammatical meanings of languages, and second, the principle that meanings need to be portrayed in a standardized semantic metalanguage based on a set of semantic primitives.

Apresjan's conception of the "naïve picture of the world" embedded in every language is best explained in his own words:

1. Each natural language reflects a specific way of perceiving and organizing (i.e. conceptualizing) the world about us. The meanings expressed in natural language form a unified system of views, a kind of collective philosophy which becomes obligatory for all speakers of that language. (...)

2. The way of conceptualizing reality (the world-view) inherent in a given language is partly universal and partly national-specific, such that speakers of different languages may view the world in slightly different ways, through the prism of their languages.

3. On the other hand, this view is "naïve" in the sense that it differs in many important particulars from a scientific picture of the world. Not

that the "naïve" notions are in any way primitive. In many cases they are no less complex or interesting than scientific notions. Take, for example, naïve notions of man's inner world. These reflect the experience of introspection over scores of generations through many millennia, and may serve as a reliable guide to this world.

4. In the naïve world picture we may identify a naïve geometry and physics of space and time (...), a naïve ethics, a naïve psychology, etc. (Apresjan 2000: 103–4)

Obviously, these ideas belong, broadly speaking, to the tradition established in linguistics by Humboldt, Sapir, and Whorf. Yet their realization in the work of Apresjan and his associates is strikingly original.

Apresjan's special emphasis is on the fact that some meanings are encoded, in a systematic way, in certain classes of words, and that speakers may be forced to express them whether or not they want to do so. For example, Russian (in contrast to French, among many languages) "forces its speakers, whenever they talk of locomotion, to specify the manner of locomotion (walking, flying crawling, and so on), although it may be irrelevant to their thought" (p. XII).

In itself, the idea that many lexical meanings have to be expressed irrespective of the speaker's intentions has its parallels in the work of other linguists and psycholinguists (e.g., Slobin 1996, 2000; Bowerman and Choi 2001). What is without parallel is its use as a driving force in large-scale lexicographic description of a particular language (in Apresjan's case, Russian), in accordance with the creed articulated in the following quote:

> The primary task of systematic lexicography is to reflect the naïve world-view which a given language embodies—its naïve geometry, physics, ethics, psychology, and so forth. The naïve pictures of each of these areas are not chaotic but form definite systems and should therefore receive a homogeneous description in a dictionary. For this purpose, generally speaking, we should first reconstruct the corresponding fragment of the naïve picture of the world on the basis of lexical and grammatical meanings. In practice, however, (...) the reconstruction and the (lexicographical) description go hand in hand and constantly provide each other with correctives. (Apresjan 2000: 104)

Turning now to the other keynote of Apresjan's research program, the notion of universal semantic primitives, I will again let Apresjan speak for himself (adding only that the idea of a "semantic metalanguage" as a basis for semantic description was put forward by the Moscow Semantic School as early as the mid-1960s). The summary paragraph of the section on "The Approach of the Moscow Semantic School to the Language of Explications" reads:

> To sum up the foregoing, the metalanguage of lexicography is a sub-language of the object language, comprising a relatively small and unified vocabulary and syntax. The basis of this metalanguage is semantic primitives. With the aid of the metalanguage, complex semantic units of the object language (grammatical as well as lexical) are reduced to a fixed structure of semantic primitives by a process of hierarchical breakdown. (Apresjan 2000: 224)

Overall, despite some important differences between Apresjan's approach and the NSM program (which Apresjan discusses in the same chapter), the closeness between them is evident. In Apresjan's own words:

> The fundamental similarity between the theories of the Moscow Semantic School and those of Anna Wierzbicka can be seen at a glance. It lies in the fact that a semantic metalanguage, understood as a language with its own vocabulary and syntax, is seen as the principal instrument of semantic description. This metalanguage is a sub-language of the object language and has nothing in common with the language of 'distinctive semantic features.' In both metalanguages a special role is allotted to semantic primitives. Both metalanguages are designed to describe both lexical and grammatical meanings. (Apresjan 2000: 224)

Aleksej Shmelev: A View from Cultural Semantics

In their recent book entitled "The constants and the variable of the 'Russian linguistic picture of the world'" (a sequel to their 2005 book "Key ideas of the Russian Linguistic Picture of the World"), Anna Zalizniak, Irina Levontina, and Aleksey Shmelev (2012: 11) write:[3]

> Every natural language reflects a certain way of experiencing and constructing the world, or a "linguistic picture of the world." The totality of ideas about the world embedded in the meanings of the words and phrases of a given language, form a certain unitary system of views and norms which presents itself as obligatory to all the speakers.

The authors emphasize that when they use the word "obligatory" (*objazatel'nyj*) they do not mean it in a deterministic sense: although the language imposes a certain "picture of the world" on its speakers, the speakers are not the slaves of this picture. By reflecting deeply on different aspects of this "picture," speakers can question them; and linguistic analysis can help speakers to be aware, and critical, of the a priori assumptions inherent in the meanings of words and expressions of the language.

To be able to speak a language one has to master certain ways of conceptualising the world reflected in that language. Because the speakers take for granted the configurations of ideas entrenched in the meanings of the words of their native language, there arises an illusion that this is simply how things are. But when different "pictures of the world" embedded in different languages are compared, often significant and by no means trivial differences come to light. (Zalizniak et al. 2012: 11)

The main object of Shmelev's and his colleagues' interest is the Russian language, and they explain their main task as "revealing those ideas about the world, human behaviour and psychological reactions, that Russian imposes on the speaker, making the speaker see the world, think and feel in particular ways" (p. 14). But since such language-specific ways of thinking and feeling are best revealed through comparisons with other languages, the authors often compare and contrast Russian meanings with those embedded in other European languages, especially French, German, and English.

A great deal of attention is also given to the linguistic evidence for the ongoing change in the "Russian linguistic picture of the world." Thus, of the two parts of the book, Part I is devoted to "Key ideas of the Russian linguistic picture of the world," and Part II, to "Linguistic change and the picture of the world." The first part is based on articles published in the mid-1990s and early 2000s. They are close in spirit, the authors say, to my own work on cultural keywords of different languages, including Russian, and they see those articles as belonging to a new direction in linguistic studies initiated by my 1992 book *Semantics, Culture and Cognition.*

Both the 2005 and the 2012 books by Zalizniak, Levontina, and Shmelev devoted to the "Russian linguistic picture of the world" are goldmines of insights into the meanings of Russian words and phrases and must be of inestimable value to anyone with a serious interest in Russian language and culture. What is particularly noteworthy about the team's approach is their interest in the motifs recurring in the meanings of many untranslatable Russian words and phrases and the emphasis on the "invisible," presuppositional character of these language-specific components of meanings.

To mention a few examples, in his introduction to the more recent book, Shmelev (2012a: 23) signals the following linguistically embodied cultural presuppositions: "unpredictable things can happen in a person's life" (e.g., *esli čto, v slučae čego, vdrug*); "in any case it is impossible to foresee everything" (e.g., *avos'*); "in order to do something, it is often necessary to mobilize one's inner resources, and this can be difficult" (e.g., *neoxota, sobirat'sja/sobrat'sja, vybrat'sja*); "a person needs a lot of space to feel good and at ease" (e.g., *prostor, dal', šir', privol'e, razdol'e*); "it is bad if a person always aims at personal profit and gain; it is good if a person can be extravagant and do things in a big way" (e.g., *meločnost', širota, razmax*); and so on. (As the Russian words quoted above are chosen as prime examples of untranslatability, I am not providing them with English glosses.) Shmelev concludes: "It appears that many ways of thinking signalled here can help [outsiders] to understand some important features of Russian [linguistic] perspective on the world and of Russian culture" (ibid.).

Since it is Russian, not English, that is at the center of Shmelev and his colleagues' attention, they do not seek to explore the "English linguistic picture of the world"; but the implications of their work for the theme of *Imprisoned in English* are clear enough. As they emphasize, *every* language carries with it certain ways of seeing the world, as well as certain implicit norms of thinking, feeling, and acting. By exploring recent semantic influences of English on the Russian lexicon, Shmelev and colleagues often throw a great deal of light on some tacit cultural assumptions embedded in English. As Shmelev (2012b) writes in his chapter entitled "A Russian look at 'western' concepts: linguistic evidence," "Investigating the conflict of values embedded in different languages and the way of solving these conflicts in loan words, the linguist can reveal some specific aspects of each of the linguistic pictures of the world" (p. 409).

Some obvious and self-explanatory examples mentioned by Shmelev include the disappearance of the pejorative semantic component from the meanings of the words *biznesman* ("businessman"), *ambicioznyj* ("ambitious"), and *kar'era* ("career") in present-day Russian, under the semantic influence of English. A less obvious but no less instructive case in point is the semantic transformation of the word *problema* ("problem"), studied in detail in Anna Zalizniak's chapter devoted to this word.

The work of Shmelev and his colleagues shares with that of Apresjan's "Moscow Semantic School" and with that of NSM researchers an emphasis on the need to explore hundreds of meanings under the microscope of semantic analysis. This meticulous attention to lexicographic detail, combined with a large scale lexical and lexico-grammatical analysis, is a feature uniting these three approaches to linguistics.

18

Bilingualism, Life Writing, Translation

Aneta Pavlenko: A View from Bilingualism

Aneta Pavlenko, a psycholinguist and applied linguist at Temple University in Pennsylvania, is the author of, inter alia, *Emotions and Multilingualism* (2005), and editor of *Bilingual Minds* (2006) and *Thinking and Speaking in Two Languages* (2011, ed). The preface to the first of these books calls it "a part of a life-long project of rewriting 'monolingual' linguistics to fit the real world—messy, heteroglossic, and multilingual" (p. XII). This lifelong project challenges what Pavlenko sees as the central assumption of mainstream linguistics ("at least in North American academia") that "the focus of language-related inquiry should be on the minority of the world's population—monolingual or predominantly monolingual speakers" (ibid.). A Russian-English bilingual and a "language migrant" herself, Pavlenko sees bilingualism as a key to the understanding of the relation between thinking and speaking, and she urges that a "multilingual lens" should be used at every juncture of linguistics.

As a graduate student at Cornell University in 1992, Pavlenko found her inspiration in a "mysterious comment" made many decades earlier by Edward Sapir:

> To pass from one language to another is psychologically parallel to passing from one geometrical system of reference to another. The environing world which is referred to is the same for either language; the world of points is the same in either frame of reference. But the formal method of approach to the expressed item of experience, as to the given point of space, is so different that the resulting feeling of orientation can be the same neither in the two languages nor in the two frames of reference. Entirely distinct, or at least measurably different, formal adjustments have to be made and these differences have their psychological correlates. (Sapir 1949 [1924]: 153); Pavlenko 2011a: 1.

As Pavlenko recalls, these words captured the disorientation of her own transition from Russian to English. But while it was a disappointment that Sapir did not elaborate on what those psychological correlates might be, in her own research she continued to meditate on Sapir's (and also Whorf's) ideas and to distinguish them, in her own mind, from the widespread simplistic "sound-bite juxtaposition of 'strong' linguistic determinism to 'weak' linguistic relativity." She also came to the conclusion that (as argued by Penny Lee in her 1996 book on Whorf) "the real authors of the Sapir-Whorf hypothesis [are] North American psychologists Roger Brown and Eric Lenneberg" (Pavlenko 2011a: 2), who distorted Sapir's and Whorf's complex and profound ideas concerning the relations between languages and ways of thinking in their eagerness to translate them "into testable research designs and hypotheses" (Pavlenko 2011a: 19).

> To begin with, they [Brown and Lenneberg] shifted the focus of the inquiry from interpretive categories of thought or concepts to cognitive processes, such as perception or memory, which Sapir and Whorf were not particularly interested in. Secondly, they privileged the idea of thought potential (and, by implication, what *can* be said) over Whorf's concerns with habitual thought (and thus by definition with what *is* said). Most importantly, they replaced relativity as a way of thinking about languages with the 'testable' idea of linguistic determinism, which does not appear in either Sapir's or Whorf's writings. (ibid.)

According to Pavlenko, the questions asked by Brown and Lenneberg (unlike those raised by Sapir and Whorf) presupposed monolingualism as the norm. "The possibility of languages 'determining' people's thoughts" could only be considered "in the world imagined to be monolingual" (p. 2), that is, the world in which there is no need to ask "what happens with those who grow up speaking two or more languages, or those who leave other languages later in life" (ibid.).

Accordingly, Pavlenko set herself the goal to return to Sapir's and Whorf's original emphasis on language as a guide to "social reality" and on "habitual thought," and to expand the range of inquiry into the relationship between language and thought by putting bilingual speakers in focus. Furthermore, she questioned the emphasis on psychological experiments "that measure reaction times to artificial tasks in laboratory conditions" and developed instead a methodology for tapping into bilingual minds by eliciting bilingual speakers' views and perception of how they think and feel in, and about, their different languages.

Talking to people whose minds, and ways of thinking and feeling are being investigated (rather than merely treating them as objects of psycholinguistic experiments) led Pavlenko, and her colleague Jean-Marc Dewaele, to the idea of devising a "web questionnaire" for the study of "bilingual minds" and "bilingual selves." The questionnaire, containing thirty-four closed and open-ended questions, was advertised through several "listserves" and led to the creation of a very rich database, based on responses from more than a thousand bilingual (or multilingual) speakers. Here is a sample of extracts from such responses cited in Pavlenko's 2005 book *Emotions and Multilingualism:*

> I tend to use English when I am angry, Japanese when I'm hurt or sad, both when I am happy or excited (...) My other bilingual friends who are all returnees like me said the same thing about using English when they're angry. I guess I like the sound of the swearing words since I heard it so many times during my stay in the U.S. This swearing doesn't happen so often in Japan. It's a cultural difference. (Ryoko, L1 Japanese, L2 English)
>
> [I prefer terms of endearment in] Spanish because there are more ways to refer to my son in Spanish endearingly. (Natalia, 28, L1 English, L2 Spanish, L3 French, uses mostly L1 English with children)
>
> Welsh is the language which is the one that feels natural for expressing feelings. Expressing endearment in English has a false 'acting' ring to it. I would inevitably talk to babies and animals in Welsh. (Maureen, 47, L1 Welsh, L2 English)

Asked if they felt sometimes like a different person when using a different language, many respondents answered with an emphatic and enthusiastic "yes." For example, in her chapter "Bilingual Selves" in the edited book *Bilingual Minds*, Pavlenko (2006: 11-12) cites the following responses (among many others):

> Definitely! Speaking other languages causes me to assume certain cultural perspectives that also entail certain behaviours. (Louise, 25, English-German-French-ASL-Lakota)
>
> Absolutely. I feel I can hide my emotions and myself a lot better in English. In Spanish I feel a lot more 'naked.' (Dolores, 31, Spanish-English-German-French)

In a chapter of her book *Emotions and Multilingualism* entitled "Semantic and conceptual levels: The bilingual mental lexicon" Pavlenko (2005: 111) characterizes "the status of bilingual informants in future research on language and emotions" as an issue "critical for this book as a whole," and she refers in this context to my own work:

> Wierzbicka (2003b, 2004, 2011a in press) has repeatedly argued that experiences and opinions of bilingual individuals need to be taken into consideration in research on language and emotions. Yet we continue seeing studies where the judgments of monolingual speakers of English and Japanese are used to draw conclusions about the similarity of the English shame and embarrassment to the Japanese *hazukashii* (Rusch, 2004). We also continue seeing ethnocentric arguments that privilege English emotion terms and discount the significance of cross-linguistic and cross-cultural differences (Pinker, 1997). Wierzbicka's (2003) response to Martha Nussbaum

perfectly summarizes the position taken in this book on the necessity of
using bilingual participants and informants:

If many bilingual and bicultural people say that the existence of different words for emotions *has* made a difference to the texture of their
emotional life, can a person who has *not* lived his or her life through two
languages establish *by means of argument* that such people are wrong?
([Wierzbicka 2003]: 579)

As this quote illustrates, there is a close convergence between Pavlenko's work
and my own, in relation to "linguistic relativity," the importance of bilingual
experience, terminological Anglocentrism, and the tendency to discount the
significance of cross-linguistic and cross-cultural differences, which is widespread in Anglophone social science.

Pavlenko closes her most recent volume, *Thinking and Speaking in Two
Languages*, by urging "that the time has come, at least in the fields of bilingualism and second language acquisition, to discard the narrow search for evidence
for or against linguistic relativity and to engage in broad explorations in thinking and speaking in two or more languages" (Pavlenko 2011c: 252). This is also
my own and my fellow NSM-researchers' view—and not only in relation to
bilingualism and second language acquisition, but to thinking and speaking in
general.

16. Eva Hoffman: A View from Life Writing

Eva Hoffman's cross-linguistic autobiography *Lost in Translation: A Life in
a New Language* (1989) was a groundbreaking publication in the history of
inquiry into the relations between language and thought. It broadened the
basis of that inquiry from philosophical and scholarly speculations to an examination of one's own lived experience and introduced a personal and human
dimension to a field increasingly threatened by the dehumanizing influence of a
narrowly conceived cognitive science (Shweder 2012a). Through concrete analyses illuminated by inside knowledge, it undermined the widespread assumption that English is a neutral language that one can "live in" without at the
same time inhabiting a certain conceptual world, and it brought immigrant
experience to bear on questions previously discussed mainly in the abstract and
away from the specifics of history (both personal and social).

Eva Hoffman emigrated with her family from Poland to North America
when she was 13 years old. The title of her book signals her double perspective
on her existential shift from Polish into English. In her experience, this shift
involved a lot of conceptual disruption and change, but there was also—as she
determined after a painful period of transition—a great deal of continuity. In
translating one's self, as in translating texts, there could be (she discovered) a

large measure of fidelity to the original, as well as a large measure of discontinuity and transformation.

> My American Friends (...) share so many assumptions that are quite invisible to them, precisely because they're shared. These are assumptions about the most fundamental human transactions, subcutaneous beliefs, which lie just below the stratum of political opinion or overt ideology: about how much "space," physical or psychological, we need to give each other, about how much "control" is desirable (...), about how much we need to hide in order to reveal ourselves. (Hoffman 1989: 210)

As the quotation marks over the words "space" and "control" indicate, such invisible "subcutaneous beliefs" shared by Hoffman's American friends are embedded into particular English words that have no counterparts in Polish— for example, words like *space* and *control*. In incorporating such new concepts, which underlie and cement her interlocutors' tacit agreements into her own mental lexicon requires, Hoffman feels, a shift in her "innermost ways."

> To remain outside such common agreements is to remain outside reality itself—and if I'm not to risk a mild cultural schizophrenia, I have to make a shift in the innermost ways. I have to translate myself. But if I'm to achieve this without becoming assimilated—that is, absorbed—by my new world, the translation has to be careful, the turns of the psyche unforced. To mouth foreign terms without incorporating their meanings is to risk becoming bowdlerized. A true translation proceeds by the motions of understanding and sympathy; it happens by slow increments, sentence by sentence, phrase by phrase. (Hoffman 1989: 211)

Thus, Hoffman does not say that she needed to "invent" a new self for herself— a totally new way of thinking, feeling, and seeing the world; her metaphor is that of "self-translation." This involves learning many new concepts, internalizing them, and integrating them into her inner self.

The word *control* in the quote about "My American Friends" illustrates this complex process of internalization and integration particularly well, for as Hoffman shows, the learning of the new concept of "control" is closely linked in her experience with the adoption of a new set of "cultural scripts" that the word epitomizes and serves (cf. Besemeres 1998; 2002: 62).

> Once, when my mother was very miserable, I told her, full of my newly acquired American wisdom, that she should try to control her feelings. "What do you mean?" she asked, as if this was an idea proffered by a member of a computer species. "How can I do that? They are my feelings (...)" As for me, I've become a more self-controlled person over the years—more "English," as my mother told me years ago. (...) I've learned how to use the mechanisms of my will, how to look for symptom and root cause before

> sadness or happiness overwhelm me. I've gained some control, and control is something I need more than my mother did. (Hoffman 1989: 269-270)

The project of "gaining control" is inseparable from learning, and internalizing, a new conceptual vocabulary.

> In the project of gaining control, I've been aided by the vocabulary of self-analysis, and by the prevailing assumption that it's good to be in charge. "I've got to get some control," my friends say when something troubles them or goes wrong. It is shameful to admit that sometimes things can go very wrong; it's shameful to confess that sometimes we have no control. (ibid.)

Looked at through the NSM lens, the word *control,* acquired by Hoffman together with its associated cultural scripts, means, roughly speaking, that if one doesn't want to feel something, one can think about some things for some time as one wants, and as a result one will not feel about these things in a way that one doesn't want to feel.

There is no word with such a meaning in Hoffman's native Polish, but all the ingredients of this meaning (FEEL, WANT, THINK, IF, and so on) are, of course, there. Presumably, in order to internalize the concept of "control," a newcomer to English who is a native speaker of Polish has to weld the configuration of simple concepts that are the building blocks of this complex concept into a unitary coin (cf. Goddard and Wierzbicka, In press, Chapter 9), which can then be mentally manipulated as a stable unit of cognitive and communicative currency, facilitating the acquisition of the cultural script of "emotional control."

When one reads a self-analysis such as Hoffman's, one can appreciate Aneta Pavlenko's observation that the question "does language affect thinking—yes or no?" reflects a deeply monolingual perspective. As Hoffman's exploration of her own experience beautifully shows, it is not a matter of either/or, but a matter of how and to what extent. Referring in particular to child and teenage migrants like Hoffman, Mary Besemeres, in her book *Translating One's Self* (2002: 64), speaks in this connection of "the possibility of integrating (...) [one's] experiences from within another language (...) in one's English-speaking adult life." Compared with several other language migrants discussed in *Translating One's Self*, Hoffman is "less often ambivalent about her bicultural experience than she is ambidextrous, her right hand as aware as it can be of what her left is secretly writing." (ibid.)

According to the bilingual Cuban writer Pérez Firmat (2003: 13), "the ultimate validity of the Sapir-Whorf hypothesis is irrelevant. What is crucial is that many bilinguals relate to their languages in ways that enact some version of this hypothesis." This applies to Eva Hoffman, too. At the same time it is striking that unlike many other bilingual testimonies, hers also enacts a version of the universalist hypothesis that recognizes the possibility of conceptual freedom and flexibility. It is a version that Hoffman, with a tinge of irony, calls her "translation therapy":

> But in my translation therapy, I keep going back and forth over the rifts, not to heal them but to see that I—one person singular—have been on both sides. Patiently, I use English as a conduit to go back and down; all the way down to childhood, almost to the beginning. When I learn to say those smallest, first things in the language that has served for detachment and irony and abstraction, I begin to see where the languages I've spoken have their correspondences—how I can move between them without being split by the difference. (Hoffman 1989: 273)

Obviously, not many bilingual speakers can be as "ambidextrous" as Eva Hoffman, but Hoffman's penetrating examination of her own experience lends support to the view that it *is* in principle possible "to exist not only within culture but also outside it" (Hoffman 1989: 276), and that "thinking outside a language is [not] impossible" (Coetzee 1992: 145). This is also the NSM position, which underlies *Imprisoned in English*.

Hoffman's book about "translating" her life from Polish into English (cf. Besemeres & Wierzbicka eds. 2007) compellingly shows how language-bound a person's life normally is. At the same time, it highlights the possibility of trans-lingual thought as a foundation on which cross-linguistic bridges can be built and which can serve as a virtual free zone of the mind (*before* language, *beyond* language, and, for bilingual and multilingual speakers, *in-between* languages).

17. J. M. Coetzee—A View from Translation

J. M. Coetzee, winner of the Nobel Prize for Literature, is best known for his novels, not for his writings on linguistics or translation. Yet as Carrol Clarkson, the author of *J.M. Coetzee: Countervoices* (2009: 3) points out, "An engagement with questions raised by the linguistic sciences is at the core of Coetzee's writing."

At the root of this engagement no doubt lies Coetzee's personal experience of bilingualism and of the tensions between Afrikaans and English in his own life. Presumably, the dilemmas and conflicts associated with these two languages played a role in Coetzee's choice of linguistics as a field of study during his stay at the University of Texas from 1965 through 1968, and in the continued interest in languages and translatability evident in his novels, as well as his essays and interviews. For example, in his interview with Jean Sévry in 1986 he commented: "I think there is evidence of an interest in problems of language throughout my novels. I don't see any disruption between my professional interest in language and my activities as a writer." (Coetzee and Sévry 1986: 1)

Similarly, in his opening address at the Linguistics at the Millennium conference at the University of Cape Town in 2000, he stated: "although I cannot any longer call myself an active linguist, my own approach to language has been shaped more deeply than I know by immersion in ways of thinking encouraged by linguistic science." (Coetzee 2000: 1)

Coetzee's deep personal engagement with questions arising from linguistics is at the center of his 1982 essay "Newton and the Ideal of a Transparent Scientific Language" (reprinted in Coetzee 1992), in which he reflects on Wilhelm von Humboldt's famous passage setting out the "language relativity" thesis:

> Since experience and action depend upon a man's representations, man lives in relation to objects almost exclusively as language leads him to live. By the very act of spinning language out of himself, he spins himself into language. Thus the national linguistic community [*Volk*] to which one belongs becomes a circle from which it is possible to escape only insofar as one steps into the circle of another language. (Humboldt 1963[1830-1835], p. 433-34)

Coetzee comments that the "Humboldt-Sapir-Whorf hypothesis" (he alternates this phrase with "the Whorf hypothesis") "has had a rough time at the hands of philosophers and linguists (who have argued that it is circular), and anthropologists and psychologists (who have argued that it cannot be verified experimentally)"; and yet from the point of view of literary translation, the basic truth of this hypothesis can hardly be doubted:

> There is one field, however, where the Whorf hypothesis is treated as self-evident, even when it is not explicitly known. This is the field of literary translation, where the task that faces the translator at every turn is one of carrying across from one language to another not so much words as the systems of assumptions lying behind those words (...) The translator moves back and forth between the circles of the two languages, trying to bring with him, at each move, the memory or feel of the sense he wishes to translate. The occupation of translation brings the translator continually face to face with the most immediate corollary of the Whorf hypothesis, namely that a full or total translation is impossible. (Coetzee 1992: 182)

One aspect of Coetzee's support for the Humboldtian thesis that is particularly noteworthy is his emphasis on the fact that speakers are usually not aware of their conceptual dependence on their native language:

> it is a further corollary of Whorf's position—and even more clearly of von Humboldt's—that because of the closeness of fit of particular languages with particular world views, a speaker does not become aware of the mediatory role of language between reality and mind except by a considerable intellectual act of self-distancing: there is normally an untroubled

continuity between nature as he sees it and the terms his language provides to see it in. (Coetzee 1992: 183)

Coetzee emphasizes in this context Whorf's desire "to achieve this self-distancing" and to bring to the surface of consciousness "the assumptions about the universe embedded in his own language, English" (Coetzee 1992: 183).

Thus, English—"the greatest imperial language of them all" (Coetzee 1992: 53)—is also culturally contingent, and native speakers of English, too, are usually not aware of their conceptual dependence on the lexical, grammatical, and cultural resources of their mother tongue. They may feel more at home in English than nonnative speakers, but if they don't have any existential translingual experience, they may be conceptually less flexible than those who do have it. Thus, in the essay "On the mother tongue," Coetzee (or his alter ego Señor C) muses:

> Does each of us have a mother tongue? Do I have a mother tongue? Until recently I accepted without question that, since English is the language I command best, English must count as my mother tongue. But perhaps it is not so. Perhaps—is this possible?—I have no mother tongue. (Coetzee 2007: 156)

For the readers of Coetzee's *Boyhood*, such reflections must bring to mind the tensions between English (his family's home language) and Afrikaans (the language of his extended family) that he experienced during his childhood:

> Would the whole experience be any different, any less complicated, any better, if I were more deeply sunk, by birth and upbringing, in the language I write—in other words, if I had a truer, less questionable mother tongue than English in which to work? Perhaps it is so that all languages are, finally, foreign languages, alien to our animal being. But in a way that is, precisely, inarticulate, inarticulable, English does not feel to me a resting place, a home. It just happens to be a language over whose resources I have achieved some mastery. (Coetzee 2007, p. 157)

Coetzee's observation that perhaps "all languages are, finally, foreign languages, alien to our animal being" accords well with the NSM view that what is inherent to "our animal being" is the innate and universal language of thought, and that all languages (including English) carry with them presuppositions inherited from earlier generations of speakers and therefore are not always fully adequate for what we really want to say.

Thus, Coetzee is far from accepting an extreme version of the "relativity thesis," according to which a person's thinking is determined by his or her language. While early on he came to suspect that "languages spoke people or at the very least spoke through people" (Coetzee 1992: 52), he "didn't believe for a moment that thinking outside a language was impossible" (Coetzee 1992: 145), and he spoke with admiration of Newton's "struggle not to be confined by the epistemology of Latin" (Coetzee 1992: 144) and of his "immense effort of consciousness to think outside language" (Coetzee 1992: 145).

This double emphasis on the conceptual and cultural contingency of all languages (including English) and on the possibility of thought outside particular languages reflects a perspective in which thinking about language and literature is closely linked to thinking about translation. (It is worth noting that Coetzee's Nobel-prize acceptance speech (2003) has been described as "a meditation on translation" (Barnard 2009: 86)). This double emphasis is also highly consonant with NSM research and with the central theme of *Imprisoned in English*.

Final Remarks

There are many other scholars whom I see as kindred spirits and whom I feel the need to mention here, however briefly. In linguistics, there is above all Andrzej Bogusławski, whose work is deeply germane to the NSM research program (see, e.g., *The Study in the Linguistics-Philosophy Interface,* 2007). There is Igor Mel'čuk, the pillar (next to Apresjan) of the Moscow Semantic School, the author of numerous books on semantics (most recently, *Semantics,* 2012) and, like Bogusławski, one of the deepest and most original thinkers in the history of the field. There is Donal Carbaugh, builder of bridges between communication studies, ethnography, and linguistics, the author of the classic work *Talking American: Cultural discourses on Donahue* (1988) and more recently, *Cultures in Conversation* (2005), a long-time supporter (and in his most recent work, practitioner) of NSM. There is also Istvan Kecskes, one of the world's authorities on the learning and teaching of English, the author (with Tunde Papp) of *Foreign Language and Mother Tongue* (2000), and the founder of the pioneering journal *Intercultural Pragmatics,* who devoted one of the first two issues of the journal to the NSM theory of cultural scripts.

Among psychologists, I would like to acknowledge, above all, the nestor of cognitive psychology Jerome Bruner, to whose splendid book *Acts of Meaning* (1990) I have often referred with admiration, most recently, in my paper (In press a) "Innate conceptual primitives manifested in the languages of the world." (As a whole, the paper is focused on the work of another eminent psychologist, Susan Carey (2009), whose thinking is also convergent with NSM thinking, because she posits the existence of innate "core cognition" ("the developmental foundation of human conceptual understanding" (p. 12)) and of an "innate stock of primitives") (p. 448).

The idea of an innate stock of concepts that can work as conceptual building blocks in human thinking is also present in the work of evolutionary anthropologist Doug Jones. Thus, Jones's review of "Evolutionary Psychology" in *Annual Review of Anthropology* (1999: 560) includes "a provisional list of 64 panhuman conceptual primitives" that "follows the cross-cultural lexical work of Wierzbicka and associates (Wierzbicka 1992, 1996, 1997)." Jones comments that "despite differences in aims and methods, it [this work] shows a striking convergence with other work in cognitive psychology and anthropology."[1]

Another psychologist whom I see as a fellow traveler is James Russell, founder and editor of *Emotion Review.* Russell's thinking about emotions—non-Anglocentric and sensitive to languages and cultures—was so heterodox and ahead of his discipline that it provoked Paul Ekman, the doyen of "emotionologists" at the time, to publish (in the leading journal of the discipline, the *Psychological Bulletin*) a paper titled "Strong Evidence for Universals in Facial Expressions: A Reply to Russell's Mistaken Critique" (Ekman 1994; cf. Russell 1994).

I would also like to mention here psychologist Jan Smedslund from Oslo University, whose basic ideas converge in important ways with those of NSM researchers. Smedslund is the originator of "psychologic"—an approach that seeks to "explicate and systematise parts of *commonsense psychology* (...) embedded in everyday language" (1988: VII) and that draws on NSM ("NSM provides guidelines for the selection of primitives," Smedslund 1997: 12).

Among anthropologists about whom I have not written here at length, I see a great deal of kindred thinking in the work of Catherine Lutz, Naomi Quinn, Geoffrey White, Robert LeVine, and especially the late Clifford Geertz, to whom I have recently paid tribute in my article "Translatability and the scripting of other peoples' souls" (Wierzbicka, 2013b).

Among historians, an excellent example of kindred thinking can be found in the work of David Hackett Fischer, the author of *Albion's Seed* (1989) and *Fairness and Freedom: A History of Two Open Societies, New Zealand and the United States* (2012). In this latter work, Fischer links the striking differences in the history of contact between Anglophone newcomers and the indigenous populations in these two societies with the different levels of cross-linguistic communication and understanding. Devoting a great deal of attention to Maori cultural key words such as *whakapapa* (which is "often translated as genealogy but means much more than that," p. 109) and to the culture-specific English key word *fairness,* Fischer draws on my NSM-based study of "fairness" in *English: Meaning and culture* (2006).

The list could go on but instead of continuing it, I will stop here and make two final points. Firstly, while some of the scholars quoted in this final part of the book link the NSM theory with my work alone, in fact, for well over twenty years this theory has been developed jointly by Cliff Goddard and myself, as equal partners. And secondly, as Nicholas Evans (2010b: 516) has said, "NSM practitioners have produced a vast body of semantic analyses across dozens of languages, and at present can claim to having developed the approach that has gone deepest into the possibilities of setting up a cross-linguistically valid set of basic semantic categories in which all meanings can be stated." This is so in large measure because "NSM practitioners" are a community of scholars pursuing the same research program across many diverse languages of the world and often working and thinking together.

To mention the main languages and the special areas of expertise of a number of NSM researchers (aside from Cliff Goddard, who is the cofounder of the NSM research community, and whose *Semantic Analysis* (1998/2011) is the best introduction to NSM theory and practice; see also, Table 1:

Felix Ameka has studied interactional routines, cultural attitudes, and cultural scripts in Ewe and other West African languages (see, e.g., 1987, 1999). He is the author of *Ewe: Its grammatical constructions and illocutionary devices* (2012), and editor of *Journal of African Languages and Linguistics.*

Yuko Asano-Cavanagh has investigated epistemic modality and the language of pain in Japanese. (see, e.g., 2009, 2011, 2012).

Helen Bromhead has studied epistemic expressions in sixteenth- and seventeenth-century English, documenting a distinct epistemic ethos of truth, faith, and certainty (2009). She has also carried out an in-depth cross-linguistic study of ethnogeographical categorization (see, e.g., 2013).

Zuzanna Bułat Silva is a specialist in Portuguese and Spanish working at Wrocław University in Poland. Her book *Fado: A Semantic Approach* (2008) is an excellent example of the use of NSM for cross-linguistic cultural semantics. (see also 2012)

Anna Gladkova has developed a full Russian version of NSM and has published a book, *Russian Cultural Semantics* (2010a), and many studies in contrastive cultural semantics comparing Russian and English. (See, e.g., 2007, 2010b).

Jean Harkins has carried out a detailed cross-linguistic study of the concept of "want" (1995). She has worked on Australian Aboriginal languages and is the author of *Bridging Two Worlds: Aboriginal English and Cross-cultural Understanding* (1994). She is also the coeditor of *Emotions in Crosslinguistic Perspective* (Harkins and Wierzbicka eds. 2001).

Rie Hasada has delved into many areas of cultural semantics of Japanese, with special reference to emotions, values, nonverbal communication, and the interactional style in Japanese. (See, e.g., 1998, 2002, 2008).

Sandy Habib has worked on Arabic and Hebrew NSM and has investigated, in particular, the domain of "supernatural semantics," with a focus on concepts such as "God," "angel," "heaven," and "hell" in English, Arabic, and Hebrew (see, e.g., 2011a, 2011).

Marie-Odile Junker's work is focused on the Algonquian language East Cree. Working with East Cree consultants, she developed techniques for studying endangered languages and endangered meanings from an indigenous perspective, through Cree-based NSM. (See, e.g., 2003, 2008).

Carsten Levisen is the author of *Cultural Semantics and Social Cognition: A Case Study of the Danish Universe of Meaning* (2012; see also his article on Danish social cognition In Press). His current research is on European-based creoles in the Pacific region and on NSM-based "cognitive creolistics".

Sophie Nicholls has developed a Kriol-based analysis of cultural scripts in Kriol (a creole language used in Northern Australia), with a view to facilitating understanding between Aboriginal and non-Aboriginal people in Australia's Northern Territory (see, e.g., In press).

Bert Peeters is a pioneer in the cultural semantics of French and a leading representative of NSM work in the Francophone world (see, e.g., 2010). His 2006 book *Semantic Primes and Universal Grammar: Evidence from the Romance Languages* is a groundbreaking publication in Romance linguistics and comparative semantics.

Carol Priestley has done a great deal of work on the Papuan language Koromu. Her experience of living in remote communities in Papua New Guinea has given her exceptionally good access to the insider's conceptual and cultural perspective. (see, e.g., 2008, 2012a and b).

Ryo Stanwood (who sadly died in 2010) did outstanding work investigating the semantics of Hawaii Creole English, and made a significant contribution to Creole studies and cross-linguistic semantics (see 1997, 1999).

Adrien Tien has applied NSM to the study of child language in Mandarin. He is the author of *Semantic and Conceptual Development During the First Four Years* (2010).

Catherine Travis has investigated cultural values and interactional style in Colombian Spanish. Her book *Discourse Markers in Colombian Spanish* (2005) is a landmark in semantically based investigations of interpersonal interaction.

Sophia Waters's work is in the area of intercultural semantics with a special interest in Australian English and French (see, e.g., 2012, 2013).

Jock Wong has published extensively on speech practices in Singapore English, showing how deeply a "local" English such as Singapore English can differ, conceptually and culturally, from Anglo English (see, e.g., 2004a, 2004b).

Zhengdao Ye has done groundbreaking work on the cultural semantics of Chinese across a wide range of areas, including emotions, facial expressions, values, social interaction, and cultural scripts (see, e.g., 2004, 2007).

Kyung-Joo Yoon has developed a full Korean version of the Natural Semantic Metalanguage, published in 2006 in Seoul as *Constructing a Korean Natural Semantic Metalanguage.* She has also studied various aspects of Korean cultural semantics (see, e.g., 2004, 2006).

This list, too, could go on, but I will stop here, referring the reader to the NSM Homepage: <http://www.griffith.edu.au/humanities-languages/school-languages-linguistics/research/natural-semantic-metalanguage-homepage> (See also, Table 1).

TABLE 1.
Selection of Languages Studied in the Nsm Framework, with Full Metalanguage Studies Marked with † (Full References Given on the NSM Homepage)

Language Family/Type	Language(s)	Sources (Not Necessarily Exhaustive)
Austronesian	Malay†, Mbula†, Longgu, Samoan	Goddard (2001a, 2001b, 2002), Bugenhagen (2001, 2002), Hill (1994), Mosel (1994)
Indo-European	Spanish†, Danish†, French†, Polish†, Russian†	Travis (2002, 2004, 2006), Levisen (2012), Peeters (2006, 2010), Wierzbicka (2002b), Gladkova (2007, 2010)
Semitic	Amharic†, Arabic†, Hebrew†	Amberber (2008), Habib (2011a, 2011b)
Finno-Ugric	Finnish†	Vanhatalo et al. (in press)
Sinitic	Chinese (Mandarin)†, Cantonese	Chappell (2002), Ye (2006, 2007, 2010), Tong et al. (1997), Tien (2009), Leung (2012), Wakefield (2011)
Algonquian	East Cree†	Junker (2003, 2008), Junker and Blacksmith (2006)
Niger-Congo	Ewe	Ameka (1994, 2006, 2009)
Japonic	Japanese†	Hasada (1998, 2001, 2008), Asano-Cavanagh (2009, 2010)
Korean	Korean†	Yoon (2006, 2008)
Tai-Kadai	Lao†	Enfield (2002)
Papuan	Koromu†, Kalam, Makasai	Priestley (2002, 2008, 2012a, 2012b), Pawley (1994), Brotherson (2008)
Pama-Nyungan (Australia)	Pitjantjatjara/Yankunytjatjara, Arrernte	Goddard (1991, 1994), Bromhead (2011a), Harkins and Wilkins (1994), Harkins (2001)
Non-Pama-Nyungan (Australia)	Bunuba	Knight (2008)
Creoles	Hawaii Creole English, Roper Kriol†	Stanwood (1997, 1999), Nicholls (2009)

NOTES

Chapter 1

1. The title of Part I of this book comes from a famous quote from the founder of modern linguistics, Wilhelm von Humboldt: "each language draws a circle around the people to whom it adheres" (1903-36, v. 7: 60). Humboldt recognized, however, that "a mid-point around which all languages revolve, can be sought and really found" (ibid.). The inner core of all languages which can give us a basis for a culture-independent metalanguage corresponds, in many ways, to Humboldt's "mid-point."

Chapter 5

1. For more precise definitions, see my 2007 article "Bodies and their parts."
2. The word *stopy* (which is not colloquial) refers to feet conceptualized as part of the legs, not as part of the body (see Wierzbicka 2007). So, for example, in the English translations of the Gospels Jesus was washing the Apostles' feet, whereas in the Polish translations he was washing their *nogi* (legs) rather than *stopy* (roughly, feet).
3. In his NSM-based study of Lao, Enfield (2002: 145) wrote about NSM: "No other descriptive metalanguage (formal or otherwise) insists on this level of cross-translatability, and so it is apparently the closest thing to a real standard of comparison available for cross-linguistic semantic comparison." Referring to the two volumes of *Meaning and Universal Grammar: Theory and empirical findings* (Goddard and Wierzbicka, eds. 2002), Enfield wrote (2002: 246):

> "The Natural Semantic Metalanguage provides a stable and methodologically useful cross-linguistic frame of reference for discovering and stating meaning, both in the laboratory and in the field. As the descriptive chapters in this set of studies demonstrate, the NSM provides a genuine solution to a fundamental problem of linguistics and anthropology—where to begin in describing what things mean."

Chapter 7

1. Anthropologist Robert LeVine (2001: xi) writes:

> Anthropologists waged intermittent guerrilla warfare against psychological universalism during much of the twentieth century. From the days of Malinowski (1927) and Mead (1928) onward, field data from non-Western societies have been used to attack and revise generalizations issued by Western psychologists and psychoanalysts. But American and European psychologists and psychoanalysts have rarely seen the need to take seriously these challenges from abroad, convinced as they are that their clinical

or experimental methods give them access to the deepest levels of generically human biopsychology. In recent years, however, some developmental and social psychologists, under the banner of cultural psychology, have paid increasing attention to the possibility that the plasticity of human development and the varying environmental conditions under which it occurs, make knowledge of human diversity central to psychological understanding (Bruner 1990, 1996; Cole 1996; Greenfield and Cocking 1994; Kitayama and Markus 1994; Miller 1997; Shweder et al. 1998; Stevenson and Stigler 1992; Valsiner 2000).

LeVine sees these developments in cultural psychology as encouraging, commenting, however, that "this new and vigorous attack" on psychological universalism blind to the cultural and linguistic diversity is still resisted and ignored by mainstream psychologies" (p. xii). A decade later, things have clearly improved. Nonetheless, according to Russell et al. (2011: 363) the program of scientific research based on basic emotion theory is still "central to discourse on emotions."

Chapter 9

1. It is interesting to note that in Hilary Mantel's splendid novels *Wolf Hall* (2009) and *Bring Up the Bodies* (2012), in which she tries to imagine the world-thought of sixteenth-century England, the words *cooperation* and *cooperate* play an important role. This is an anachronism, which illustrates how difficult it is for a modern "Anglo" to imagine an earlier epoch when English speakers didn't think in such terms.

Chapter 10

1. The new meaning of the English word *science,* which excludes the humanities, appears to be derived from that of the word *scientist*: (derived in turn from phrases like "real sciences" in 19th century Britain). In his book *The Age of Wonder*, Richard Holmes (2008: 449) speaks in this context of "a passionate discussion of semantics" which engulfed the British Association for the Advancement of Science (BAAS) reported by the geologist William Whewell in the *Quarterly Reveiw* of 1834:

> Formerly the 'learned' embraced in their wide grasp all the branches of the tree of knowledge, mathematicians as well as philosophers, physical as well as antiquarian speculators. But these days are past...This difficulty was felt very oppressively by the members of the BAAS at Cambridge last summer. There was no general term by which these gentlemen could describe themselves with reference to their pursuits.
>
> 'Philosophers' was felt to be too wide and lofty a term, and was very properly forbidden them be Mr. Coleridge, both in his capacity as philologer and metaphysician. 'Savans' was rather assuming and besides too French; but some ingenious gentlemen [in fact Whewell himself] proposed that, by analogy with 'artist', they might form 'scientist'—and added that there could be no scruple to this term since we already have such words as 'economist' and 'atheist' - but this was not generally palatable.

Chapter 13

1. In his chapter "Vocabularies and theories" in *The Meaning of Primate Signals,* Harré (1984: 96) commented on "the use of scientific rhetoric" in primatological literature: "e.g. 'displayed the same behaviours' for 'did the same things.'" Such rhetoric is objectionable for two reasons: its narrow behaviorism and its use of unnecessarily complex academic English.

2. In his book *Dying Words,* Nicholas Evans (2010a) has expressed a view that the Australian language Dalabon doesn't have words for know and think, and the Australian language Kayardild, for want. As argued in detail in Goddard and Wierzbicka, To appear, in relation to know and think, and in Wierzbicka In press, in relation to want, these claims are in our view unsustainable.

Chapter 14

1. Comparing his own idea of a universal language based on the "Alphabet of Human Thoughts" with the languages invented by his contemporaries such as John Wilkins, Leibniz wrote:

> For their [i.e. Wilkins and his followers'] language or script only allows a convenient form of communication to be set up between people divided by language; but the true *Characteristica Realis,* as I conceive of it, ought to be considered one of the most apt tools of the human mind, as it would have unrivalled power with respect to the development of ideas, storing those ideas, and distinguishing between them. (Gerhardt (ed.) 1960-1 Vol. 7:7)

Thus, in Leibniz's view, a language based on simple and clear concepts can force the speakers to say only things that are fully understandable (and not only seemingly so), and be a tool for thinking and for comparing and elucidating ideas. *Mutatis mutandis,* these are the goals of the NSM program in general, and the notion of Minimal English in particular (cf. Wierzbicka 2012; Goddard and Wierzbicka In press).

2. In his 2010 book *Globish,* Robert McCrum, coauthor of the television series *The Story of English,* has adopted the term "Globish" (which, he says, Nerrière has invented "in a moment of inspiration") for his own purposes: not as a name for a simplified form of communication between nonnative speakers and learners of English, but as a characterization of English in its current global role: "the world-wide dialect of the third millennium" (p. 8), "the universal lingua franca, a global means of communication that is irrepressibly contagious, adaptable, populist and subversive" (p. 15).

Chapter 15

1. I would like to stress that, as already mentioned, for more than twenty years, Cliff Goddard and I have been developing the NSM program as equal partners, so it is inaccurate to link this program with my name alone, as, for example, Shweder and D'Andrade do.

2. As another approach that he finds particularly helpful, Dowrick mentions the analysis of emotions developed by psychologist James Russell, based on the recognition of good and bad feelings.

Chapter 16

1. I made a similar point myself in my 1999 book *Emotions Across Languages and Culture,* where I wrote:

> the word *emotion* is not as unproblematic as it seems; and by taking the notion of "emotion" as our starting point we may be committing ourselves, at the outset, to a perspective which is shaped by our own native language, or by the language currently predominant in some academic disciplines rather than taking a maximally "neutral" and culture-independent point of view. (p. 2)

Chapter 17

1. Wray and Grace (2007) affirm (citing Dixon and Aikhenvald (2002) as their source) that "many languages do not have a word for 'word.'" According to NSM research, however, this claim is unfounded (Goddard 2011b).

2. In his book *Dying Words*, Nicholas Evans (2010a) has expressed a view that the Australian language Dalabon doesn't have words for know and think. As argued in detail in Goddard and Wierzbicka, To appear, this claim is unsustainable.

3. I have singled out Aleksey Shmelev's name for the title of this section to keep the symmetry with the titles of the other sections. In fact, however, Shmelev, Zalizniak, and Levontina are a team and this section is devoted to the work of all three.

Final Remarks

1. The list of NSM primes is also partially reproduced by semiotician Umberto Eco (1999: 150). Eco writes:

> Wierzbicka (1996), who backs up her hypotheses with a vast recognition of different languages, persuasively maintains the existence of certain *primes* common to all cultures. In her view, these are notions such as I, Someone, Something, This, Other, One, Two, Many, Much, Think, Want, Feel, Say, Do, Happen, Good, Bad, Small, Big, When, Before, After, Where, Under, No, Some, Live, Far, Near, If, and Then (my summarized list is incomplete).

REFERENCES

Ajo, Frances et al. 2010. Native speakers as documenters: A student initiative. Grenoble, Lenore and Furbee, N. Louanna (eds). *Language documentation: Practice and values.* 275–288.

Alpher, Barry. 1982. Dalabon dual subject prefixes, kinship categories, and generation skewing. In J. Heath, F. Merlan and A. Rumsey, eds., *Languages of Kinship in Aboriginal Australia.*, 19–30. Sydney: Sydney University Press.

Amberber, Mengistu. 2008. Semantic primes in Amharic. In: Cliff Goddard (ed.), *Cross-Linguistic Semantics.* Amsterdam: John Benjamins, 83–119.

Ameka, Felix. 1994. Ewe. In Goddard and Wierzbicka, (eds), 57–86.

Ameka, Felix. 2006. 'When I die, don't cry': the ethnopragmatics of "gratitude" in West African languages. In Cliff Goddard (ed.) *Ethnopragmatics: Understanding Discourse in Cultural Context*, 231–266. Berlin: Mouton de Gruyter.

Ameka, Felix Kofi. 2009. Access rituals in West African communities: An ethnopragmatic perspective. In *Ritual Communication*, ed. Gunther Senft and Ellen B. Basso, 127–152. NY: Berg.

Ameka, Felix Kofi. 2012. *Ewe: Its grammatical construction and illocutionary devices.* Munich: LINCOM.

Anderson, J. R. and Matsuzawa, T. 2006. Yawning: An opening into Empathy?. In Matsuzawa, Tomonaga, and Tanaka, (eds.), 233–245.

Apresjan, Jurij D. 2000. *Systematic Lexicography.* Translated by Kevin Windle. Oxford: Oxford University Press.

Authur, Jay. 1999. Jay Arthur on dictionaries of the default country. Lingua Franca. ABC Radio National. 12 June.

Asano-Cavanagh, Yuko. 2009. A semantic analysis of Japanese epistemic markers: *chigainai* and *hazuda*. *Language Sciences* 31(5): 837–852.

Asano-Cavanagh, Yuko. 2010. Semantic analysis of evidential markers in Japanese: *rashii, yooda* and *sooda*. *Functions of Language* 17 (2): 153–180.

Asano-Cavanagh, Yuko. 2011. An analysis of three Japanese tags: *ne, yone and daroo*. *Pragmatics and Cognition* 19(3), 448–475.

Asano-Cavanagh, Yuko. 2012. Expression of *kawaii* ('cute'): Gender reinforcement of young Japanese female school children. *Joint AARE, APERA International Conference Proceedings, 5/12/2012.* Sydney: Australian Association for Research in Education (AARE).

Asquith, Pamela J. 1984. The inevitably and utility of anthropomorphism in description of primate behaviour. In Harré and Reynold (eds.) *The Meaning of Primate Signals*, 138–174. Cambridge: Cambridge University Press.

Austin, Peter K. (ed.). 2003–2010. *Language Documentation and Description.*Vols. 1–9. London: Hans Rausing Endangered Languages Project, School of Oriental and African Studies.

Avis, J. & Harris, P. L. 1991. Belief-desire reasoning among Baka children: evidence for a universal conception of mind. *Child Development* 62, 460–467.

Bacon, Francis. 1860. "Novum Organum." In *The Works of Francis Bacon*. Vol. 4, ed. James Spedding, Robert Leslie Ellis, and Douglas Denon Heath. New York: Garrett Press.

Bakhtin, Mikhail. 1963 [1929]. *Problemy poetiki Dostoevskogo* (Problems of Dostoevsky's poetics). Moscow: Sovetskij pisatel'.

Barnard, Rita. 2009. Coetzee in/and Afrikaans. *Journal of Literary Studies* 25:4, 84–105.

Barrett, Lisa Feldman. 2006. Solving the emotion paradox: Categorization and the experience of emotion. *Personality and Social Psychology Review*, 10(1): 20–46.

Barsalou, Lawrence. 2003. Situated simulation in the human conceptual system. *Language and Cognitive Processes* 18(5-6): 513–562.

Bartmiński, Jerzy. 2005. *Aspects of Cognitive Ethnolinguistics*. London: Equinox.

Bassetti, Benedetta and Vivian Cook. 2011. In *Language and Bilingual Cognition*, ed. Vivian Cook and Benedetta Bassetti, 143–190. Hove, UK: Routledge.

Bauman, Richard & Charles Briggs. 2003. *Voices of modernity: Language ideologies and the politics of inequality*. Cambridge; New York: Cambridge University Press.

Bellah, Robert N., Richard Madsen, William M. Sullivan, Ann Swidler and Steven M. Tipton. 1985. *Habits of the Heart: Individualism and Commitment in American Life*. Berkeley: University of California Press.

Benveniste, Emile. 1971. *Problems in General Linguistics*. Translated by M. E. Meek. Coral Gables, FL: University of Miami Press.

Berlin, Brent and Paul Kay. 1969. *Basic Color Terms: Their Universality and Evolution*. Berkeley: University of California Press.

Berlin, Brent. 1992. *Ethnobiological Classification*. Princeton, NJ: Princeton University Press.

Berlin, Isaiah. 1976. *Vico and Herder: two studies in the history of ideas*. London: Hogarth.

Berlin, Isaiah. 1980. *Personal impressions*. London: The Hogarth Press.

Besemeres, Mary. 1998. Language and self in cross-cultural autobiography: Eva Hoffman's *Lost in Translation*. *Canadian Slavonic Papers*. XL, 3-4. 327–344.

Besemeres, Mary. 2002. *Translating One's Self: Language and Selfhood in Cross-Cultural Autobiography*. Oxford: Peter Lang.

Besemeres, Mary and Anna Wierzbicka (eds.). 2007. *Translating Lives: Living with Two Languages and Cultures*. St. Lucia: University of Queensland Press.

Bickerton, Derek. 2009. *Adam's tongue: How humans made language*. New York: Hill and Wang.

Biro, Dora, Susana Carvalho and Tetsuro Matsuzawa. 2010. Tools, Traditions, and Technologies: Interdisciplinary Approaches to Chimpanzee Nut Cracking. In E. V. Lonsdorf, S. R. Ross and T. Matsuzawa, eds., 141–155. *The Mind of the Chimpanzee: ecological and experimental perspectives*. Chicago: The University of Chicago Press.

Blount, Benjamin. 1984. The language of emotions: An ontogenetic perspective. *Language Sciences* 6(1): 129–156.

Boesch, Christophe. 2009. *The Real Chimpanzee: Sex Strategies in the Forest*. Cambridge: Cambridge University Press.

Boesch, Christophe. 2012. *Wild Cultures*. Cambridge: Cambridge University Press.

Boesch, Christophe and Hedwige Boesch-Achermann. 2000. *The Chimpanzee of the Taï Forest: Behavioural Ecology and Evolution*. Oxford: Oxford University Press.

Bogusławski, Andrzej. 2007. *The Study in the Linguistics-Philosophy Interface*. Warsaw: BEL Studio.

Bowerman, Melissa and Sang-Chin Choi. 2001. Shaping Meanings for Language: universal and language-specific and the acquisition of semantic categories. In M. Bowerman and S. C. Levinson (eds.), *Language Acquisition and Conceptual Development*, 475–511. Cambridge: Cambridge University Press.

Bowern, Claire. 2008. *Linguistic Fieldwork: A practical guide*. Basingstoke; New York: Palgrave Macmillan.

Brett, Lily. 2001. *New York*. Picador: Pan Macmillan Australia.

Bromhead, Helen. 2009. *The Reign of Truth and Faith: Epistemic Expressions in 16th and 17th Century English*. Berlin: Mouton de Gruyter.

Bromhead. Helen. 2011a. Ethnogeographical categories in English and Pitjantjatjara/Yankunytjatjara. *Language Sciences* 33(1), 58–75.

Bromhead, Helen. 2011b. The bush in Australian English. *Australian Journal of Linguistics* 31, 445–471.

Bromhead, Helen. 2013. *Mountains, Rivers, Billabongs: Ethnogeographical categorization in cross-linguistic perspective*. PhD Thesis. Australian National University, Canberra.

Brotherson, Anna. 2008. The ethnogeometry of Makasai (East Timor). In Cliff Goddard (ed.), *Cross-Linguistic Semantics*, 259–276. Amsterdam: John Benjamins.

Brown, G. and Harris, T. 1978. *Social Origins of Depression*. London: Tavistock Publications.

Brown, Penelope and Stephen C. Levinson. 1978. "Universals in language usage: politeness phenomena". In Esther Goody (ed.) *Questions and politeness: strategies in social interaction*. Cambridge: Cambridge University Press. 56–310.

Brown, Penelope and Stephen C. Levinson. 1987. *Politeness: Some universals in language usage*. Cambridge; New York: Cambridge University Press.

Bruner, Jerome. 1990. *Acts of Meaning*. Cambridge, MA: Harvard University Press.

Bugenhagen, Robert. 1990. Experiential constructions in Mangap-Mbula. *Australian Journal of Linguistics* (Special issue on the semantics of emotions) 10(2): 183–215.

Bugenhagen, Robert D. 2001. Emotions and the nature of persons in Mbula. In Jean Harkins and Anna Wierzbicka (eds.), *Emotions in Crosslinguistic Perspective*, 69–114. Berlin: Mouton de Gruyter.

Bugenhagen, Robert D. 2002. The syntax of semantic primitives in Mangaaba-Mbula. In Cliff Goddard and Anna Wierzbicka (eds.), *Meaning and Universal Grammar – Theory and Empirical Findings*, Volume I, 1–64. Amsterdam: John Benjamins.

Bułat Silva, Zuzanna. 2008. *Fado: A Semantic Approach*. Warsaw: Wrocławskie Wydawnictwo Owiatowe. (In Polish).

Bułat Silva, Zuzanna. 2012. *Saudade*: A key Portuguese emotion. *Emotion Review* 4(2): 203–211.

Call, Joseph and Michael Tomasello. 2008. Does the chimpanzee have a theory of mind? 30 years later. *Trends in Cognitive Science* 12: 187–192.

Call, Joseph. 2010. Trapping the Minds of Apes: Causal Knowledge and Inferential Reasoning about Object-Object Interactions. In E. V. Lonsdorf, S. R. Ross and T. Matsuzawa, eds., *The Mind of the Chimpanzee: ecological and experimental perspectives*, 75–86. Chicago: The University of Chicago Press.

Call, Joseph and Michael Tomasello (eds.). 2007. *The gestural communication of apes and monkeys*. Mahwah, New Jersey: Erlbaum.

Carbaugh, Donal. 1988. *Talking American: cultural discourses on DONAHUE*. Norwood, NJ: Ablex.

Carbaugh, Donal. 2005. *Cultures in Conversation*. Mahwah, NJ: Erlaum.

Carey, Susan. 2009. *The Origin of Concepts*. Oxford: Oxford University Press.

Carstairs G. Morris and Ravi L. Kapur. 1976. *The Great Universe of Kota: Stress, Change, and Mental Disorder in an Indian Village*. Berkeley: University of California Press.

Chappell, Hilary. 2002. The universal syntax of semantic primes in Mandarin Chinese. In Cliff Goddard and Anna Wierzbicka (eds.), *Meaning and Universal Grammar – Theory and Empirical Findings*, Volume I, 243–322. Amsterdam: John Benjamins.

Clarkson, Carrol. 2009. *J.M. Coetzee: Countervoices*. London: Palgrave Macmillan.

Clyne, Michael. 1994. *Inter-cultural communication at work*. Cambridge: Cambridge University Press.

Coetzee, J. M. 1982. Newton and the ideal of a transparent scientific language. *Journal of Literary Semantics* 11: 3–13.

Coetzee, J. M. 1992. *Doubling the Point: Essays and Interviews*. Cambridge: Harvard University Press.

Coetzee, J. M. 2000. Linguistics at the Millennium. Opening Address at the Linguistics at the Millennium Conference held at the University of Cape Town, January 2000.

Coetzee, J. M. 2003. *He and His Man: The 2003 Nobel Prize Lecture in Literature Online*.

Coetzee, J. M. 2007. *Diary of a Bad Year*. Melbourne: Text.

Coetzee, J. M. and J. Sévry. 1986. An Interview with J.M. Coetzee. *Commonwealth* 9 (Autumn 1986): 1–7.

Cohen, R. 2001. Language and conflict resolution: The limits of English. *International Studies Review*. 2 (1), 245–64.

Cole, M. 1996. *Cultural psychology: A once and future discipline*. Cambridge, MA: Harvard University Press.

Collin, Richard. 2012. Moving Political Meaning across linguistic frontiers. *Political Studies. Collins Cobuild English Language Dictionary*. 1987. London: HarperCollins.

Collins Wordbanks. <http://wordbanks.harpercollins.co.uk/auth/?>

Conklin, Harold. 1964 [1955]. Hanunóo colour categories. In Dell H. Hymes, ed., *Language in Culture and Society*, 189–192. New York: Harper Row.

Cook Vivian and Benedetta Bassetti (eds). 2011. *Language and Bilingual Cognition*. Hove, UK: Routledge.

Cook, Vivian. 2009. *All in a Word*. London: Melville House.

Cook, Vivian. 2011a. Relating language and cognition: The speaker of one language. In V. Cook and B. Bassetti (eds.) 3–22.

Cook, Vivian. 2011b. Linguistic Relativity and Language Teaching. In V. Cook and B. Bassetti (eds.) 509–518.

Corballis, Michael. 2002. *From and to mouth: The origins of language*. Princeton: Princeton University Press.

D'Andrade, Roy. 1995. *The Development of Cognitive Anthropology*. Cambridge: Cambridge University Press.

D'Andrade, Roy. 2001. A Cognitivist's View of the Units Debate in Cultural Anthropology. *Cross Cultural Research* 35(2): 242–257.

Dalrymple, Mary, Makoto Kanazawa, Yookyun Kim, Sam Mchombo and Stanley Peters. 1998. Reciprocal expressions and the concept of reciprocity. *Linguistics and philosophy* 21: 159–210.

Darwin, Charles. 1872. *The expression of the emotions in man and animals*, third edition. [With an Introduction, Afterword and Commentaries by Paul Ekman]. London: HarperCollins.

Davidson, Donald. 2001. *Subjective, Intersubjective, Objective*. Oxford: Clarendon Press.

Davidson, Ian. 2010. The colonization of Australia and its adjacent islands and the evolution of modern cognition. *Current Anthropology* 51(1): S177–S189.

Davis, Wayne, A. 1998. *Implicature: Intention, convention and principle in the failure of Gricean Theory*. Cambridge: Cambridge University Press.

Dawkins, Richard. 2006. *The God Delusion*. New York: Houghton Mifflin.

de Tocqueville, Alexis. 1966 [1848]. *Democracy in America*: New York: Harper & Row.

De Waal, Frans, 1984. Comment: Two eyes of Science. In Harré and Reynold (eds). 107–109.

De Waal, Frans, 1996. *Good Natured: The Origins of Right and Wrong in Humans and Other Animals*. Cambridge, MA: Harvard University Press.

De Waal, Frans. 2003. "Social Syntax: The If-Then Structure of Social Problem Solving." In Frans. de Waal and B. L. Tyack, eds., *Animal Social Complexity: Intelligence, Culture, and Individualized Societies*, 230–248. Cambridge, MA: Harvard University Press.

Dixon, R. M. W. and A. Y. Aikhenvald. 2002. Word: a typological framework. In R. M. W. Dixon & A. Y. Aikhenvald, eds., *Word: A Cross-linguistic Typology*, 1–41. Cambridge: Cambridge University Press.

Dixon, Thomas. 2003. *From Passions to Emotions: The Creation of a Psychological Category*. Cambridge: Cambridge University Press.

Dixon, Thomas. 2008. *The Invention of Altruism. Making Moral Meanings in Victorian Britain*. Oxford: British Academy, Oxford University Press.

Donald, Merlin. 2001. *A Mind So Rare: The Evolution of Human Consciousness*. New York: Farrar Strauss and Giroux.

Dowrick, Christopher. 2004. *Beyond Depression: A New Approach to Understanding and Management*. Oxford: Oxford University Press.

Dugatkin, Lee Alan. 1997. *Cooperation Among Animals: An Evolutionary Perspective*. Oxford: Oxford University Press.

Dumont, L. 1970. *Homo Hierarchius: The caste system and its implications*. Chicago: University of Chicago Press.

Durst, Uwe. 2001. Why Germans don't feel "anger." In Jean Harkins & Anna Wierzbicka, eds., *Emotions in Crosslinguistic Perspective*, 119–152. Berlin: Mouton de Gruyter.

Dwyer, Arienne M. 2010. Models of successful collaboration. In Grenoble, Lenore and Furbee, N. Louanna (eds). *Language documentation: Practice and values*. 193–212.

Eco, Umberto. 1999. *Kant and the Platypus*. London: Secker & Warburg.

Eco, Umberto. 2003. *Rat or Mouse. Translation as Negotiation*. London: Weidenfeld and Nicolson.

Eelen, Gino. 2001. *A Critique of Politeness Theories*. Manchester: St. Jerome Publishing.

Ehlich, Konrad. 2005. On the historicity of politeness. In Richard Watts, Sachiko Ide, and Konrad Ehlich, eds., *Politeness in Language*, 71–108. Berlin: Mouton de Gruyter.

Ekman, Paul. 1972. Universal and cultural differences in facial expressions of emotions. In *Nebraska Symposium on Motivation 1971*, ed. J. K. Cole, 207–293. Lincoln: University of Nebraska Press.

Ekman, Paul. 1973. *Darwin and Facial Expression: A Century of Research in Review*. New York: Academic.

Ekman, Paul. 1975. The universal smile: face muscles talk every language. *Psychology Today*, September: 35–39.

Ekman, Paul. 1980. *The Face of Man: Expressions of Universal Emotions in a New Guinea village*. New York: Garland STPM.

Ekman, Paul. 1992. An argument for basic emotions. *Cognition and Emotion* (Special issue on basic emotions) 6(3/4): 169–200.

Ekman, Paul. 1994. Strong evidence for universals in facial expressions: A reply to Russell's mistaken critique. *Psychological Bulletin* 115(2): 268–287.

Ekman, Paul. 2003. *Emotions Revealed: Recognizing Faces and Feelings to Improve Communication and Emotional Life*. New York Henry Holt and Company.

Ekman, Paul & Daniel Cordaro. 2011. What Is Meant by Calling Emotions Basic. *Emotion Review* 3(4): 364–370.

Ekman, Paul and Richard Davidson. 1994. Epilogue—Affective science: A research agenda. In Ekman and Davidson eds., 409–430.

Ekman, Paul and Richard Davidson (eds.) 1994. *The Nature of Emotion: Fundamental questions*. Oxford: Oxford University Press.

Ekman, Paul, and W.V. Friesen. 1971. Constants across cultures in the face and emotion. *Journal of personality and social psychology*. 17: 124–29.

Enfield, N. J. 2002. Combinatoric properties of Natural Semantic Metalanguage in Lao Emotions. In Goddard & Wierzbicka, eds. vol. 2, 145–256.

Enfield, N. J. 2011. Description of reciprocal situations in Lao. In *Reciprocals and Semantic Typology*, ed. Nicholas Evans, Alice Gaby, Stephen C. Levinson, and Asifa Majid, 129–149. Amsterdam: John Benjamins.

Enfield, N. J. and Stephen C. Levinson (eds.). 2006. *Roots of Human Sociality: Culture, cognition and interaction*. Oxford; New York: Berg.

Evans, Nicholas. 1985. *Kayardild: The Language of the Bentinck Islanders of North West Queensland*. PhD Thesis, Australian National University.

Evans, Nicholas. 1995. *A Grammar of Kayardild with Historical-comparative Notes on Tangkic*. Berlin: Mouton de Gruyter.

Evans, Nicholas. 2010a. *Dying Words: Endangered Languages and What They Have to Tell Us*. Chitchester, UK: Wiley-Blackwell.

Evans, Nicholas. 2010b. Semantic Typology. In *The Oxford Handbook of Linguistic Typology*, ed. Jae Jung Song, 504–533. Oxford/New York: Oxford University Press.

Evans, Nicholas, Francesca Merlan & Maggie Tukumba. 2004. *A first dictionary of Dalabon (Ngalkbon)*. Maningrida: Maningrida Arts and Culture.

Evans, Nicholas and Hans-Jürgen Sasse. 2003. Searching for meaning in the Library of Babel: Field semantics and problems of digital archiving. In Barwick, Linda and Jane Simpson (eds). *Researchers, communities, institutions and sound recordings*. 1–42.

Evans, Nicholas and David Wilkins. 2001. The complete person: networking the physical and the social. In *Forty years on: Ken Hale and Australian languages*, Jane Simpson, David Nash, Peter Austin, and Barry Alpher, eds., 493–521. Canberra: Pacific Linguistics.

Everett, Daniel L. 2005. Reply. *Current Anthropology* 46(4): 641–646.

Everett, Daniel. 2012. *Language: The Cultural Tool*. New York: Pantheon Books.

Fabrega, Horacio. 1974. *Disease and social behavior: An interdisciplinary perspective*. Cambridge, MA: The MIT Press.

Fabrega, Horacio. 1997. *Evolution of Sickness and Healing*. Berkeley: University of California Press.

Fabrega, Horacio. 1997. *Origins of Psychopathology: The Phylogenetic and Cultural Basis of Mental Illness*. Piscataway: Rutgers University Press.

Fabrega, Horacio. 2002. *Origins of Psychopathology: The Phylogenetic and Cultural Basis of Mental Illness*. Piscataway: Rutgers University Press.

Fabrega, Horacio. 2012. Ethnomedical Implications of Wierzbicka's Theory and Method. Emotion Review. *Emotion Review* 4(3): 318–319.

Fabrega, Horacio. In press. *Conditions of Psychiatric Interest in Early Human History*.

Fabrega, Horacio, Forthcoming. Early Evolution of Medicine.

Fenton, S. and A. Sadiq (eds.). 1993. *The Sorrow in my Heart: Sixteen Asian Women Speak About Depression*. London: Commission for Racial Equality.

Fernández-Armesto, Felipe. 1998. *Truth: A history and guide for the perplexed*. London: Black Swan.

Firmat, Pérez. 2003. *Tongue ties: Logo-eroticism in Anglo-Hispanic literature*. New York: Palgrave Macmillan.

Fischer, David Hackett. 1989. *Albion's seed: Four British folkways in America*. New York: Oxford University Press.

Fischer, David Hackett. 2012. *Fairness and Freedom: A history of two open societies: New Zealand and the United States*. New York: Oxford University Press.

Freud, Sigmund. 1954. *The origins of psychoanalysis*. New York: Basic Books.

Furbee, N. Louanna. 2010. Language documentation: Theory and practice. In: Grenoble, Lenore and Furbee, N. Louanna (eds). *Language documentation: practice and values.* 3–24.

Garton Ash, Timothy. 2011. Germans, More or Less. *New York Review of Books*, February 24, 2011.

Geertz, Clifford. 1973. Thick description: Toward an interpretive theory of culture. In Clifford Geertz, *Interpretation of culture*, 3–30. New York: Basic.

Geertz, Clifford. 1974. From the native's point of view: On the nature of anthropological understanding. *Bulletin of the American Academy of Arts and Sciences*: 28:1 26–45.

Geertz, Clifford. 2000. *Available light: Anthropological reflections on philosophical topics*. Princeton, NJ: Princeton University Press.

Gellner, Ernest. 1981. General introduction: relativism and universals. In *Universals of Human Thought: The African Evidence*, Barbara Bloom Lloyd and John Gay eds., 1–20. Cambridge: Cambridge University Press.

Gentner, Dedre and Lera Boroditsky. 2001. Individuation, relativity and early word learning. In *Language acquisition and conceptual development*, Melissa Bowerman and Stephen C. Levinson eds., 215–256. Cambridge: Cambridge University Press.

Gentner, Dedre. 1982. Why nouns are learned before verbs: linguistic relativity versus natural partitioning. In *Language Development, vol. 2: Language, Thought, and Culture*, ed. S. A. Kuczaj II, 301–334. Hillsdale, NJ: Lawrence Erlbaum.

Gerdts, Donna B. 2010. Beyond expertise: The role of the linguist in language. In Grenoble, Lenore and Furbee, N Louanna (eds). 173–192.

Gergen, Kenneth J. 1991. *The saturated self: dilemmas of identity in contemporary life*. New York: Basic Books.

Gerhardt, C. I. 1960–61 [1890] *Die philosophischen Schriften von Gottfried Wilhelm Leibniz*, Vols 1–7. Hildesheim: Georg Olms.

Gladkova, Anna. 2007. Universal and language-specific aspects of "propositional attitudes": Russian vs. English. In: Andrea C. Schalley and Drew Khlentzos (eds), *Mental States: Volume 2: Language and Cognitive Structure*. Amsterdam: John Benjamins, 61–83.

Gladkova, Anna. 2008. Tolerance: New and traditional values in Russian in comparison with English. In Cliff Goddard (ed.), *Cross-linguistic Semantics*, 301–329. Amsterdam: John Benjamins.

Gladkova, Anna. 2010. "Sympathy," "compassion," and "empathy" in English and Russian: A linguistic and cultural analysis. *Culture & Psychology* 16(2): 267–285.

Gladkova, Anna. 2010a. *Russkaja kul'turnaja semantika: emocii, cennosti, zhiznennye ustanovki* [Russian cultural semantics: Emotions, values, attitudes.] Moscow: Languages of Slavonic Cultures. (in Russian)

Gladkova, Anna. 2010b. "Sympathy," "compassion," and "empathy" in English and Russian: A linguistic and cultural analysis. *Culture & Psychology* 16(2): 267–285.

Goddard, Cliff. 1991. Testing the translatability of semantic primitives into an Australian Aboriginal Language. *Anthropological Linguistics* 33(1), 31–56.

Goddard, Cliff. 1994. Lexical primitives in Yankunytjatjara. In Goddard and Wierzbicka (eds). 229–262.

Goddard, Cliff. 1996. *Pitjantjatjara/Yankunytjatjara to English Dictionary*, 2nd edn. Alice Springs: Institute for Aboriginal Development.

Goddard, Cliff. 1998. *Semantic Analysis*. Oxford: Oxford University Press.

Goddard, Cliff. 2007. A response to NJ Enfield's review of Ethnopragmatics (Goddard, ed. 2006). *Intercultural Pragmatics* 4(4), 531–538.

Goddard, Cliff. 2001a. *Sabar, ikhlas, setia* – patient, sincere, loyal? A contrastive semantic study of some "virtues" in Malay and English. *Journal of Pragmatics* 33, 653–681.

Goddard, Cliff. 2001b. *Hati*: A key word in the Malay vocabulary of emotion. In Jean Harkins and Anna Wierzbicka (eds), *Emotions in Crosslinguistic Perspective*, 171–200. Berlin: Mouton de Gruyter.

Goddard, Cliff. 2002. The search for the shared semantic core of all languages. In Cliff Goddard and Anna Wierzbicka (eds.), *Meaning and Universal Grammar – Theory and Empirical Findings*, Vol. I, 5–41. Amsterdam: John Benjamins.

Goddard, Cliff. 2009. The "communication concept" and the "language concept" in everyday English. *Australian Journal of Linguistics* 29(1), 11–25.

Goddard, Cliff. 2010. Cultural scripts: applications to language teaching and intercultural communication. *Studies in Pragmatics* (Journal of the China Pragmatics Association) 3, 105–119.

Goddard, Cliff. 2011a. *Semantic Analysis*, 2nd ed. Oxford: Oxford University Press.

Goddard, Cliff. 2011b. The lexical semantics of "language" (with special reference to "words"). *Language Sciences*, 33(1): 40–57.

Goddard, Cliff. Forthcoming. Introduction to the special issue on social cognition. *Australian Journal of Linguistics*.

Goddard, Cliff. In press. On "disgust." In *Emotion in Context*, ed. F. Baider & Georgeta Cislaru. Amsterdam: John Benjamins.

Goddard, Cliff (ed.). 2006. *Ethnopragmatics: Understanding Discourse in Cultural Context*. Berlin: Mouton de Gruyter.

Goddard, Cliff (ed.). 2008. *Cross-linguistic Semantics*. Amsterdam: John Benjamins.

Goddard, Cliff, Anna Wierzbicka and Horacio Fabrega. Forthcoming. Evolutionary Semantics.

Goddard, Cliff and Anna Wierzbicka. 2008. Contrastive semantics of physical activity verbs: "Cutting" and "chopping" in English, Polish, and Japanese. *Language Sciences*.31(1): 60–96.

Goddard, Cliff and Wierzbicka, Anna. 1994. *Semantic and lexical universals: Theory and empirical findings*. Amsterdam: John Benjamins.

Goddard, Cliff and Wierzbicka, Anna (eds). 2007. Semantic Primes and cultural scripts in language teaching and intercultural communication. In Sharifian, Farzad and Palmer, Gary (eds.), *Applied cultural linguistics: Inplications for second language learning and intercultural communication*. Amsterdam: John Benjamins. 104–124.

Goddard, Cliff and Anna Wierzbicka. In press a. *Words and meanings: Studies in lexical and cultural semantics*. Oxford: Oxford University Press.

Goddard, Cliff and Anna Wierzbicka. In press b. Lexical universals and semantic fieldwork.

Goddard, Cliff and Anna Wierzbicka (eds.). 2004. Special Issue on "Cultural Scripts." *Intercultural Pragmatics* 1(2): 153–274.

Goddard, Cliff and Anna Wierzbicka (eds.), 2002. *Meaning and Universal Grammar: Theory and empirical findings*, 2 vols. Amsterdam: John Benjamins.

Goodenough, Ward H. 1970. *Description and Comparison in Cultural Anthropology*. Cambridge: Cambridge University Press.

Goody, Esther (ed.). 1978. *Questions and Politeness: Strategies in social interaction*. Cambridge: Cambridge University Press.

Grenoble, Lenore A. 2010. Language documentation and field linguistics: The state of the field. In Grenoble and Furbee.. pp. 289–310.

Grenoble, Lenore A. and N. Louanna Furbee. 2010. *Language Documentation: Practice and Values*. Amsterdam: John Benjamins.

Grice, H. P. 1975. Logic and Conversation. In *Syntax and semantics 3: Speech acts*, ed. Peter Cole and Jerry M. Morgan, 41–58. New York: Academic Press.

Griffiths, P.E. (1997). *What emotions really are: The problem of psychological categories*. Chicago: University of Chicago Press.

Habib, Sandy. 2011a. "Angels can cross cultural boundaries." *RASK, International Journal of Language and Communication* 34: 49–75.

Habib, Sandy. 2011b. "Ghosts, fairies, elves, and nymphs: Towards a semantic template for non-human being concepts." *Australian Journal of Linguistics* 31: 411–443.

Hale, Kenneth L. 1959 Unpublished field notes. MIT Archives.

Hale, Kenneth L. 1966. Kinship reflections in syntax: some Australian languages. *Word* 22(1/4): 319–324.

Hale, Kenneth L. 1974. *An elementary dictionary of the Warlpiri language*, ms.

Hale, Kenneth L. 2001. Interview quoted in Kenneth Hale Obituary. *The economist*. November 1. Online. Accessible from: http://www.economist.com/node/842137.

Hargrave, Susanne. 1982. A report on colour term research in five Aboriginal languages. In *Work Papers of SIL-AAB Series B8*, 201–226. Darwin: Summer Institute of Linguistics Australian Aborigines Branch.

Harkins, Jean. 1994. *Bridging Two Worlds*. Santa Lucia: University of Queensland Press.

Harkins, Jean and David P. Wilkins. 1994. Mparntwe Arrernte and the search for lexical universals. In Goddard and Wierzbicka (eds). 285–310.

Harkins, Jean and Anna Wierzbicka (eds). 2001. *Emotions in Crosslinguistic Perspective*. Berlin: Mouter de Gruyter.

Harman, Oren. 2010. *The Price of Altruism: George Price and the Search for the Origins of Kindness*. London: Vintage.

Harrap's Standard German and English Dictionary. 1963. Harrap.

Harré, Rom. 1984. "Vocabularies and theories." In Harré and Reynold (eds.) *The Meaning of Primate Signals*, 90–106. Cambridge: Cambridge University Press.

Harré, Rom. 1986. *The Social Construction of Emotion*. New York. John Wiley & Sons.

Harré, Rom. 2012. Methods of Research: cultural/discursive psychology. In *Psychology for the Third Millennium: Integrating Cultural and Neuroscience*, ed. Rom Harre and Fathali M Moghaddam, 22–36. London: Sage.

Harré, Rom and Fathali M. Moghaddam. 2012. Psychoneurology: The program. In *Psychology for the Third Millennium: Integrating Cultural and Neuroscience*, ed. Rom Harre and Fathali M Moghaddam, 2–21. London: Sage.

Harris, Roy. 1982. *The Language Myth*. St. Martin's Press: New York.

Hasada, Rie. 1998. Sound symbolic emotion words in Japanese. In *Speaking of Emotions: Conceptualisation and expression*, ed. Angeliki Athanasiadou and Elżbieta Tabakowska, 83–98. Berlin: Mouton de Gruyter.

Hasada, Rie. 2001. Meanings of Japanese sound-symbolic emotion words. In: Jean Harkins and Anna Wierzbicka (eds), *Emotions in Crosslinguistic Perspective*. Berlin: Mouton de Gruyter. 221–258.

Hasada, Rie. 2002. "Body part" terms and emotion in Japanese. *Pragmatics and Cognition* 10(1): 107–128.

Hasada, Rie. 2008. Two virtuous emotions in Japanese: *Nasakeljoo* and *jihi*. In: Cliff Goddard (ed.) *Cross-Linguistic Linguistics*. Amsterdam: John Benjamins, 331–347.

Hastings, James (ed.). 1908-1927. *Encyclopaedia of Religions and Ethics*, 12 vols. New York: Charles Scribner's Sons.

Hauser, Marc. 2006. *Moral Minds: How Nature Designed Our Universal Sense of Right and Wrong*. New York: Harper Collins.

Hellwig, Birgit. 2010. Meaning and translation in linguistic fieldwork. *Studies in Language* 34(4): 802–831.

Henderson, John and Veronica Dobson. 1994. *Eastern and Central Arrernte to English dictionary*. Alice Springs, N. T.: Institute for Aboriginal Development.

Hill Deborah. 1994. Longgu. In Goddard and Wierzbicka (eds). 1994. 311–329.

Hinton, Leanne. 2001. Language revitalization: An overview. In Hinton, Leanne and Ken Hale (eds) *The green book of language revitalization in practice*. 3–18.

Hinton, Leanne. 2001. The Karuk language. In Hinton, Leanne and Ken Hale (eds). *The green book of language revitalization in practice*. 191–194.

Hinton, Leanne and Ken Hale (eds.). 2001. *The green book of language revitalization in practice*. San Diego; London: Academic Press.

Hirata, S. 2006a. Chimpanzee Learning and Transmission of Tool Use to Fish for Honey. In Matsuzawa, T., Tomonaga, M., & Tanaka, M. (eds). *Cognitive Development in Chimpanzees*. 201–213. Tokyo: Springer.

Hirata, S. 2006b. Tactical Deception and Understanding of Others in Chimpanzees. In Matsuzawa, T., Tomonaga, M., & Tanaka, M. (eds). *Cognitive Development in Chimpanzees*. 265–278. Tokyo: Springer.

Hochschild, Arlie Russell. 1983. *The managed heart: commercialization of human feeling*. Berkley: University of California Press.

Hoffman, Eva. 1989. *Lost in Translation: A life in a new language*. New York: Dutton.

Holmes, Richard. 2008. *The Age of Wonder: How the Romantic Generation discovered the beauty and terror of science*. London: Harper.

Horton, Robin. 1993. *Patterns of Thought in Africa and the West: Essays on magic, religion and science*. Cambridge: Cambridge University Press.

Hryniewicz, Wacław. 2012. *God's Spirit in the World: Ecumenical and Cultural Essays*. Washington DC: Council for Research in Values and Philosophy.

Humble, T. 2006. "Ant Dipping in Chimpanzees: An Example of How Microecological Variables, Tool Use, and Culture Reflect the Cognitive Abilities of Chimpanzees." In Matsuzawa, T., Tomonaga, M., & Tanaka, M. (eds). *Cognitive Development in Chimpanzees*. 452–475. Tokyo: Springer.

Humboldt, Carl Wilhelm von. 1903–36. *Wilhelm von Humboldts Werke*. Ed. Albert Leitzmann. 17 vols. Berlin: B. Behr.

Humboldt, Carl Wilhelm von. 1963. *Schriften zur Sprachphilosophie*. 5 vols. Stutgart: J. G. Cotta.

Ide, Sachiko. 1989. Formal forms and discernment: Two neglected aspects of universals of linguistic politeness. *Multilingua* 8(2/3): 223–248.

Izard, Carroll. 1971. *The Face of Emotions*. New York: Appleton-Century-Croft.

James, William. 1890. *The Principles of Psychology*, vol. 2. New York: Macmillan.

Johnson-Laird, Philip & Keith Oatley. 1989. The language of emotions: An analysis of a semantic field. *Cognition & Emotion* 3: 81–123.

Jones, D. 1999. "Evolutionary Psychology." *Annual Review of Anthropology*. 28: 553–575.

Junker, Marie-Odile. 2003. A Native American view of the "mind" as seen in the lexicon of cognition in East Cree. *Cognitive Linguistics* 14(2-3): 167–194.

Junker, Marie-Odile. 2008. Semantic primes and their grammar in a polysynthetic language: East Cree. In *Cross-Linguistic Semantics*, ed. Cliff Goddard, 163–204. Amsterdam: John Benjamins.

Junker, Marie-Odile and Blacksmith, Louise. 2006. Are there emotional universals? Evidence from the Native American Language East Cress. *Culture and Psychology*.

Kachru, Braj. 1985. Standards, codification and sociolinguistic realism: The English Language in the outer circle. In R. Quirk and H. G. Widdowson, eds. *English in the World: Teaching and learning the language and literatures*. Cambridge: Cambridge University Press. 11–30.

Kachru, Braj. ed. 1992. *The Other Tongue: English across cultures*. Urbana: University of Illinois Press. 2nd ed.

Kay, Paul, Brent Berlin, Luisa Maffi, and William Merrifield. 1997. Color naming across languages. In C.L. Hardin and L Maffi. *Colour Categories in Though and Language*. Cambridge: Cambridge University Press. 21–56.

Kay, Paul. 2004. NSM and the Meaning of Colour Words. *Theoretical Linguistics* 29(3): 237–248.

Kay, Paul and Rolf G. Kuehni. 2008. Why colour words are really … colour words. *Journal of the Royal Anthropological Institute* 14: 886–887.

Kay, Paul and Terry Regier. 2007. Color naming universals: The case of Berinmo. *Cognition* 102: 289–298.

Kecskes, Istvan and Tünde Papp. 2000. *Foreign Language and the Mother Tongue*. Mahwah, NJ: Lawrence Erlbaum.

Keesing, Roger. 1984. Rethinking mana. *Journal of Anthropological Research*. 40: 137–156.

Keesing, Roger M. 1994. Radical cultural difference: Anthropology's myth? In *Language Contact and Language Conflict*, ed. Martin Pütz, 3–24. Amsterdam: John Benjamins.

Kitayama, Shinobu and Markus, Hazel (eds). 1994. *Emotion and culture: Empirical studies of mutual influences*. Washington, DC: American Psychological Association.

Kluckhohn, Clyde. 1953. Universal categories of culture. In *Anthropology today: An encyclopedic inventory*, ed. A. Kroeber, 507–523. Chicago: University of Chicago Press.

Knight, Emily. 2008. Hyperpolysemy in Bunuba, a polysynthetic language of the Kimberley, Western Australia. In Cliff Goddard, ed., *Cross-Linguistic Semantics*, 205–223. Amsterdam: John Benjamins.

Kolnai, Aurel. 2004 [1929]. *On disgust*. Edited and with an Introduction by Barry Smith & Carolyn Korsmeyer. Chicago/La Salle: Open Court. [Original *Der Ekel*, in *Jahrbuch für Philosophie und phänomenolgische Forschung* Vol. 10, 1929].

Krauss, Michael. 1992. The world's languages in crisis. *Language* 68(1): 4–10.

Kronenfeld, David B. 1996. *Plastic Glasses and Church Fathers. Semantic Extension from the Ethnoscience Tradition*. New York: Oxford University Press.

Labov, William. 1973. The boundaries of words and their meanings. In *Ways of Analyzing Variation in English*, CJ. N. Bailey and Roger Shuy (eds), Washington DC: Georgetown University Press. 340–373.

Larina, Tatiana. 2009. The category of politeness and the style of communication: A comparison of English and Russian linguo-cultural tradition. Moscow: Jazyki Slavjanskix Kul'tur. [In Russian].

Laughren, Mary, Kenneth Hale and Warlpiri Lexicography Group. 2006. *Warlpiri-English Encyclopaedic Dictionary. Electronic files*. St. Lucia: University of Queensland.

Lazarus, Richard. 1995. Vexing research problems inherent in cognitive-mediational theories of emotion and some solutions. *Psychological Inquiry* 6(3): 183–196.

Lee, Penny. 1996. *The Whorf Theory Complex: A Critical Reconstruction*. Amsterdam: John Benjamins.

Leech, Geoffrey. 2005. Politeness: Is there an East-West Divide? *Journal of Foreign Languages* 6, 1–30.

Lefevere, André. 1977. *Translating Literature: The German tradition from Luther to Rosenzweig*. Amsterdam: Van Gorcum. [Chapter: Arthur Schopenhauer, "Equivalence and atomisation of the original," 98–101].

Leung, Helen. 2012. The semantics of Cantonese utterance particle laa1. *Proceedings of the 2011 conference of the Australian Linguistic Society*. ANU Research Collections. https://digitalcollections.anu.edu.au.

LeVine, Robert. 2001. Japan as front line in the cultural psychology wars. In *Japanese Frames of Mind: Cultural Perspectives on Human Development*, eds. Hidetada Shimizu and Robert A. LeVine, xi–xxii. Cambridge: Cambridge University Press.

Levisen, Carsten. 2012. *Cultural Semantics and Social Cognition: A Case Study on the Danish Universe of Meaning*. Berlin: Mouton de Gruyter.

Levisen, Carsten. In press. Danish Pig-talk: A Study in Semantic Diversity and Social Cognition. *AJL special issue* special issue on social cognition, edited by Cliff Goddard.

Levy, Robert I. 1973. *Tahitians: Mind and Experience in the Society Islands*. Chicago: University of Chicago Press.

Levy, Robert. 1983. Introduction: self and emotions. *Ethos* 11.3: 128–34.

Levy, Robert I. 1984. Emotion, knowing and culture. In Richard A. Shweder and Robert A. LeVine, eds., *Culture Theory: Essays on mind, self, and emotions*, 214–237. Cambridge: Cambridge University Press.

Levy-Brühl, Lucien. 1979. *Fonctions mentales dans les sociétés inférieures* (How natives think). Translation by Lilian A. Clare. New York: Arno Press.

Locke, John. 1959 [1690]. *An Essay Concerning Human Understanding*. Oxford: Clarendon Press.

Longman Dictionary of Contemporary English. (1987). 2nd ed. Harlow: Longman.

Lucy, John A. 1992. *Grammatical Categories and Cognition*. Cambridge: Cambridge University Press.

Lucy, John A. 1997. The linguistics of "color." In *Color categories in thought and language*, ed. C. L. Hardin and L. Maffi, 320–346. New York: Cambridge University Press.

Lucy, John A. 2011. Language and cognition: The view from anthropology. In *Language and Bilingual Cognition*, ed. Vivian Cook and Benedetta Bassetti, 43–68. Hove, UK: Routledge.

Lutz, Catherine. 1983. Ethnopsychology compared to what? Explaining behaviour and consciousness among the Ifaluk. In *Person, self and experience: Exploring Pacific ethnopsychologies*, ed. GM White & J. Kirkpatrick, 35–79. Berkeley: University of California Press.

Lutz, Catherine. 1988. *Unnatural Emotions: Everyday Sentiments on a Micronesian Atoll and Their Challenge to Western Theory*. Chicago: University of Chicago Press.

Majid. Asifa. 2010. Words for parts of the body. In *Words and the Mind: How words capture human experience*, ed. Barbara Malt and Phillip Wolff, 58–71. New York: Oxford University Press.

Malouf, David. 2003. Made in England: Australia's British Inheritance. *Quarterly Essay* 12: 1–66.

Malinowski, Bronisław. 1927. *Sex and repression in a savage society*. New York: Harcourt Brace.

Malt, Barbara C., Steven A. Sloman, and Silvia P. Gennari. 2003. Universality and language specificity in object naming. *Journal of Memory and Language* 49: 20–42.

Mandler, George. 1975. *Mind and Emotion*. New York: John Wiley and Sons.

Mantel, Hilary. 2009. *Wolf Hall*. London: Fourth Estate.

Mantel, Hilary. 2012. *Bring Up the Bodies*. London: Fourth Estate.

Mark, David M. and Andrew G. Turk, A. G. 2003. Landscape Categories in Yindjibarndi: Ontology, Environment, and Language. In W. Kuhn, M. Worboys & S. Timpf eds., *Spatial Information Theory: Foundations of Geographic Information Science*, In LNCS 2825, 28–45. Berlin: Springer.

Mark, David M., Andrew G. Turk and David Stea. 2007. "Progress on Yindjibarndi ethnophysiography" In S. Winter, M. Duckham, L. Kulik and B. Kuipers eds., *Spatial Information Theory: 8th International Conference, Melbourne Australia September 2007 Proceedings, LNCS 4736*, 1–19. Berlin: Springer.

Mason, Te Haunihiata. 2008. The Incorporation of *Mātauranga Māori* or Māori Knowledge into *Te Mātāpuna*, the First Monolingual Māori Dictionary for Adults. In Amery, R. and J. Nash (eds.). *Warra wiltaniappendi Strengthening languages: Proceedings of the Inaugural Indigenous Languages Conference (ILC) 2007*. Adelaide: University of Adelaide SA. 35–39.

Matsumoto, Yoshiko. 1988. Reexamination of the universality of face: politeness phenomena in Japanese. *Journal of Pragmatics* 12, 403–426.

Matsuzawa, T., Tomonaga, M., & Tanaka, M. (eds). 2006. *Cognitive Development in Chimpanzees*. Tokyo: Springer.

McCrum, Robert. 2010. *Globish: How the English Language Became the World's Language*. New York: Norton.

Mead, Margaret. 1928. *Coming of Age in Samoa*. New York: William Morrow.

Mel'čuk, Igor. 2011. Preface in I. Boguslavskij (ed) *Slovo I Jazyk (Word and Language)*. (Festschrift for Apresjan). Moscow: Jazyki Slavjanskix Kul'tur, 14–17.

Mel'čuk, Igor. 2012. *Semantics: From Meaning to Text*. Amsterdam: John Benjamins.

Miller, William Ian. 1997. *The Anatomy of Disgust*. Cambridge, MA: Harvard University Press.

Moorfield, John C. 2005. *Te aka. Maori-English, English-Maori dictionary and index*. Auckland: Pearson/Longman.

Mosel, Ulrike. 1994. Samoan. In: Goddard and Wierzbicka, (eds). 331–360.

Munn, Nancy D. 1973. *Walbiri Iconography: Graphic representation and cultural symbolism in a Central Australian Society*. Ithaca: Cornell University Press.

Nerrière, Jean Paul. 2004. *Parlez Globish?* Paris: Eyrolles.

Nicholls, Sophie. 2010. Referring Expressions and Referential Practice in Roper Kriol (Northern Territory, Australia). PhD Thesis. University of New England, Armidale, NSW.

Nicholls, Sophie. In press. Cultural Scripts in Roper Kriol. *Australian Journal of Linguistics*.

Noble, William. 1996. *Human Evolution, Language and Mind: A Psychological and Archaeological Inquiry*. Cambridge: Cambridge University Press.

Noble, W., and Iain Davidson. 1996. *Human Evolution, Language and Mind: A Psychological and Archaeological Inquiry*. Cambridge: Cambridge University Press.

Obama, Barak. 2006. *The Audacity of Hope: Thoughts on Reclaiming the American Dream*. Melbourne: Text.

Obeyesekere, Gananath. 1985. Depression, Buddhism, and the work of culture in Sri Lanka. In *Culture and Depression: Studies in the Anthropology and Cross-Cultural Psychiatry of Affect and Disorder*, ed. Arthur Kleinman and Byron Good, 134–152. Berkeley: University of California Press.

Oxford English Dictionary. OED Online. www.oed.com.

Ogden, Charles Kay. 1930. *Basic English: A General Introduction with Rules and Grammar*. London: Paul Treber.

Oxford Russian-English Dictionary. 1980. Oxford: Oxford University Press.

Parker, David. 2004. Global English, Culture, and Western Modernity. (A revised version of Parker 2001). In *English and Globalization: Perspectives from Hong Kong and Mainland China*, ed. Kwok-Kan Tam, Timothy Weiss, 23–42. Hong Kong: The Chinese University of Hong Kong.

Pavlenko, Aneta. 2005. *Emotions and Multilingualism*. Cambridge: Cambridge University Press.

Pavlenko, Aneta. 2006. Bilingual Selves. In *Bilingual Minds: Emotional Experience, Expression, and Representation*, ed. Aneta Pavlenko, 1–33. Tonawanda, NY: Multilingual Matters.

Pavlenko, Aneta. 2011a. Introduction: Bilingualism and Thought in the 20th Century. In Pavlenko (ed) 1–28.

Pavlenko, Aneta. 2011b. (Re-)naming the World: Word-to-Referent Mapping in Second Language Speakers. In Pavlenko (ed) 198–236.

Pavlenko, Aneta. 2011c. Thinking and Speaking in Two Languages: Overview of the field. In Pavlenko (ed) 237–257.

Pavlenko, Aneta (ed). 2006. *Bilingual Minds: Emotional Experience, Expression, and Representation.* Tonawanda, NY: Multilingual Matters.

Pavlenko, Aneta (ed). 2011. *Thinking and Speaking in Two Languages.* Tonawanda, NY: Multilingual Matters.

Pavlenko, Aneta and Barbara Malt. 2011. Kitchen Russian: Cross-linguistic differences and first-language object naming by Russian–English bilinguals. *Bilingualism: Language and Cognition* 14: 19–46.

Pawley, Andrew. 1994. Kalam exponents of lexical and semantic primitives. In Goddard and Anna (eds), 87–422.

Peeters, Bert (ed). 2006. *Semantic Primes and Universal Grammar: Empirical evidence from the Romance languages.* Amsterdam: John Benjamins.

Peeters, Bert. 2010. "La métalangue sémantique naturelle: acquis et défis." In (Mémoires de la Société de linguistique de Paris, N.S., 18), ed. J. François, 75–101. Leuven: Peeters.

Pesmen, Dale. 2000. *Russia and Soul: An Exploration.* Cornell: Cornell University Press.

Phillipson, Robert. 1992. *Linguistic Imperialism.* Oxford: Oxford University Press.

Pinker, Steven. 1994. *The Language Instinct.* New York: W. Morrow and Co.

Pinker, Steven. 1997. *How the mind works.* New York: W.W. Norton.

Pinker, Steven. 2007a. *The stuff of thought: Language as a window into human nature.* New York: Viking.

Pinker, Stephen. 2007b. Critical discussion: Toward a consilient study of literature. *Philosophy and Literature* 31: 161–177.

Pinker, Steven. 2012. *The Better Angels of Our Nature: Why violence has declined.* New York: Penguin.

Ponsonnet, Maia. 2010. Unpublished material. Australian National University.

Porpora, Douglas V. 2001. *Landscapes of the Soul: The loss of moral meaning in American life,* New York: Oxford University Press.

Premack, D. & Woodruff, G. 1978. Does the chimpanzee have a theory of mind? *Behavioral Brain Sciences* 1, 515–526.

Priestley, Carol. 2002. Insides and emotion in Koromu. *Pragmatics & Cognition.* 10(1/2), 243–270.

Priestley, Carol. 2008. The semantic of "inalienable possession" in Koromu (PNG). In *Cross-Linguistic Semantics,* ed. Cliff Goddard, 277–300. Amsterdam: John Benjamins.

Priestley, Carol. 2009. A grammar of Koromu (Kesawai), a Trans New Guinea language of Papua New Guinea. Unpublished PhD thesis. The Australian National University.

Priestley, Carol. 2012a. Koromu temporal expressions: Semantic and cultural perspectives. In *Space and Time in Languages and Cultures: Language, Culture, and Cognition,* ed. L. Filipović & K.M. Jaszczolt, 143–166. Amsterdam: John Benjamins.

Priestley, Carol. 2012b. The expression of potential event modality in the Papuan language of Koromu. In Ponsonnet, M., Dao, L. and Bowler, M. (eds), *Proceedings of the 42nd Australian Linguistic Society Conference – 2011.* ANU Research Collections. [http://hdl.handle.net/1885/9422].

Prinz, Jesse. 2012. *Beyond human nature: How culture and experience shape the human mind.* n.p.: Allen Lane.

Proust, Marcel. 1982. *A search for lost time. Swann's way*. Translated by James Grieve. Canberra: Australian National University.

Radcliffe-Brown, A. R. 1930–1931 *The Social Organization of Australian Tribes*. Sydney: Oceania Monographs.

Rathmayr, Renate. 1999. Metadiscours et realité linguistiquel'example de la politesse russe. *Pragmatics* 91, 75–96.

Regier, Terry, Paul Kay, Aubrey L. Gilbert, and Richard B. Ivry. 2010. Language and thought: Which side are you on, anyway? In *Words and the Mind: How words capture human experience*, ed. Barbara Malt and Phillip Wolff, 165–182. New York: Oxford University Press.

Roberson, Debi, Ljubica Damjanovic & Mariko Kikutani. 2010. Show and Tell: The Role of Language in Categorizing Facial Expression of Emotion. *Emotion Review* 2(3): 255–260.

Romney, A. K., and R.G. D'Andarde. 1964. Cognitive aspects of English kin terms. *American Anthropologist*. 68:3:2 146–170.

Rosaldo, Michelle. 1980. *Knowledge and Passion: Ilongot notions of self and social life*. Cambridge: Cambridge University Press.

Rosaldo, Michelle. 1982. The things we do with words: Ilongot speech acts and speech act theory in philosophy. *Language and Society* 11, 203–237.

Rusch, C. 2004. Cross-cultural variability of the semantic domain of emotion terms: An examination of English *shame* and *embarrass* with Japanese *hazukashii*. *Cross-Cultural Research*. 38, 3, 236–248.

Russell, James A. 1994. Is there universal recognition of emotion from facial expressions? A review of the cross-cultural studies. *Psychological Bulletin* 115(1): 102–141.

Russell, James A., Erika L. Rosenberg & Marc D. Lewis. 2011. Introduction to a Special Section on Basic Emotion Theory. *Emotion Review* 3-4: 363.

Russon, Anne E. 2004. "Great Ape Cognition Systems." In Russon & Begun, eds. 76–100.

Russon, Anne E. & David R. Begun, eds. 2004. *The Evolution of Thought: Evolutionary Origins of Great Ape Intelligence*. Cambridge: Cambridge University Press.

Sacks, Oliver. 1996. *The Island of the Colour-blind*. Sydney: Picador.

Sacks, Oliver. 2013. "Speak, memory." *New York Review of Books*, vol. LX, no. 3, pp. 20–21.

Samarin, William J. 1967. *Field linguistics; a guide to linguistic field work*. New York: Holt, Rinehart and Winston.

Sanz, Crickette M. & David B. Morgan. 2010. "The Complexity of Chimpanzee Tool Use Behaviours." In: E.V. Lonsdorf, S. R. Ross and T. Matsuzawa, eds. *The Mind of the Chimpanzee: ecological and experimental perspectives*. 127–140. Chicago: The University of Chicago Press.

Sapir, Edward. 1949. Selected writings in language, culture and personality (David Mandelbaum, ed.). Berkeley: University of California Press.

Schaffer, Frederic. 1998. *Democracy in Translation: Understanding Politics in an Unfamiliar Culture*. Ithaca, NY: Cornell University Press.

Scherer, Klaus. 1994. Towards a concept of "modal emotions." In Paul Ekman and Richard Davidson, eds., 25–31.

Schopenhauer, Arthur. 1977 [1815]. Equivalence and the Atomization of the Individual. In *Translating Literature: The German Tradition from Luther to Rosenweig*, André Lefevre, 98–101. Amersterdam: Van Gorcum.

Scott, Kim. 2007. Strangers at Home. In *Translating Lives: Australian stories of language migration*, ed. Mary Besemeres and Anna Wierzbicka, 1–11. St. Lucia: University of Queensland Press.

Searle, John. 1975. Indirect Speech Acts. In *Syntax and semantics, Vol. 3: Speech acts*, Peter Cole and Jerry Morgan, eds., 59–82. New York: Academic Press.

Searle, John R. 1995. *The Construction of Social Reality*. New York: Free Press.

Shimizu, Hidetada and LeVine, Robert (eds). 2001. *Japanese Frames of Mind: Cultural Perspectives on Human Development*. Cambridge: Cambridge University Press.

Shmelev, Aleksej. 2012a. Možno li ponjat' russkuju kul'turu čerez klučerez ključevye slova russkogo jazyka? In. A. Zalizniak, I. Levontina & A Shmelev (eds), pp. 17–23.

Shmelev, Aleksej. 2012b. Russkij vzgljad na "zapadnye" koncepty: jazykovje dannye. In. A. Zalizniak, I. Levontina & A Shmelev 2012, pp. 395–409.

Shweder, Richard A. 1991. *Thinking through cultures: expeditions in cultural psychology*. Cambridge, MA: Harvard University Press.

Shweder, Richard A. 1994. "You're not sick, you're just in love": Emotion as an interpretive system. In P. Ekman and R. J. Davidson (eds) *The Nature of Emotion*, 32–44. New York: Oxford University Press.

Shweder, Richard A. 2003. *Why do men barbecue?: Recipes for cultural psychology*. Cambridge, MA: Harvard University Press.

Shweder, Richard A. 2004. Deconstructing the emotions for the sake of comparative research. In *Feelings and Emotions: The Amsterdam Symposium*, ed. Antony S. R. Manstead, Nico Frijda, and Agneta Fischer, 81–97. Cambridge: Cambridge University Press.

Shweder, Richard A. 2012a. Anthropology's disenchantment with the cognitive revolution. *Topics in Cognitive Science* 4: 354–361.

Shweder, Richard. 2012b. Cultural Psychology of Natural Kinds. *Emotion Review* 4, 4. 382–384.

Shweder, Richard. 2012c. Relativism and universalism. In D. Fassin (ed.) *A companion to moral anthropology*. Chichester, UK: Blackwell, 85–102.

Shweder, Richard A. 2013. Understanding Souls: A Commentary on Anna Wierzbicka's Natural Semantic Metalanguage. *The Australian Journal of Anthropology*. 24(1): 22–26.

Shweder, Richard A. & Jonathan Haidt. 2000. The Cultural Psychology of Emotions: Ancient and New. In *Handbook of Emotions*, 2nd ed., ed. M. Lewis & J. M. Haviland-Jones, 379–414. New York: Guilford Press.

Shweder, Richard A., Jonathan Haidt, Randall Horton and Craig Joseph. 2008. The Cultural psychology of the emotions: ancient and renewed. In *Handbook of Emotions*, 3rd ed, ed. Michael D. Lewis, Jeannette M. Haviland-Jones, and Lisa Feldman Barrett. New York: The Guilford Press.

Simons, Gary F., and Lewis, M. Paul. 2013. The world's languages in crisis: a 20-year update. Presented at the 26th Linguistics Symposium: *Language death, endangerment, documentation and revitalization*. Milwaukee: University of Wisconsin.

Simpson, Jane. 2006. How do we know what they see? (available online: http://blogs.usyd.edu.au/elac/2006/09/how_do_we_know_what_they_see_f.html, accessed January 11, 2013).

Slobin, Dan. 1996. From "thought to language" to "thinking for speaking." In J. Gumperz and S. Levinson (eds) *Rethinking Linguistic Relativity*. 70–96. Cambridge: Cambridge University Press.

Slobin, Dan. 2000. Verbalized events: A dynamic approach to linguistic relativity and determination. In S. Niemeier and R. Dirven (eds) *Evidence for Linguistic Relativity*. 107–138. Amsterdam: John Benjamins.

Smedslund, Jan. 1988. *Psycho-Logic*. Berlin: Springer.

Smedslund, Jan. 1997. Is the "psychologic" of trust universal? In *The Language of Emotions*, ed. Susanne Niemeier & René Dirven, 3–13. Amsterdam: John Benjamins.

Smith, Zadie. 2009. *Changing My Mind: Occasional Essays*. New York: Penguin Press HC.

Spiro, Melvin. 1994. Some reflections on cultural determinism and relativism with special reference to emotion and reason. In Richard Shweder and Robert A LeVine, eds. *Culture theory: essays on mind, self, and emotion*, 323–346. Cambridge: Cambridge University Press.

Stanwood, Ryo E. 1997. The primitive syntax of mental predicates in Hawaii Creole English: A text-based study. *Language Sciences* 19(3): 209–217.

Stanwood, Ryo E. 1999. On the Adequacy of Hawai'i Creole English. PhD dissertation. University of Hawai'i.

Stolt, Birgit. 2012. *Lasst uns fröhlich springen!*. Berlin: Weidler.

Tannen, Deborah. 1981. New York Jewish conversational style. *International Journal of the Sociology of Language* 30: 133–149.

Tattersall, Ian. 2012. *Masters of the Planet: seeking the origins of human singularity*. New York: Palgrave Macmillan.

Taylor, Charles. 1989. *Sources of the Self: The making of the modern identity*. Cambridge, MA: Harvard University Press.

Terkourafi, Marina. 2011. From Politeness$_1$ to Politeness$_2$: Tracking norms of im/politeness across time and space. *Journal of Politeness Research* 7(2): 159–185.

Thieberger, Nicholas, ed. 2012. *The Oxford Handbook of Linguistic Fieldwork*. Oxford: Oxford University Press.

Tien, Adrian. 2009. Semantic prime HAPPEN in Mandarin Chinese: In search of a viable exponent. *Pragmatics & Cognition* 17(2): 356–382.

Tien, Adrian. 2010. *Lexical Semantic of Children's Mandarin Chinese during the First Four Years*. Munich: LINCOM.

Todd, Olivier. (1996). *Albert Camus—Une Vie*. Paris: Gallimard.

Tomasello, Michael. 1999. *The cultural origins of human cognition*. Harvard: Harvard University Press.

Tomasello, Michael. 2012. *A Natural History of Human Thinking*. MS MPI-EVA, Leipzig (6-12).

Tomasello, M. & Call, J. 1997. *Primate Cognition*. Oxford: Oxford University Press.

Tomasello, Michael with Carol Dweck, Joan Silk, Brian Skyrms and Elizabeth Spelke. 2009. *Why we cooperate*. Cambridge, MA: MIT Press.

Tomasello, Michael & Joseph Call. 2010. "Chimpanzee Social Cognition." In: Lonsdorf Elizabeth, Stephen R. Ross, Tetsuro Matsuzawa. *The mind of the chimpanzee*. Chicago: University of Chicago Press. 235–250.

Tong, Malindy, Yell, Michael and Goddard, Cliff. 1997. Semantic primitives of time and space in Hong Kong Cantonese. *Language Sciences* 19(3), 245–261.

Travis, Catherine. 2002. La Metalengua Semántica Natural: The Natural Semantic Metalanguage of Spanish. In Cliff Goddard and Anna Wierzbicka (eds.), *Meaning and Universal Grammar – Theory and Empirical Findings*, Volume I, 173–242. Amsterdam: John Benjamins.

Travis, Catherine. 2004. The ethnopragmatics of the diminutive in conversational Colombian Spanish. *Intercultural Pragmatics* 1(2), 249–274.

Travis, Catherine. 2005. *Discourse Markers in Colombian Spanish*. Berlin: Mouton De Gruyter.

Travis, Catherine. 2006. The communicative realization of confianza and calor humano in Colombian Spanish. In: *Ethnopragmatics: Understanding Discourse in Cultural Context*, ed. Cliff Goddard, 199–230. Berlin: Mouton de Gruyter.

Underhill, James. 2012. *Ethnolinguistics*. Cambridge: Cambridge University Press.

Valsiner, Jaan. 2000. *Culture and human development*. Thousand Oak, CA: Sage Publications.

van Brakel, Jaap. 1993. Emotions: A cross-cultural perspective on forms of life. In W. M. Wentworth and J. Ryan, eds., *Social Perspectives on Emotions*, vol. 21–22. Greenwich USA: JAI Press.

van Brakel, Jaap. 1994. The ignis fatuus of semantic universalia: the case of colour. *British Journal for the Philosophy of Science*. 45: 770–783.

van Brakel, Jaap. 2004. The empirical stance and the colour war. *Divinatio*. 20. 7–26.

Vanhatalo, Ulla, Anna Idström and Heli Tissari. In press. The foundations of the Finnish based Natural Semantic Metalanguage.

von Hippel, William and Sally Dunlop. 2005. Aging, Inhibition, and Social Inappropriateness. *Psychology & Aging*. 20(3); 519–523.

Wakefield, John C. 2011. *The English Equivalents of Cantonese Sentence-Final Particles: A Contrastive Analysis*. (PhD Thesis). The Hong Kong Polytechnic University.

Waters, Sophia. 2012. "It's rude to VP": The cultural semantics of rudeness. *Journal of Pragmatics* (Special Issue on (Im)politeness in English edited by Michael Haugh and Klaus Schneider) 44: 1051–1062.

Waters, Sophia. 2013. *The Cultural Semantics of Sociality Terms from Australian English with Contrastive Reference to French*. PhD thesis. Armidale: University of New England.

Watts, Richard J. 2002. From polite language to educated language: the re-emergence of an ideology. In Richard Watts and Peter Trudgill, eds., *Alternative Histories of English*, 155–172. London: Routledge.

Watts, Richard J. 2003. *Politeness*. Cambridge: Cambridge University Press.

Watts, Richard. 2005. Linguistic politeness and politic verbal behaviour: Reconsidering claims for universality. In Watts et al: 43–70.

Watts, Richard. 2005, Sachiko Ide, and Konrad Ehlich, eds., *Politeness in Language*, Berlin: Mouton de Gruyter.

Whiten, Andrew & David Erdal. 2012. The human socio-cognitive niche and its evolutionary origins. *Philosophical Transactions of the Royal Society B—Biological Sciences* 367(1599): 2119–2129.

Whorf, Benjamin Lee. 1956. *Language, thought and reality: Selected writings of Benjamin Lee Whorf*. J. B. Carroll (ed.). New York: Wiley.

Wierzbicka, Anna. 1972. *Semantic primitive*. Frankfurt: Athenäum.

Wierzbicka, Anna. 1984. Cups and mugs: Lexicography and conceptual analysis. *Australian Journal of Linguistics* 4(2): 205–255.

Wierzbicka, Anna. 1985a. *Lexicography and Conceptual Analysis*. Ann Arbor: Karoma. [ch. 5].

Wierzbicka, Anna. 1985b. Different cultures, different languages, different speech acts: Polish vs. English. *Journal of Pragmatics* 9: 145–178.

Wierzbicka, Anna. 1985c. Oats and wheat: The fallacy of arbitrariness. In: John Haiman (ed), *Iconicity in syntax*. Amsterdam: John Benjamins. 311–342.

Wierzbicka, Anna. 1986. Human emotions: Universal or culture-specific? *American Anthropologist* 88(3): 584–594.

Wierzbicka, Anna. 1988. *The semantics of grammar*. Amsterdam: John Benjamins.

Wierzbicka, Anna. 1989. Soul and mind: Linguistic evidence for ethnopsychology and cultural history. *American Anthropologist* 91(1): 41–58.

Wierzbicka, Anna. 1990. Human emotions: Universal or culture-specific? *American Anthropologist* 88(3): 584–594.

Wierzbicka, Anna. 1991/2003. *Cross-cultural Pragmatics: The Semantics of Human Interaction*. Berlin: Mouton de Gruyter.

Wierzbicka, Anna. 1992. *Semantics, Culture and Cognition: Universal human concepts in culture-specific configurations*. New York: Oxford University Press.

Wierzbicka, Anna. 1994. Emotion, language and "cultural scripts". In Kitayama and Markus (eds.). 130–198

Wierzbicka, Anna. 1996. *Semantics: Primes and Universals*. Oxford: Oxford University Press.

Wierzbicka, Anna. 1997. *Understanding Cultures through their Key Words: English, Russian, Polish, German, Japanese*. New York: Oxford University Press.

Wierzbicka, Anna. 1998. Angst. *Culture & Psychology* 4(2): 161–188.

Wierzbicka, Anna. 1999. *Emotions Across Language and Cultures: Diversity and Universals*. Cambridge: Cambridge University Press.

Wierzbicka, Anna. 2001. *What Did Jesus Mean? Explaining the Sermon on the Mount and the parables in simple and universal human concepts*. New York: Oxford University Press.

Wierzbicka, Anna. 2002a. Russian Cultural Scripts: The thoery of cultural scripts and its applications. *Ethos* 30(4)): 401–432.

Wierzbicka, Anna. 2002b. Semantic primes and universal grammar in Polish. In: Cliff Goddard and Anna Wierzbicka (eds), *Meaning and Universal Grammar – Theory and Empirical Findings*. Vol. II. Amsterdam: John Benjamins. 65–144.

Wierzbicka, Anna. 2003a. Jewish cultural scripts and the interpretation of the Bible. *Journal of Pragmatics*. 36(3): 575–599.

Wierzbicka, Anna. 2003b. Emotion and culture: arguing with Martha Nussbaum. *Ethos*. 31(4): 577–600.

Wierzbicka, Anna. 2005. There are no "colour universals," but there are universals of visual semantics. *Anthropological Linguistics* 47(2): 217–244.

Wierzbicka, Anna. 2006a. *English: Meaning and Culture*. New York: Oxford University Press.

Wierzbicka, Anna. 2006b. Anglo scripts against "putting pressure" on other people and their linguistic manifestations. In *Ethnopragmatics: Understanding Discourse in Cultural Context*, Cliff Goddard (ed.), 31–63. Berlin: Mouton de Gruyter.

Wierzbicka, Anna. 2007. Bodies and their parts: An NSM approach to semantic typology. *Language Sciences*, 29(1): 14–65. [ref ch. 5].

Wierzbicka, Anna. 2008a. Why there are no "colour universals" in language and thought. *Journal of the Royal Anthropological Institute* 14(2): 407–425.

Wierzbicka, Anna. 2008b. Rejoinder to Paul Kay and Rolf G. Kuenhi. *Journal of the Royal Anthropological Institute* 14(4): 887–889.

Wierzbicka, Anna. 2008c. A Conceptual Basis for Intercultural Pragmatics and World-wide Understanding. In *Developing Contrastive Pragmatics: Interlanguage and Cross-cultural Perspective*, ed. Martin Pütz and JoAnne Neff-van Aertselaer, 3–45. Berlin: Mouton de Gruyter.

Wierzbicka, Anna. 2009a. Language and metalanguage: key issues in emotion research. *Emotion Review* 1(1): 3–14.

Wierzbicka, Anna. 2009b. "Reciprocity": an NSM approach to linguistic typology and social universals. *Studies in Language* 33(1): 103–175.

Wierzbicka, Anna. 2009c. Pragmatics and cultural values: The hot center of Russian discourse. In Fraser, Bruce and Turner, Ken (eds.) *Language in life, and a life in language: Jacob Mey – a festschrift*. Bingley, UK: Emerald 423–434.

Wierzbicka, Anna. 2010a. *Experience, Evidence and Sense: The hidden cultural legacy of English*. New York: Oxford University Press.

Wierzbicka, Anna. 2010b. "Story"—An English cultural keyword and a key interpretive tool of Anglo culture. *Narrative Inquiry* 20(1): 153–181.

Wierzbicka, Anna. 2011a. Bilingualism and cognition: The perspective from semantics. In *Language and Bilingual Cognition*, ed. Vivian Cook and Benedetta Bassetti, 191–218. Hove, UK: Routledge.

Wierzbicka, Anna. 2011b. Defining "the humanities." *Culture and Psychology*. 17(1): 31–46.

Wierzbicka, Anna. 2012a. Polskie słowa-wartości w perspektywie porównawczej. Część. II. Prawość i odwaga. *Etnolingwistyka* 24: 19–46.

Wierzbicka, Anna. 2012b. Cultural change reflected in different translations of the New Testament. In Terttu Nevalainen and Elizabeth Traugott, eds., *The Oxford Handbook of the History of English*, 434–445. Oxford: Oxford University Press.

Wierzbicka, Anna. 2012c. Is "pain" a human universal? Conceptualisation of "pain" in English, French and Polish. *Colloquia Communia* 1(92): 29–53.

Wierzbicka, Anna. 2012d. The semantics of "sex" in a cross-linguistic and cross-cultural perspective. In Ju. Apresjan, I. Boguslavsky, M.-C. L'Homme, L. Iomdin, J. Milicevic, A. Polguere and L. Wanner (eds.). *Meaning, Texts and other Exciting Things. a Festschrift to Commemorate the 80th Anniversary of Professor Igor Alexandrovich Mel'cuk*, 641–649. Moscow: Jazyki slavjanskoj kultury.

Wierzbicka, Anna 2012e. Is pain a human universal?: A cross-linguistic and cross-cultural perspective on Pain. *Emotion Review* 4(3): 307–317.

Wierzbicka, Anna. 2012f. Is 'pain' a human universal? Conceptualisation of 'pain' in English, French, and Polish. *Colloquia Communia*. 1(92): 29–53.

Wierzbicka, Anna. 2013a. Understanding others requires shared concepts. *Pragmatics & Cognition* 20(2): 356–379.

Wierzbicka, Anna. 2013b. Translatability and the scripting of other peoples' souls. *The Australian Journal of Anthropology* 2.

Wierzbicka, Anna. In press a. Innate conceptual primitives manifested in the languages of the world and in infant cognition. In Stephen Laurence and Eric Margolis, *Concepts: New Directions*. Cambridge, MA: MIT Press.

Wierzbicka, Anna. In press b. Deconstructing "colour", exploring indigenous meanings. In D. Young (ed.), *Rematerializing Colour*. Wantage, UK: Sean Kingston.

Wilson, William H. and Kauanoe Kamanā. 2001. "Mai Loko Mai O Ka 'I'ini: Proceeding from a dream": The 'Aha Pūnana Leo connection in Hawaiian language revitalisation. In Hinton, Leanne and Ken Hale (eds). 147–178.

Wittgenstein, Ludwig. 1953. *Philosophical Investigations*. New York: MacMillan.

Wong Jock. 2004a. The particles of Singapore English: A semantic and cultural interpretation. *Journal of Pragmatics* 9: 739–793.

Wong Jock. 2004b. Redublication of nominal modifiers in Singapore English: A semantic and cultural interpretation. *World Englishes* 23(3): 339–354.

Wray, Alison and George Grace. 2007. The consequences of talking to strangers: Evolutionary corollaries of socio-cultural influences on linguistic form. *Lingua* 117: 543–578.

Ye, Zhengdao. 2004. The Chinese folk model of facial expressions. A linguistic perspective. *Culture & Psychology* 10(2): 195–222.

Ye, Zhengdao. 2006. Why the 'inscrutable' Chinese face? Emotionality and facial expression in Chinese. In Cliff Goddard (ed.) *Ethnopragmatics: Understanding Discourse in Cultural Context*, 127–169. Berlin: Mouton De Gruyter.

Ye, Zhengdao. 2007. Taste as a gateway to Chinese cognition. In *Mental States: Volume 2: Language and Cognitive Structure*, ed. Andrea C. Schalley & Drew Khlentzos, 109–132. Amsterdam: John Benjamins.

Ye, Zhengdao. 2010. Eating and drinking in Mandarin and Shanghainese: A lexical-conceptual analysis. In E. Christensen, E. Schier & J. Sutton (eds.), *ASCS09: Proceedings of the 9th Conference of the Australasian Society for Cognitive Science*, 375–83. Sydney: Macquarie Centre for Cognitive Science.

Yoon, Kyung-Joo. 2004. Not just words: Korean social models and the use of honorifics. *Intercultural Pragmatics* 1(2): 189–210.

Yoon, Kyung-Joo. 2006. *Constructing a Korean Natural Semantic Metalanguage*. Seoul: Hankook Publishing Co.

Yoon, Kyung-Joo. 2008. The Natural Semantic Metalanguage of Korean. In: Cliff Goddard (ed.), *Cross-Linguistic Semantics*. Amsterdam: John Benjamins, 121–162.

Zalizniak, Anna, Irina Levontina & Aleksej Shmelev. 2005. *Kljuchevye idei russkoj jazykovoj kartiny mira*. [Key ideas of the Russian linguistic picture of the world.] Moscow: Jazyki Slovjanskix Kul'tur.

Zalizniak, Anna, Irina Levontina & Aleksej Shmelev. 2012. *Konstanty: peremennye russkoj jazykovoj kartiny mira*. [The Constants and Variables of the Russian Linguistic Picture of the World]. Moscow: Jazyki Slavjanskix Kul'tur.

Zlatev. Jordan. 2008. *The Shared Mind: Perspectives on Intersubjectivity*. Amsterdam: John Benjamins.

Žuravleva, Elena. 2008. Pokolenija russkogo seksa [The generations of Russian sex]. *Liga svobodnyx gorodov* [A League of Free Towns]. http://www.freetowns.ru/ru/projects/demography/-/love_poll (accessed July–August 2008).

INDEX